FEMALE SCHOLARS

A Tradition Of Learned Women Before 1800

edited by J.R. BRINK

EDEN PRESS

WOMEN'S PUBLICATIONS

Montréal Canada

FEMALE SCHOLARS: A TRADITION OF LEARNED WOMEN
BEFORE 1800, edited by J.R. Brink

© 1980 Eden Press Women's Publications
245 Victoria Avenue, Montréal, Canada H3Z 2M6
and
St. Albans, Vermont 05478 U.S.A.

ISBN: 0-920792-02-2

Printed in Canada at Ateliers des Sourds, Montréal
Dépot légal - première trimestre 1980
Bibliothèque nationale du Québec

CONTENTS

ACKNOWLEDGMENTS

I would like to express my appreciation to Arizona State University for supplying research funds which assisted in financing the preparation of this collection. I am also indebted to Teresa Trotter and Valerie Bennett for their typing and to Rebecca Jones for her assistance in proofreading.

To the Center for Reformation Research and to the Southeastern Institute of Medieval and Renaissance Studies, sponsored by Duke University and the University of North Carolina, Chapel Hill, I am especially grateful for summer fellowships in 1977 and 1978. These Institutes provided the interdisciplinary stimulation which made possible this collection.

Both with advice and encouragement Sherri Clarkson of Eden Press Women's Publications has assisted in guiding this project to completion.

LIST OF ILLUSTRATIONS

v

For Lilly Byrum Wise and Elinor Faith Brink

INTRODUCTION

The biographical and critical studies which follow are a preliminary response to the question so frequently asked by modern feminists—"Where do the sleeping giants lie?" Some of the women who appear in these essays might be approached from a literary perspective, but most are scholarly women who, like Anna Maria van Schurman, devoted themselves to theology and linguistics or, like Mercy Otis Warren, were interested in political and social history. Rather than outlining broad historical and social trends, these studies focus upon the lives of individual learned women in relation to the times in which they lived. The subtitle, *A Tradition of Learned Women Before 1800*, was added after the book was compiled. It states the fascinating and provocative hypothesis suggested by this collection: during the late Medieval and Early Modern periods, there was a tradition of female scholarship.

The collection as a whole is international and interdisciplinary in scope because the tradition itself was international. Learned women, conscious of being "exceptions," made every effort to establish contacts with contemporary women who lived in other countries and also to study the work of their predecessors regardless of nationality. This does not mean that they were "feminists" in any modern sense of the term; few of the women considered here either showed an interest in or tried to improve the status of women. They did advocate equal education for women, although frequently with severe qualifications. Still, because they were excluded from academic and public life, they were strongly attracted to the work of other scholarly women.

TRADITION OF FEMALE SCHOLARSHIP

Beginning with the Dutch scholar Anna Maria van Schurman (1607 - 1678), it is possible to outline this tradition. In 1638 Schurman, possibly the most

1

famous female scholar of the early seventeenth century, wrote a Latin treatise in a scholastic format debating the question, "whether the study of letters is fitting to a Christian woman." Her defense of female education was widely read and later appeared in French and English translations. Her British counterpart Bathsua Makin (1608? - 1675?), tutor to the daughters of Charles I, corresponded with Schurman as did the French scholar Marie le Jars de Gournay, close friend of Montaigne and author of *L'Egalité des Hommes et des Femmes* (1622). Christine of Sweden, that paragon of females whom even John Milton acknowledged to be intellectually superior, reportedly visited Schurman in Utrecht. Christine corresponded with Descartes and with Anne Dacier, the famous seventeenth-century French classical scholar, inviting them to settle in Sweden. Although Christine successfully recruited Descartes, she was unable to persuade Anne Dacier to join her court.

In 1684 the academy of Ricovatri at Padua chose Madame Dacier to be one of its members. Like Anna Maria van Schurman, Dacier served as a model for later female scholars. In 1712 the British scholar Dr. George Hickes cited her as an outstanding example of female scholarship and compared the work of Elizabeth Elstob (1683 - 1756), his own protégé, with her achievements:

> I suppose you may have seen Mrs. Elstob. . . . The publication of the MSS. she hath brought (the most correct I ever saw or read) will be . . . the credit of our country, to which Mrs. Elstob will be counted abroad, as great an ornament in her way as Madame Dacier is in France (British Museum, Harl. MS. 7524, n.45).

Elizabeth Elstob, author of the first Anglo-Saxon grammar in English, was familiar with and admired the work of her Dutch predecessor Anna Maria van Schurman, referring critics of her work to Schurman's defense of female scholarship. The descendants of former pupils of Bathsua Makin were among the subscribers to the works of Elstob. One of them, Lady Elizabeth Hastings, tried to relieve the poverty of the great Anglo-Saxon scholar by offering her a position as headmistress of a female charity school which she sponsored.

INTELLECTUAL MODELS

Less information survives from the Middle Ages and the early Renaissance, making it more difficult to trace fully the connections among learned women.

Even in the absence of a well-defined tradition, however, there are fascinating indications of literary and social influence. Marguerite de Navarre (1492 - 1549) supplied a model of learning and piety to a whole generation of women who followed her. Elizabeth I of England translated one of Marguerite's devotional works while she was acquiring the knowledge of languages which was to make her, like Marguerite, a queen famous for her learning.

A little-known Spanish writer, Maria de Zayas y Sotomayor (1590?–1661?), whose works have not yet been translated into English, was probably influenced by the *Heptaméron* (1549) of Marguerite de Navarre. Maria de Zayas, in turn, may have influenced the French writer of a later generation, Madame de Lafayette. Madame de Lafayette, author of *La Princesse de Clèves* (1678), was the closest friend of Madame de Sévigné (1626 - 1696), the great correspondent, whose letters provide a social history of her age.

While the existence of a large correspondence makes it easy to document the friendship of Abigail Adams and Mercy Otis Warren (1728 - 1814), there are other kinds of connections and influence that are more difficult to assess. It is possible that respect for female learning became a tradition in certain families. Caterina (Cornaro) Corner (1454? - 1510) received her early education at a Benedictine Convent in Padua. Later, in his *Gli Asolani* her kinsman Pietro Bembo portrayed Caterina as the gracious ruler of a court circle distinguished by learning and culture. It was a descendant of the Corner family who became the first woman to receive a university degree. On 25 June 1678 the Venetian Elena Lucrezia Cornaro Piscopia was awarded a degree by the University of Padua. Tempting as the possibility of a connection is, it would be very difficult to document. Moreover, if the tradition of educating women passed from mother to daughter and the mother's family name was not preserved, evidence of a tradition would soon be lost unless every generation produced a famous female scholar.

Two women considered in this collection emphasize their own isolation. Christine de Pisan (1364 - 1430?), whose works were very popular in her own day, successfully functioned as a professional writer, but her writings indicate that she regarded herself as an isolated phenomenon. Likewise, Sor Juana Inés de la Cruz (1651 - 1695), an important figure in Spanish and Latin American literary tradition, describes herself in her autobiography as a scholar without a teacher and a student without fellow scholars. In these and other instances, it may be premature to accept a woman's expressed feelings of

3

isolation as demonstrable fact unless we have a detailed knowledge of her social milieu.

SOCIAL TRENDS AND INDIVIDUAL ACHIEVEMENT

The impact of religious movements and of socioeconomic trends upon women who lived before 1800 is increasingly a matter of debate. On the one hand, it is suggested that the Protestant Reformation adversely affected a strong tradition of female learning existing in the Middle Ages and administered through the Roman Catholic convent schools. On the other hand, it is also argued that the development of Protestantism stimulated vernacular translations of the Bible, placing increased emphasis upon literacy and so opening new doors for women as well as men of the less privileged classes. An earlier view, that one of the glories of the Renaissance was that women and men enjoyed equal status, is being questioned by those who doubt that there was a renaissance for women.

It may be easier, in fact, to identify trends than it will be to assess and interpret the impact of social and economic change on individual achievement. This is certainly true of learned women. This study suggests as many questions as it answers. Perhaps the single most interesting question raised by these essays is—what motivated these women to engage in intellectual pursuits? It is tempting to consider what family circumstances produced them and what historical factors influenced their development or thwarted their promise. Tantalizing as such questions are, generalizations are difficult and possibly misleading. The majority of these women, for example, were widowed while still relatively young or else remained single, but since the majority of gifted unmarried women did not become scholars, marital status does not by itself explain the achievements of these women.

Similarly, we would expect the percentage of learned aristocratic women to be much greater than that of middle or lower class women. Even to the logical expectation that class and economic status would be significant, there are notable exceptions: Christine de Pisan supported herself and her family by her scholarship; Bathsua Makin and Elizabeth Elstob came from what we would today call middle-class backgrounds.

4

DEFINING SCHOLARSHIP

Supposing that sufficient data survive for a reliable study of the effects of sex, marital status, and class on female scholarship, there is the additional problem of defining what is meant by "scholar." The English "Bluestockings," who were perceived as cultivated by their contemporaries, were certainly gifted, but were they in every case scholars? The lack of a term for learned women, parallel to the common use of "gentleman scholar" and "man of letters" for men, underlines the difficulty of this kind of study.

There was never a widespread acceptance of "lady scholar"; the term itself sounds awkward. The roughly equivalent expression was probably "bluestocking," and yet, according to the *Oxford English Dictionary*, it was coined to refer to men and then used for women. During the late eighteenth century and increasingly in the nineteenth, to be a "bluestocking" was to be suspiciously unfeminine. It was used as a derogatory term to describe the affectation of learning and to refer to women who were careless in dress, neglectful of domestic chores—in short to refer to women who were not fulfilling a traditional social role. Even William Hazlitt, himself a "gentleman scholar," was to use the term pejoratively, announcing: "I have an utter aversion to *bluestockings*. I do not care a fig for any woman who even knows what an *author* means" (*Table Talk*, II, VII, 168).

There were times and places in which female learning was more encouraged than others, but the woman scholar was for the most part an oddity, labeled "unnatural" as frequently by women as men. In spite of this prejudice against learned women, there are a surprising number of "sleeping giants." The dilemma of the scholar interested in learned women who lived before the nineteenth century is not that there are too few names, but that so little biographical information is readily accessible. Johan van Beverwijck's work on Anna Maria van Schurman and George Ballard's biographies of learned British women are of assistance to the modern scholar, but the endless catalogs of famous and infamous women in the works of Christine de Pisan, Boccaccio, Chaucer, and others tell us little.

Although this collection suggests that there was an international tradition, the picture presented here is far from complete. There are notable and numerous omissions, ranging from Christine of Sweden to the English Mary Sidney, Countess of Pembroke; from the Italian Nogarola Isotta to the French scientist and metaphysician Madame du Châtelet; from the German Olympia Morata to the Canadian Marie de l'Incarnation. Studies of these and many other women are needed if we are to understand fully the status, achievements, and circumstances of women who lived before 1800.

J.R. Brink
Arizona State University
December 1979

CHRISTINE DE PISAN: FIRST PROFESSIONAL WOMAN OF LETTERS (1364–1430?)

LESLIE ALTMAN

The scholar investigating the position of women in the Middle Ages quickly discovers that the evidence is inconclusive, even self-contradictory. What evidence exists—legal documents, manuals of behavior, literary portrayals—refers primarily to women of the upper classes and so excludes from consideration the vast majority of medieval women. Even for the upper classes, variations in time, from the twelfth to the fifteenth centuries, and in locale make generalization difficult. Theoretical discussions of the position of women by theologians present another difficulty. Among clerics, two mutually exclusive ideas seem to have existed simultaneously, antifeminism and woman worship: on the one hand, woman is despised in the person of Eve; on the other, she is exalted in the person of Mary.

One common thread in both religious and secular writings is the notion that woman is fundamentally different from man, either far better or far worse. This view of woman as an alien being may be a result of the phenomenon about which Chaucer's Wife of Bath complains, the men wrote the books:

> By God! if wommen hadde writen stories,
> As clerkes han withinne hire oratories,
> They wolde han writen of men moore wikkednesse
> Than al the mark of Adam may redresse.[1]

There are, of course, exceptions. The *lais* of Marie de France survive, as do the letters of Héloise, the troubadour poetry of Beatrice de Die, the autobiographical accounts of mystics, such as Dame Julian of Norwich and Margery

7

Kempe, and other religious writings by learned nuns.[2] One writer stands out because she supported herself and her family by her pen: Christine de Pisan (1364 - 1430?), one of the most prolific secular writers of the period and the unique professional woman writer.

The study of Christine's life and works provides some direct evidence regarding the position of women in the Middle Ages. Unfortunately, the general reader is faced with some formidable difficulties. She has written two major works concerned with women, *Le Livre de la Cité des Dames* and *Le Livre des Trois Vertus*, but both are still in manuscript.[3] Some of Christine's work has been translated into English, but these translations date from the fifteenth and early sixteenth centuries. Bryan Anslay's translation of *La Cité des Dames* in 1521, called *The Boke of the Cyte of Ladyes*, is difficult to locate, and its Gothic print is not easy for the non-specialist to decipher.[4] Nevertheless, the struggle is rewarding. Christine's works provide fresh insight from a uniquely female perspective into the actual social position of women in France at the end of the fourteenth century; both *La Cité des Dames* and *Le Livre des Trois Vertus* deserve attention as sources of specific and practical information about the lives of women of all classes. Her success as a professional writer is also testimony to the possibilities open to a woman of ability.

Christine's writings, unlike those of most medieval writers, provide a substantial amount of information about her own life. Two works, *Le Livre de la Mutacion de Fortune* and *La Vision-Christine*,[5] provide autobiographical accounts, probably designed in part to inform patrons of her background. Christine was born in Venice in 1364, the first child of Tommaso da Pizzano, later gallicized to Thomas de Pizan or Pisan. Thomas himself was probably born at Pizzano near Bologna, where he studied medicine and theology at the University and where he may have taught.[6] He married the daughter of Tommaso di Mondini, Councillor of the Republic of Venice, and at the time of Christine's birth in 1364, Thomas de Pisan was himself a Councillor in Venice. That same year Charles V of France invited Thomas to serve his court as astrologer and physician. Thomas returned his wife and infant daughter to Bologna, and five years later in 1369 he transported them to Paris to be with him.

Christine lived with her parents at the court of Charles V for ten years. No record exists of her having had any formal education during this period: the court, however, would have been intellectually stimulating and a center of culture because Charles was a learned man who surrounded himself with men of intellect. It was during this period that Jean, Duke of Berry, brother of the king, began his famous collection of works of art.[7]

Christine wrote of her early life that although her mother did not believe in education for women, her father enjoyed her quickness of mind and did not discourage her from reading. He did not educate her as he would have educated a son, but her education was superior to what a female would usually receive. In *Le Livre de la Mutacion de Fortune* Christine objects to the custom of not educating women:

> Plus par coustume que par droit.
> Se droit regnoit, riens n'y perdroit
> La femmelle, ne que le filz (ll. 419-21).

That is, if right rather than custom prevailed, neither the daughter nor the son would lose the chance to be educated.

In 1379 at the age of fifteen Christine was married to Etienne du Castel, who at the time served Charles V as secretary. When the king died the following year, Etienne continued to serve the new king, Charles VI, in the same capacity. Thomas de Pisan, however, lost his influence at court and with it his regular income. Christine's parents and her two younger brothers became dependent on her husband. In addition, in 1381 Christine gave birth to the first of three children, a daughter. Two sons followed, one of whom probably died young, as only his birth is noted.[8] The youngest child, Jean, was born in 1385. Then in 1389, while on a trip to Beauvais with the king, Etienne became ill and died, leaving her at twenty-five without support for her three young children; since her father had also died, her mother and two younger brothers were likewise dependent on her.

Christine's situation would be difficult in any time. Furthermore, in trying to settle her husband's affairs she lacked an advisor or patron to consult; instead she was faced with an indifferent or even hostile court administration. Three pages of *La Vision-Christine* are devoted to men who counting on her ignorance of her husband's affairs and perhaps her naiveté and grief tried to deceive her.[9] Responsible court officials were less interested in the financial problems of one family than in the growing instability of the French state. Christine, once respected as the daughter of the famous astrologer-physician, was forced to apply for favor in a public manner and thus expose herself to the rudeness and scorn of the court. She lost some of her possessions,

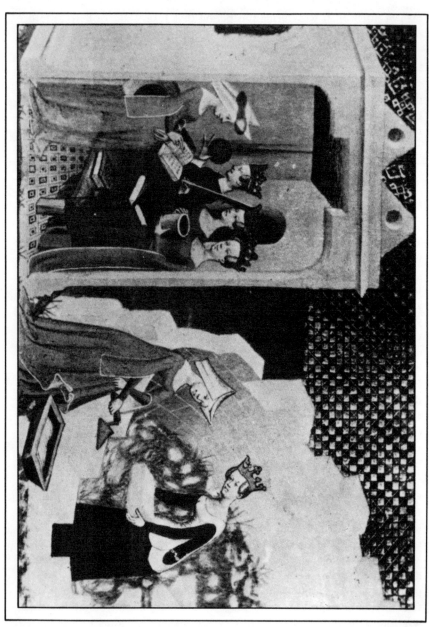

Christine is pictured reading, visited by the Trois Vertus (left); and helping Raison to build the walls of the Cité des Dames (right).

10

borrowed money, and was finally obliged to bring lawsuits to recover her inheritance.

The experience of being a woman in a man's world seems to have affected Christine's attitudes about the role of women in society. During this period of domestic, legal, and financial difficulties, she turned to writing; her earliest poems are written during the period following her husband's death. In a long poem (23, 636 lines) begun in 1400 and finished in 1403, *Le Livre de la Mutacion de Fortune*, Christine describes how her happiness ended with her husband's death and how Fortune turned her into a man so that she could fend for herself:

> . . . de femelle devins masle
> Par Fortune, qu'ainsy le voult;
> Si me mua et corps et coult
> En homme naturel parfaict,
> Et jadis fus femme, de fait
> Homme suis, je ne ment pas,
> Assez le demonstrent mes pas (ll. 142-48)

> [. . . from female I became male
> By Fortune, who wanted it thus;
> So (she) changed me, both body and will,
> Into a natural, perfect man;
> Formerly, I was a woman; now
> I am a man, I do not lie,
> My stride demonstrates it well enough.]

That Christine believed her ability to survive depended upon a "mutation" from woman to man testifies to the prevailing social attitudes about women, particularly the view that women were physically weak and subordinate to men, an assumption Christine shared.

Le Livre de la Mutacion de Fortune also provides evidence that Christine had embarked on a wide-ranging program of self-education. After an autobiographical introduction, *Le Livre* becomes a compendium of information, beginning with a description of the castle of Fortune and its inhabitants, a description which includes the famous men of the period, among them Richard II of England and the nobility of France. The poem then considers the branches of learning and the history of the world from the Creation to the present, concluding with descriptions of Edward III of England, Charles V and Charles

VI of France, and her patron, Louis, Duke of Orléans, brother of Charles VI. Christine emphasizes the instability of Fortune and the error of men who put their faith in things of this world, repeating a theme that runs through medieval literature.[10] Her suggestion, however, that Fortune can alter one's sexual identity seems unique.

The variety of Christine's sources in this poem is evidence of her learning. Christine's biographer Marie-Josèphe Pinet has disparaged her, stating that although one is first impressed by the bulk of the learning from history, mythology, and philosophy, gradually one comes to realize that "Christine had read much, retained quite a lot, but not always understood her authorities."[11] Pinet's analysis of sources further suggests that Christine knew little Latin and no Greek, and that with the possible exception of Boethius she read most of her Latin sources in French translations, such as Guillaume de Tignonville's *Diz des Philosophes*. According to Pinet, her chief contribution to the advancement of learning was her recommendation in *Le Livre de Prudence* that her readers read Dante.

Whatever the extent of her classical learning, hers was a remarkable achievement in self-education. Christine made use of whatever books were available—those she inherited from her father and her husband as well as those she could use at the Louvre, which at that time contained over 1200 volumes. In addition, Jean Gerson, Chancellor of the University of Paris, who supported her in her attack on *Le Roman de la Rose*, might well have allowed her to use the University collection.[12] Two miniatures in one manuscript of *Le Livre des Trois Vertus* are evidence of her public image. In each she is surrounded by books: the first shows her in her library, holding a book in her hand with a dozen or more books visible; the second shows her asleep in her study with half a dozen books behind her.[13]

As a professional writer, she was unquestionably successful. The variety and quality of extant manuscripts have led A.T.P. Byles, who edited Caxton's translation of her book on chivalry, *Le Livre des Faits d'Armes et de Chevalerie* to conclude:

> So great was the demand for copies of her works by the wealthy nobles of France and Burgundy that she never appears to have found any difficulty in supporting herself and her family by her pen. The sumptuous manuscripts of *Le Livre des Faits d'Armes* . . . are an obvious indication of her renown.[14]

Her poetry was also well-known in England. The Lancastrian Henry IV invited Christine to live at his court. The most popular of her works in her own day, *L'Epistre d'Othéa, la déesse, à Hector*, was translated into English three times in the century after its publication. The Yorkist Anthony Woodville, Earl of Rivers, brother-in-law to Edward IV, translated Christine's *Enseignments Moraux* and *Proverbes Moraux*, which were printed together in 1478 by Caxton as *The Morale Proverbes of Christine*.[15]

It is not an easy thing to assess historically the nature of this remarkable woman's achievements. Recent "revisionist" interpretations of the Middle Ages have suggested that this was "the last period in which women enjoyed lives that were nearly parallel to those of men," but this conclusion seems to ignore an important phenomenon of the period, the antifeminist rhetoric of the church.[16] For the early Church Fathers the problems with women began with Genesis. Because Eve was made from Adam's rib, it followed that woman was an afterthought, that she was created to help man, and that she was made in man's image, not God's. Furthermore, the Fall suggested woman's moral weakness and her disastrous effect on man. This negative view of woman was confirmed by Old Testament stories of evil women (Lot's wife, Potiphar's wife, Jezebel) and of weak men construed as victims of women (Samson, David, Solomon).

The New Testament added to the implicit warning about the dangers of women a disparagement of sexual relations in general and marriage in particular. The doctrines of Saint Paul, especially in 1 Corinthians 7, 11, and 13, and Ephesians 5 and 22, form the foundations of the medieval Christian view of women. Paul held that marriage was inferior to virginity and that the husband was head of his wife as Christ was head of the Church, an analogy which suggested that when a woman disobeyed her husband, she sinned. The early Church Fathers, basing their commentaries on Paul, wrote not only that marriage is inferior to virginity, but also that sexual intercourse is justified only in marriage and only within marriage when it is directed toward the begetting of children, or when it has the effect of keeping the spouse from seeking illicit relationships. Some commentators suggested that without the Fall there would have been no sexual intercourse, viewing sexual desire as part of the punishment for the sin of Adam and Eve. The orthodox view was articulated by St. John Chrysostom: "a necessary evil, a natural temptation, a desirable calamity, a domestic peril, a deadly fascination and a painted ill."[17] For one who had taken a vow of celibacy, no doubt the definition approached accuracy. Further evidence of the Church's negative view of women can be found in

13

developing institutional practices: women were considered unfit to receive the sacrament with uncovered heads; they were forbidden to be priests; and priestly celibacy was institutionalized at the Lateran Council of 1215.

Accompanying and perhaps mitigating this developing antifeminism was another phenomenon, an awakening interest in the Virgin Mary. Beginning in the twelfth century, Mary was more frequently represented in poetry and in the visual arts; tales of miracles of the Virgin became increasingly popular; and she became known as the Queen of Heaven, operating on a more sympathetic and emotional level than Father, Son, and Holy Spirit. Despite orthodox objections (Aquinas insisted that Mary was conceived in sin and redeemed by her Son) the events of the Virgin's life were celebrated as festivals and began to play an important part in Church ritual. The effect of this development upon the status of women in the secular world is difficult to assess. Marina Warner has suggested that "in the very celebration of the perfect human woman, both humanity and women were subtly denigrated."[18] Difficult as it is to weigh the relative influence of the antifeminist rhetoric and of the idealization of Mary, one area of sexual egalitarianism conceded by the Church is a surprise to post-Victorian moderns: women's sexual needs were thought to be as compelling as those of men. The medieval theory of sexuality was that both men and women were driven toward sexual relations by their physiology. Although such a concession would not raise the status of women, medieval women may have been free to behave more naturally than their Victorian counterparts.

Two secular traditions, the codes of courtly love and chivalry, may also have affected the status of women. The idea of a code of courtly love was first proposed in 1883 by Gaston Paris, who based his analysis on Chrétien de Troyes' tale of *Le Chevalier de la Charette* (c. 1170), on troubadour love poetry, and on the book of Andreas Capellanus called *De Arte Honeste Amandi* (c. 1185).[19] In essence these works suggest that there existed in the Middle Ages a code of behavior for lovers based on three principles: that love is a wonderful kind of suffering; that love increases the virtue of the lover, particularly by service to his lady; and that love cannot exist between husband and wife because of the compulsion implied by the marriage contract. Whether the code of courtly love reflects actual practice (whether, in fact, Andreas' book is even partially serious) is not clear.[20] The number of courtly lovers we find in medieval literature, Troilus and Criseyde, Lancelot and Guinevere, Tristan and Isolde, to name the most famous examples, suggests that courtly love, by exalting the ennobling effect of romantic love, may have worked against antifeminist rhetoric.

Similarly, the code of chivalry, which seems to have evolved in the eleventh and twelfth centuries as a restraint on the barbarism of knightly warfare, may have counteracted the disparagement of women by emphasizing the virtues of courtesy to ladies and protection of the weak. Because of their exaggerated devotion to the ideal of womanhood, one suspects, however, that these codes of behavior were probably as irrelevant to medieval women as the disputations of celibate monks. Neither code was intended to affect the relationship between husband and wife, the most significant of all relationships for most women; nor did either code concern itself with women of the lower classes.

For this reason manuals of behavior written for actual women are of particular importance, and it is interesting to compare the manuals written by men for women in their households with the works of Christine, who supplies a female perspective. Two well-known examples, contemporary with Christine, are the book of advice to his young wife by the Ménagerie de Paris (c. 1329-94) and the book of advice to his three daughters by Geoffrey de la Tour-Landry (1371).[21] Both works emphasize obedience to her spouse as the chief wifely virtue. The Knight of the Tour-Landry heartily recommends wife-beating as a cure for disobedience: in order to teach his daughters the importance of obedience, he tells two stories of women who were permanently disfigured by broken noses inflicted by justly annoyed husbands. Both authors assume that women are weaker than men and that they must be protected, even if protection entails force. Because of their moral weakness women should be sheltered from the corrupting influence of commerce with the world; because of their intellectual weakness they must also be kept ignorant to preserve their innocence. Both books, however, are directed to women of the upper classes; the pictures that they give are incomplete. Even so, they are probably more realistic than those we receive from medieval romances and Church doctrine.

In contrast to these two works written by men for women are the works Christine wrote with the explicit purpose of defending, describing, or teaching women. Her earliest work specifically concerned with women is a poem entitled *L'Epistre du Dieu d'Amour* (1399), later paraphrased by Thomas Hoccleve as *The Letter of Cupid* (1402).[22] The poem is an attack on antifeminist writers, written in the form of a king's reply to a public request—a form Christine would have known from direct experience. Cupid, King of Love, in response to a request from all gentle ladies, admonishes the writers who speak ill of women. The two antifeminist writers Christine specifically attacks are Ovid for the *Ars Amatoria* and Jean de Meun for *Le Roman de la Rose*. *L'Epistre du Dieu d'Amour* chooses a middle ground between the exaggerated attacks and defenses that are typical of the period.[23] Basing her discussion on logic and common sense, Christine makes a series of valid and clever points. She begins by arguing that it is ignorant, rude, and ungrateful to condemn women, as all men are given birth, nourished, and buried by women. She insists that one should not generalize that all women are evil because a few are: because Satan fell, are all angels evil? Arguing against the antifeminist writers, she says that Ovid's *Art of Love* should be called the "Art of Deception." She points out that if women are weak-willed and unstable of affection, as Ovid suggests, then it should not have been necessary for him to write an entire book instructing men on how to deceive them. Regarding *Le Roman de la Rose* and other antifeminist works she says:

> . . . les livres ne firent
> Pas les femmes, ne les choses n'i mirent
> Que l'en y list contre elles et leurs meurs;
> . . .
> Mais se femmes eussent les livres fait
> Je scay de vray qu'autrement fust du tait. (ll. 409-10, 418-19).

> [Women did not write the books
> Nor put the things in them
> That one reads there against them and their morals;
> . . .
> but if women had written the books
> I truly know they would have done otherwise.]

Like Geoffrey Chaucer, who portrayed the Wife of Bath as making the same observation, Christine is aware that men do not always present a reliable view of the other sex.

Christine is equally eloquent when she describes the role of women in Christian history. She notes that women did not betray Christ, as the Apostles did, that Christ himself was born of woman, and that Mary sits on the left hand of God, next to her Son. She also writes a lawyerlike brief for the defense of Eve, arguing that Eve did not deceive Adam because she did not intend to deceive Adam; rather she disobeyed God, as Adam did, as nearly all of us do daily. The learned Isotta Nogarola of Verona was later to take up the same issue in the fifteenth century.

16

L'Epistre du Dieu d'Amour is an early foray into "feminist" polemics, leading directly to the public debate over the morality of Jean de Meun's *Le Roman de la Rose* in 1401.[24] The evidence of the debate, which was essentially an exchange of letters, suggests that by 1401 Christine was sufficiently well-established as a professional writer to defend publicly the female sex against antifeminist clerks, in particular Jean de Meun, the "true catholic, solemn master, doctor in theology, and excellent philosopher," as one of her opponents described him.[25]

In 1405 Christine produced the two works that are of particular interest to the modern reader: *Le Livre de la Cité des Dames* and *Le Trésor de la Cité des Dames* or *Le Livre des Trois Vertus*. According to Pinet, Christine wrote these two works because she was again near financial ruin, and, since the death of Philip, Duke of Burgundy, without a patron. Pinet further suggests that the feminine subject of these two works is designed to appeal to potential female patronesses. *La Cité des Dames* has no dedication but does mention all the great ladies of the court: Isabelle, the queen; and the wives of the Dukes of Burgundy, Berry, and Bourbon. *Le Livres des Trois Vertus* is dedicated to the wife of the Dauphin, the Duchess of Guienne. Whatever her precise motivation for writing them, because of the breadth of subject matter, Christine, in effect, offers these works to women of all classes.

The first book, *Le Livre de la Cité des Dames*, is a dream vision: the poet herself is reading the *Lamentations of Matheolus*, an antifeminist tract, and wondering why clerks write evil of women. Christine falls into a reverie which is interrupted by three allegorical ladies, who appear to her in a ray of light and command her to help them build a city for women who are without defense and without champions. The three figures are Reason, Righteousness (or Integrity), and Justice. Reason will build the foundations and the walls; Integrity will build the houses, palaces, and temples; and Justice will build the towers, battlements, and gates: that is, the City of Ladies will be built by Reason, peopled by Integrity, and defended by Justice. The book has three sections, each ostensibly concerned with building parts of the city, but actually consisting of Christine's conversations with each of the three allegorical personages in turn. In each section Christine asks questions about women, and the allegorical figure responds with explanations and illustrative *exempla*.

Christine begins, for example, by asking Reason how men and women differ. Reason's answer is, as one might expect, logical: women have weaker bodies, but nature compensates them for their physical weakness by making their spirits, and therefore their moral sensibilities, more refined than those of men. The body is not the source of virtue; reason is. Some of God's creatures are more inclined to reason and thence to virtue than others. Christine pursues this issue and asks Reason if God ever made a woman so noble as to achieve a higher understanding of philosophical matters. Reason responds that experience of diverse things is the greatest teacher and that because women have almost exclusively domestic experience, they have little knowledge of higher or abstract learning. Learning is difficult; some are quicker than others, but sex is *not* determinative.[26]

The first section of *La Cité des Dames* argues for women's natural capabilities; the second attempts to educate women by means of examples of righteousness; the third is essentially a history of famous women and their contributions to society. The bulk of all three sections is devoted to retelling the stories of famous women and in this respect *La Cité des Dames* resembles Boccaccio's *De claris mulieribus* and Chaucer's *Legend of Good Women*; from the former many of the stories are drawn.[27] Christine uses two contemporary women as prime examples of women's capabilities: Novella of Bologna and Anastaise. The first of these was the daughter of Johannes Andrea, a teacher at the University of Bologna. Novella was so learned that she taught her father's students in his absence, but she did so behind a veil, so that her beauty would not distract the students. The second, Anastaise, was a skillful illuminator of manuscripts, the most successful at her craft in her time. Christine mentions that she herself used Anastaise's talents, paying a high price for her illuminations. *La Cité des Dames* also includes mythological examples of women's learning and craftmanship, among others Nichostrate, inventor of the Latin alphabet and grammar, and Minerva, inventor of armor.

Christine's conviction that women should be educated, already mentioned in *Le Livre de la Mutacion de Fortune*, is reiterated in *La Cité des Dames*. Here she insists that women are as capable of being taught as men and therefore have an equal right to be taught. If one customarily put girls in school and taught them the arts and sciences, as one does with boys, she writes, then they would learn as well as boys. Their bodies may be weaker, but their attention is greater when it is applied.[28] *La Cité des Dames*, however, is not feminist propaganda. Christine's "feminism" is grounded in medieval philosophy: women are different from men. Each sex has its task and performs its duties according to its nature and its inclination as well as according to custom. She believes that because men are more powerful than women, they alone have the strength to execute the laws. Since by custom women cannot appear in

18

public except discreetly, women have no role in government nor in public life; both custom and nature forbid it. Even so, Christine acknowledges that the work of men and women is not always distinguishable and goes so far as to praise women who do men's work better than men do.[29]

Le Trésor de la Cité des Dames, or *Le Livre des Trois Vertus*, the second of the books devoted to women, is divided into three sections, but in this case the division follows a social hierarchy: the first book is devoted to the high aristocracy, princesses and noble ladies; the second, to women who live at court; the third, to women of the towns, bourgeoisie, commons, and laboring classes. The first section forms more than half of the book. Since *Le Livre des Trois Vertus* is dedicated to the Dauphine, its emphasis on the aristocracy is logical, but its inclusion of all classes seems to be unique. Rather than considering the rights of the husband, Christine is concerned with those of wives. Her advice to a wife married to a bad husband is to be quiet about her problem in order to avoid injury to the husband's reputation and thence to the wife's. If the husband is unfaithful, the wife should ignore the infidelity and try to make herself more attractive to him, for the sake of his soul and his reputation, and especially for the good name of the children. She stresses as well the importance of a woman learning to function as the head of the household in the case of the temporary absence or death of her husband. Her own bitter experience following her husband's death had taught her the dangers of ignorance of worldly affairs.

Because *Le Livre des Trois Vertus* is a didactic work of practical advice, the education of women is discussed as a practical matter.[30] She insists that it is vital to teach women to calculate so that they can keep their household accounts properly. The experience of virtually uninterrupted warfare during her lifetime had demonstrated the importance of a woman learning as much as possible about defending the manor in the case of attack. The education of a woman should teach her feudal law, estate management, household management and budgeting, medicine, farming, crop management, marketing and labor relations.[31] Although women might have neither public rights nor responsibilities, *Le Livre des Trois Vertus* suggests that in practice women of all classes were often equally responsible with men for the operations of daily life.

In her last known work, *Le Dittié de Jehanne d'Arc*, Christine returns to the subject of women. Composed in 1429, the year of Joan's triumph over the English, the poem is religious in tone, praising God for having provided a sixteen-year-old girl from Arc as an instrument to deliver France from its enemies and its internal political problems. In its concern for the political situation of France and in its obvious delight that France was destined to be saved by a woman, *Le Dittié de Jehanne d'Arc* is a fitting conclusion to the work of Christine de Pisan:

Hee! quel honneur au femenin
Sexe! Que Dieu l'ayme il appert,
Quant tout ce grant peuple chenin,
Par qui tout le regne est desert,
Par femme est sours et recouvert,
Ce que C^m hommes fait n'eussent,
Et les traictres mis a desert!
A peine devant ne le creussent.

[Oh! What honour for the female sex! It is perfectly obvious that God has special regard for it when all these wretched people who destroyed a whole kingdom—now recovered and made safe by a woman, something 5000 men could not have done—and the traitors [have been] exterminated. Before the event they would scarcely have believed this possible.

Une fillete de XVI ans
(N'est-ce pas chose fors nature?),
A qui armes ne sont pesans,
Ains semble que sa norriture
Y soit, tant y est fort et dure!
Et devant elle vont fuyant
Les ennemis, ne nul n'y dure.
Elle fait ce, mains yeulx voient.

A little girl of 16 (is not this something quite supernatural?) who does not even notice the weight of the arms she bears—indeed her whole upbringing seems to have prepared her for this, so strong and resolute is she! And her enemies go fleeing before her, not one of them can stand up to her. She does this in full view of everyone.][32]

In spite of the admiration, even pride, this medieval woman experienced at the achievement of Joan of Arc, her works remain products of the medieval world, based on assumptions regarding differences between the sexes which do not readily lend themselves to a revival by modern feminists. The works of Christine de Pisan assume that each individual has a purpose, a social and political destiny determined by sex. Her contemporary Eustache Deschamps praised her "virility," and a modern French critic has even called her the first female "man of letters."[33] Significantly, and perhaps ironically, she either saw her own career as dependent on her "mutation" from woman to man or realized the necessity of presenting it in this light to her contemporaries. Christine's works and her success as a writer, nevertheless, suggest that the experience of medieval women may have been different from the images derived from literature and theology, and for this reason reexamination of her works should be of value.[34]

In assessing her contribution to female learning, it is important to remember that those seventeenth-century female scholars who followed Christine—the Dutch Anna Maria van Schurman, English Bathsua Makin, and Mexican Sor Juana Inés de la Cruz—also qualified their advocacy of female learning by excluding women from public life. Her works and her example served to inspire these and other women, who, like Christine, would define themselves as scholars and intellectuals and who would, as did this medieval woman, transcend social and personal circumstances to insist that education by right, if not by custom, belonged to both sexes.

NOTES

[1] Wife of Bath's Prologue, ll. 693-96, from *The Works of Geoffrey Chaucer*, ed. F.N. Robinson, 2nd ed. (Boston: Houghton Mifflin, 1957).

[2] For useful general discussions of the position of women, see Eileen Power, "The Position of Women," in *The Legacy of the Middle Ages*, ed. G.C. Crump and E.F. Jacob (Oxford: Clarendon, 1926); Doris Mary Stenton, *The English Woman in History* (London: Allen & Unwin, 1957); and Eileen Power, *Medieval Women*, ed. M.M. Postan (Cambridge, England: Cambridge University Press, 1975).

[3] Susan Groag Bell, *Feminist Studies*, 3 (1976), 184, n. 3, reports that an edition of *Le Livre de la Cité des Dames* by Monika Lange, University of Hamburg, is forthcoming; Charity Cannon Willard, Ladycliff College, is editing *Le Livre des Trois Vertus*.

[4] Bryan Anslay's book is available in the British Library; it is being edited by Maureen Cheney-Curnow, University of Montana.

[5] *Le Livre de la Mutacion de Fortune, par Christine de Pisan*, ed. Suzanne Solente, 5 vols. (Paris: Société des Anciens Textes Francais, 1959); *Lavision-Christine*, ed. Sister Mary Louise Towner (Washington, D.C.: Catholic Univ. of America, 1932). Citations to these works are in the text. Translations are my own unless otherwise indicated in the notes.

[6] See Enid McLeod, *The Order of the Rose: The Life and Ideas of Christine de Pizan* (Totowa, N.J.: Rowman and Littlefield, 1976), pp. 13ff. for information on Thomas de Pisan.

[7] Suzanne Solente, *Christine de Pisan, Extrait de L'Histoire Littéraire de la France* (Paris: Imprimerie Nationale, 1969), XL, 9.

[8] Marie-Josèphe Pinet, *Christine de Pisan (1364-1430): Etude Biographique et Littéraire* (Paris: H. Champion, 1927), p. 49.

[9] Ibid., p. 25.

[10] See Howard R. Patch, *The Goddess Fortuna in Mediaeval Literature* (Cambridge, Mass.: Harvard University Press, 1927), for a discussion of the theme of Fortune.

[11] Pinet, p. 435. For another view of Christine's scholarship and her use of sources, see P.G.C. Campbell, *L'Epistre d'Othéa: Etude sur les Sources de Christine de Pisan* (The Hague: Mouton, 1958).

[12] On the books to which Christine would have had access, see McLeod, pp. 77-78, and Pinet, pp. 32ff.

[13] Bibliothèque Royale de Belgique, MS. 9236, reproduced in Mathilde Laigle, *"Le Livre des Trois Vertus" de Christine de Pisan et son Milieu Historique et Littéraire* (Paris: H. Champion, 1912).

[14] *The Book of Fayttes of Armes and of Chyvalrye*, 2nd ed., EETS, O.S. 189 (London, 1937), p. xii.

[15] According to Enid McLeod (p. 177, n.3), this translation by Rivers was reprinted in a limited edition by William Blades in 1859.

[16] *The Female Spectator: English Women Writers Before 1800*, ed. Mary R. Mahl and Helene Koon (Old Westbury, New York: Feminist Press, 1977), p. 5. For analysis of an extreme antifeminist, see J.N.D. Kell, *Jerome: His Life, Writings, and Controversies* (New York: Harper and Row, 1975), pp. 179-94. For a more liberal view, see R.B. Tollinton, *Clement of Alexandria: A Study in Christian Liberalism* (London: Williams and Norgate, 1914), pp. 270-302. For a general discussion of clerical antifeminism and its roots, see Carolly Erickson, *The Medieval Vision: Essays in History and Perception* (Oxford: Oxford University Press, 1976), pp. 189ff.

[17] Quoted in Vern L. Bullough, *The Subordinate Sex: A History of Attitudes Toward Women* (Urbana: University of Illinois Press, 1973), p. 188.

[18] Marina Warner, *Alone of All Her Sex: The Myth and the Cult of the Virgin Mary* (New York: Alfred Knopf, 1976), p. xxi.

[19] Gaston Paris, "La Conte de la Charette," *Romania*, 12 (1883), 459-534.

[20] For a reexamination of courtly love, see *The Meaning of Courtly Love*, ed. F. X. Newman, Papers of the First Annual Conference of the Center for Medieval and Early Renaissance Studies, 17-18 March 1967 (Albany, N.Y., 1968).

[21] *The Goodman of Paris*, trans. Eileen Power (London: G. Routledge & Sons, 1928) and *The Book of the Knight of the Tour-Landry*, trans. Thomas

Wright, EETS, O.S. 33 (London, 1868).

[22] *The Letter of Cupid to Lovers, His Subjects*, in *Hoccleve's Works*, ed. Frederick J. Furnivall, EETS, E.S. 61 (London, 1892-1925), pp. 72-92 and 243-49. For extracts from Christine's text, see also EETS, E.S. 73, pp. 20-34.

[23] For an excellent study of medieval satire and defense of women, see Frances Lee Utley, *The Crooked Rib: An Analytical Index to the Argument about Women in English and Scots Literature to the End of the Year 1568* (1944; rpt. New York: Octagon, 1970).

[24] On the quarrel over *Le Roman de la Rose*, see Ernest Langlois, "Le Traité de Gerson contre *Le Roman de la Rose*," *Romania*, 45 (1918-1919), 23-48; and C.F. Ward, "The Epistles of the *Romance of the Rose* and Other Documents of the Debate" Diss. University of Chicago 1911.

[25] Quoted in McLeod, p. 66.

[26] See Rose Rigaud, *Les Idées Feministes de Christine de Pisan* (Neuchatel: Imprimerie Attinger Frères, 1911), p. 97.

[27] For Christine's debt to Boccaccio, see A. Jeanroy, "Boccace et Christine de Pisan," *Romania*, 48 (1919), 93-105.

[28] See Laigle, p. 121, and Rigaud, passim.

[29] Christine elsewhere argues that education is significant only to the degree that it improves the soul. Knowledge without virtue, in fact, is dangerous. See Laigle, p. 187.

[30] On Christine's educational ideas, see Astrik L. Gabriel, "The Educational Ideas of Christine de Pisan," *Journal of the History of Ideas*, 16 (1955), 3-22.

[31] On the practical education of women, see Eileen Power, "The Position of Women," in *The Legacy of the Middle Ages*, n.2 above.

[32] Quoted in Angus J. Kennedy and Kenneth Varty, "Christine de Pisan's *Dittié de Jehanne d'Arc*," *Nottingham Mediaeval Studies*, 18 (1974), 29-55, and 19 (1975), 53-76. The quotation from the poem is from the first article, p. 44. The translation by Kennedy and Varty is from the second article, p. 70.

[33] The comment of Deschamps is quoted in Pinet, p. 38; the anonymous French critic is quoted in Power, *Medieval Women*, p. 32.

[34] Carolly Erickson, in *The Medieval Vision* (cited above, n.16), argues that the experiences of individual women are "at odds with abstract restrictions of theology, law, literature, and folklore" (p. 207). See also Charity C. Willard, "A Fifteenth-Century View of Women's Roles in Medieval Society: Christine de Pizan's *Livre des Trois Vertus*," in *The Role of Woman in the Middle Ages*, ed. R. T. Morewedge (Albany: State Univ. of New York Press, 1975), pp. 90-120.

CATERINA CORNER, QUEEN OF CYPRUS*
(1454? - 1510)

LOUISE BUENGER ROBBERT

A contemporary of Christopher Columbus, of Lorenzo the Magnificent, of Martin Luther, and of Lucrezia Borgia, Caterina Corner was born in Venice, married the King of Cyprus, ruled Cyprus as a widow for sixteen years, and after her abdication, retired to Asolo, a northern Venetian territory where she established her court as a center of Renaissance learning and culture.[1] Literary tradition and legend suggest that she first came into prominence when her uncle, Andrea Corner, a wealthy Venetian businessman and confidante of Cypriote kings, was exiled to Cyprus and dropped a small portrait of the youthful Caterina before James the Bastard, King of Cyprus. He picked up the portrait, fell in love with the young woman, and would not rest until he had made arrangements to marry Caterina. While probably not true, this legend justifies in romantic terms the mutually profitable alliance between Cyprus and Venice during the fifteenth century.

Caterina was born in Venice on 24 November 1454 or 1456, St. Catherine's Day. The large and important Corner family traced its lineage back to the *Cornelii gens* of imperial Rome and formed one of the twelve founding families of Venice, according to tradition. In the fourteenth century the Corner family had become one of the wealthiest families in Venice with large investments on Cyprus in sugar plantations and salt. The assessments of taxation in Venice in 1379 reveal that Federico Corner had more disposable wealth than any other Venetian; his net worth is given as 60,000 Venetian pounds. A Marco Corner reigned as Doge of Venice from 1365 to 1368. Marco Corner, father of Caterina, and his brother, Andrea, descended from a

*Copyright, 1979, Louise Buenger Robbert

collateral line, equally famous for its wealth and social position in Venice and similarly influential in Venetian government and foreign affairs.

Caterina inherited an equally rich heritage from Fiorenza, her mother, who brought Levantine distinction into the Corner palace on the Grand Canal. Fiorenza grew up on the Aegean island of Naxos, the daughter of Nicolo Crispo, Duke of Naxos, and Valenza, who was born a Greek princess. From her grandmother Valenza, Caterina inherited the imperial Byzantine blood of Emperor John Comnenos of Trebizond. How much of the Byzantine scholarship in Greek letters was preserved in Naxos is not known. That the Crispo dukes of the Archipelago appreciated and encouraged scholarship is shown by their hospitality to Cyriacus of Ancona, a famous traveler, archeologist, and merchant, who visited Andros and other Aegean islands to copy inscriptions shortly before his death in 1452. The island rulers "not only received him courteously, but also ordered excavations to be made for his benefit."[2] Thus Greek and Latin-Italian cultures blended in the person of Caterina Corner.

Caterina grew up in the heart of Venice. At the age of ten she began to attend a convent school run by Benedictine nuns in Padua. We do not know any further details of her education, but from her patronage of learning in her later life at Asolo it seems likely that she was exposed to letters, art, music, and other accomplishments of the wealthy and cultivated. The Corner families brilliantly educated their sons in the Renaissance humanist tradition; no fewer than five of them figure prominently in the literary salons of early sixteenth-century Venice. The brothers Marco, Francesco, and Andrea Corner participated in the salon of John Lascaris, Monsignore della Casa. Marcontonio and Benedetto Corner were among the learned gathering in the house of Domenico Venier. The most prominent Italian humanist of the generation after Caterina Corner was her relative Pietro Bembo who was later to reside at her court in Asolo.

In 1468 when Caterina was fourteen years old, King James II of Cyprus asked for her hand in marriage. Although the betrothal contract was signed in November of that year, the marriage did not take place until 1472. Because the Venetian Republic traditionally had prohibited its doges and their families from marrying foreign royalty, Caterina was formally adopted as a daughter of the Republic so that her royal marriage would enhance the importance of the entire state, not just a private family. The marriage ended tragically within a few months when her husband James became ill of dysentery and died nine days later on 7 July 1473. He had reigned for eleven years. He named as his heirs his widow and their unborn child, and, if they should die, his three bastard children. Caterina gave birth to their son, James III, a few weeks after her husband's death.

Her position in Cyprus was insecure, and she was surrounded by conspiracies and plots. Before their marriage, James had fought long and hard to gain the throne of Cyprus. As the bastard son of King John of Cyprus, James in his youth had been ordained Archbishop of Nicosia. His half-sister Charlotte succeeded to the throne of Cyprus in 1458, while James escaped to Egypt where he persuaded the Mameluke Sultan to give him military assistance. With Mameluke troops and loyal Cypriote followers, he began a successful campaign to conquer the island, and by 1462 had taken the throne from Charlotte and her weak husband, Louis of Savoy. After James' death in 1473, Charlotte of Lusignan unsuccessfully attempted to unseat Queen Caterina. Although Charlotte was supported by the Knights of St. John on Rhodes, her brother-in-law the Duke of Savoy, and the pope, she never regained possession of the island.

A more serious threat to Queen Caterina involved many of the highly placed Catalans who were members of the Council of Regency. Four months after the death of King James, they conspired to remove her uncle, Andrea Corner, who was the head of the Council of Regency, to take the young prince away from his mother, and to control the queen. The conspirators hoped to secure the regency and the future succession of the throne for Karla, the bastard daughter of the late King James, whom they had affianced to Don Alonzo, bastard son of King Ferdinand of Naples. The conspiracy was initially successful. Andrea Corner, Caterina's uncle, and her cousin Marco Bembo were murdered. The conspirators controlled events so thoroughly that the bodies were not recovered for several days, and then only after dogs had eaten them. Not only was her son taken from her, but Caterina also had to watch her physician murdered in her presence as he begged for mercy.

Because of quarrels among themselves, the conspirators lost ground at the court, and many had fled Cyprus by January of 1474. In March two Venetian councilors for civil affairs and a proveditor for military affairs came to Cyprus to assist Queen Caterina. That the people of Cyprus supported the queen is indicated by the tumultuous demonstrations of loyalty to her, especially in the capital city of Nicosia. The representatives of Venice remained with her, ostensibly to advise her. A series of her letters remains from this period in which she complains to Venice that her freedom of movement is being impaired by these Venetian representatives. She also implores the Venetian authorities to exert pressure so that her son might be returned to her, but in the heat of the following summer, she suffered another loss. Her son died of malaria around his first birthday in August, 1474. Marco Corner, her father, joined her in Cyprus shortly afterward. His presence seems to have eased the friction caused by the interference on the part of the Venetian councilors and proveditor.

Queen Caterina's rule on Cyprus in these years played a part in the power struggle between Venice and the Ottoman Turks. In this long war, Venice had lost strategic Negroponte in the Aegean to the Turks in 1470 and Scutari in Albania in 1471. In 1472 Caterina's marriage had given Venice access to the Cypriote ports, which became important Venetian naval bases. In 1479 Venice sued the Ottoman Turkish Sultan in Istanbul for peace. As the price of peace, Venice acquiesced in the loss of Negroponte and Scutari, paid a huge tribute, but renewed the Venetian commercial privileges in the Ottoman Empire. The Venetian fleet prevented the landing of Turks and Turkish pirates on Cyprus, and Cyprus was spared the massacres, enslavements, and looting from which many other Aegean islands were suffering.

It was yet another conspiracy, this time to marry Caterina herself into the royal house of Naples, which caused Venice to intervene and force Caterina to abdicate. Venetian foreign policy would not tolerate the marriage of Caterina, because the kingdom of Cyprus would go to her children, enabling Naples, or some other foreign power, to gain a foothold in this important island kingdom. No less melodramatic than the earlier conspiracy, this plot ended with one of the chief conspirators swallowing diamonds after he had been apprehended by the Venetian fleet. Before sending a formal letter to Caterina asking her to abdicate, the Venetian Council of Ten asked Giorgio Corner, brother of Caterina, to go to Cyprus and to persuade her to retire to Venice where they promised that she would be given jurisdiction over a pleasant mainland territory and receive a stipend of 8,000 ducats a year, equal to her allowance while queen.[3]

Reluctant to leave her rich kingdom, she asked her brother if it would not be sufficient if she promised to turn the island over to the Venetian Republic after her death. Giorgio Corner replied with a lengthy speech in which he summarized the dangers of her position in Cyprus, her vulnerability to the Turks, and concluded with appeals to her loyalty to Venice and even her affection for him:

It is much better not to be forced by the Turks but rather to accept a little house or a diminuation of life-style from Venice. . . . Fortune is changeable, many-sided, and sudden; not always can one predict the plans one's enemies make nor make preparations in time. . . . Above all, she should consider that even if no necessity compels her, it is important for her to make her own name everlastingly glorious by donating a very noble kingdom to her fatherland. Then in the annals of history it would be written that the city of Venice was honored and increased by the kingdom of Cyprus through the act of one of its own citizens. In all lands and countries she would always be known and named queen.[4]

After having carefully mentioned her relatives and her ties to the city where she had her first communion, he concluded with even more emotional arguments:

[He reminds her that] he is not only her brother, but a brother she has always trusted. He himself not only implores her to understand that men will believe, not that *she* did not wish the Republic to persuade her, but that *he* did not wish to persuade her. And in this case all the city will hate him. . . . No prayer could she make more pleasing to the Majesty of God, no greater sacrifice, no more acceptable act, than to offer, voluntarily, this gift to Venice. It is self-evident that this action is the will of God, the wish of her country, the [means of preserving] the well-being of the Republic.[5]

The queen broke out in tears, and in a pretty compliment to her brother's oratory, replied that Venice ought rather to receive the island of Cyprus from her brother than from herself. She agreed to abdicate and to accept the terms proposed by Venice.

Caterina's return to Venice and her abdication were eased by the splendor of her reception upon her return. The doge came out to the Lido and invited her on board the *Bucintoro*, his lavishly decorated ceremonial barge. After she again formally abdicated, ceding Cyprus to the Republic, the Council of Ten gave her jurisdiction over the castle of Asolo and its territory for the remainder of her life. As Lady of Asolo, her jurisdiction would be limited by Venetian foreign policy, by Venetian restrictions upon trade and commerce, and by a

29

prohibition that she could not change the real estate and service obligations of the people in her tiny domain.

During the last third of her life Caterina Corner, Queen of Cyprus and Lady of Asolo, became a patron of the arts. Very little remains from her own writing except for a few private letters written while she was in Cyprus, but she encouraged and subsidized scholarship and painting. The most important intellectual product of her court in Asolo is Pietro Bembo's Arcadian dialogue, *Gli Asolani*. Related to Caterina, Bembo was born in Venice in 1470 and accompanied his father to Florence where the elder Bembo held office as ambassador to Lorenzo the Magnificent. In Florence, Bembo continued his study of the classics and was admitted to the circle of the Platonic Academy in the Medici palace. Later he went to Sicily to perfect his Greek under the tutelage of Constantine Lascaris. After his return to Venetian territory, he displeased his father by preferring the life of a poet, scholar, and courtier to a career in government service, the usual profession of a Venetian nobleman. This young man in his twenties, who was to become the leading Italian humanist of the first half of the sixteenth century, chose to visit and reside at Caterina's court in Asolo.

Not much remains of the palace inhabited by Caterina, but according to Bembo the view of the mountains from her garden was spectacular. The nineteenth-century Venetian romantic writer, Pompeo Molmenti, however, has left a charming description of Caterina's garden:

> The castle overlooked a garden, very lovely and marvellously beautiful, with its broad and shady trellis of vines running down the middle, its flower beds, its green lawns, juniper hedges, groves of laurel quick with the murmur of a running stream that issued from the live rock, its little winding walks that spread their network through the pleasance.[6]

Located at the foothills of the Alps, north of the city of Treviso, the city continues today to have a population of about 5,000.

The castle of Asolo and its garden furnished the setting for Pietro Bembo's *Gli Asolani*. This work reports a series of three dialogues concerning the nature of love which take place among a group of men and women at the siesta hour in the gardens of Asolo. In Book One, Perottino replies to queries about love with a long speech demonstrating that love brings only sorrow and misery.

Book Two contains the long monologue of Gismondo who tells of the joy and completeness of love for both women and men. Book Three introduces the reader to Caterina, Queen of Cyprus, in person, who asks her maid-in-waiting about the previous discussions and then herself joins the group to hear the third and last discussion. Finally, Lavinello speaks to all of the excellence of Platonic love, recounting the wisdom revealed to him by a hermit at the top of the hill of Asolo.

From *Gli Asolani* the reader receives the unmistakable impression that at the court of Caterina women were expected to be both learned and creative. In Book II, Gismondo remarks that lovers "like sometimes to recite their poems to their ladies, sometimes to hear their ladies do the same" and that lovers find "further pleasure if they [women] will sing some song of ours [men's] or perhaps of theirs."[7] Although Gismondo later acknowledges that literary and musical creativity may occur less frequently in women than men, there is no suggestion that learning is unsuitable for women.[8]

In Book III Bembo states directly that women have minds and should devote them to literary studies, adding that if they did so, they could excel in literature and scholarship:

> For unless it is denied that women as well as men have minds, I do not know why they, any more than we, should be refused the right to seek knowledge of what one ought to flee from or pursue; and these are among the most obscure questions, around which as on their axles all the sciences revolve, questions which are the targets of all our diligence and thought. If women do not occupy all their free time with those duties which are said to be proper to them, but devote their whole leisure to literary studies and these pursuits, it makes little difference what some may say about it, for sooner or later the world will praise the women for it.[9]

In addition to the above explicit statement of the right and duty of women to engage in literature and scholarship, there are more subtle indications that female participation in intellectual activities was encouraged at Asolo. When Queen Caterina asks what has occurred in the two previous discussions, it is Berenice, her maid-in-waiting, who summarizes the speeches of Perottino and Gismondo while "always taking heed that she addressed a lady and a queen."[10] It is because of this summary that Caterina "resolved to honor that gallant company by being present at Lavinello's discourse that evening." There could be no clearer indication that Caterina encouraged female learning at her court in Asolo.

Although composed when the author was twenty-five, Bembo's *Gli Asolani* was first published by the Aldine Press in March, 1505. By the end of the sixteenth century it had gone through at least twenty-two Italian editions. The first Spanish version appeared in 1551, and the French translation, begun in 1508, appeared in 1545 and was revised six times in the century. The translator of the first English version, Rudolf B. Gottfried, calls it "one of the influential books of the Renaissance."[11] Certainly, it was a major influence on an even more important work, Baldassare Castiglione's the *Courtier*. In the *Courtier*, which is in some respects modeled upon *Gli Asolani*, Castiglione puts into the mouth of Bembo, a character in the work, an apostrophe to Platonic love. Through the *Courtier* the ideas of Bembo, influenced by his experiences at the court of Caterina, spread through Europe.

There are two particularly tantalizing hints that Queen Caterina may have influenced the development of Renaissance art and the spread of humanist learning. No less a scholar than Rudolf Wittkower has suggested that Giorgione, the Venetian painter of the High Renaissance, spent some time at the court in Asolo and that he derived inspiration for his Arcadian paintings from this experience.[12] The romantic, partly fanciful, idyllic spirit which characterizes some of Giorgione's most provocative works is also found in Bembo's *Gli Asolani*, but Giorgione's life remains shrouded in mystery, and the details may never be known.

There are also a number of suggestions that the Aldine Press, famous for its magnificent editions of the Greek classics, was connected with Caterina Corner and her court at Asolo. Aldo Manuzio, founder of the New Academy in Venice and genius of the Aldine Press, married the daughter of the printer from Asolo, Andrea Tornesani. Tornesani not only maintained his property in Asolo, but also purchased a press in Venice from Nicholas Jensen in 1479, to which Aldo came in 1490. Tornesani managed the household of his famous son-in-law in Venice; at Aldo's death, Tornesani of Asolo became the executor of his property. It is possible that the famous Aldine Press itself was inspired and even patronized by Caterina. Pietro Bembo, who was in Asolo until 1495, later joined the editorial group around Aldo Manuzio.

In addition to the Greek heritage she derived from her mother, Caterina spent much of her life in Cyprus where Greek was spoken. Charlotte, her sister-in-law and rival for her throne, used the Greek language exclusively in formal communication even after years of exile in Italy. It is unlikely that Aldo's ambitious projects of publishing a Greek grammar and editing classical Greek texts were unknown to Caterina, and she may have inspired and encouraged him to bring them to fruition. The chronological pattern of events seems to support this possibility. Caterina became Lady of Asolo in 1489; she died in Venice in 1510. Aldo Manuzio came from Bassano in 1490 to work with Tornesani, and in 1495 they began to print the complete works of Aristotle. From 1495 to 1505 the Aldine Press produced its great editions of Aristophanes, Sophocles, Herodotus, Xenophon, Euripides, Demosthenes, Plutarch, Plato, and Pindar. Aldo married in 1505 and died in 1515. His son became a priest and lived in Asolo; Aldo's brother-in-law and heir was also known as Francesco da Asolo. These and other suggestions of a connection between the circle of Caterina Corner and the Aldine Press might be further explored by modern scholarship.[13]

In spite of the security and tranquility promised her by the Republic, the last two years of Caterina's life were troubled. In 1508 her brother Giorgio, the skillful orator who had persuaded her to leave Cyprus, was named proveditor of a Venetian army raised against the Hapsburgs. During this campaign Caterina retired from Asolo on the exposed Hapsburg-Venetian border and returned to Venice. Although her brother's campaign was successful, the next year Pope Julius II organized the League of Cambrai against Venice in which much of Europe united to prevent the further expansion of Venice. The Venetian army was badly defeated by the French at Agnadello on 14 May 1509, but Venice survived the onslaught of French, Papal, and Hapsburg armies by playing off one foe against another. During these conflicts, on 10 July 1510, Caterina Corner died. Although the day of her funeral was viciously cold with rain and windstorms, the highest officials of Venice took part in the ceremonies: the Signoria, the Vice Doge, the Patriarch of Venice, and several bishops. Appropriately, the Venetian humanist, Andrea Navagero, pronounced her eulogy.

So passed into history the amazing woman who ruled Cyprus for sixteen years and who later established a court at Asolo which influenced the development of humanistic learning and literature for over a generation. Pietro Bembo, of whom one modern scholar has said, "wherever you seek to enter the literary life of the time, you find that all avenues take you to Bembo," inspired by the atmosphere of Caterina's court, wrote a series of dialogues which served as a model for the *Courtier*.[14] Caterina Corner, as the Lady of Asolo, herself supplied a model for the cultured and learned ruler who encouraged the arts; that model through *Gli Asolani* and later the *Courtier* was to influence all of Europe.

NOTES

[1] Her name is spelled "Corner" in the Venetian dialect and pronounced with an accent on the last syllable. In Italian it is written "Cornaro"; in Latin, "Cornelia." For an early study of Caterina Corner, see Horatio F. Brown, "Caterina Cornaro, Queen of Cyrpus," in *Studies in the History of Venice* (New York: E.P. Dutton & Co., 1907), I, 255-92.

[2] William Miller, *Essays in the Latin Orient* (1921; rpt. Amsterdam: Adolf M. Hakkert, 1964), pp. 171, 177.

[3] Sir George Hill, *A History of Cyprus* (1948; rpt. Cambridge: The University Press, 1972), III, 743, esp. n.3.

[4] Pietro Cardinal Bembo, "Istoria Viniziana," translated into Italian by Pietro Bembo and Carlo Gualteruzzi, in *Opere del Cardinale Pietro Bembo* (Venice, 1729; rpt. Ridgewood, New Jersey: The Gregg Press Inc., 1965), I, 14-16; Hill, *History of Cyprus*, III, 745, reports that this speech appears in five other chronicles. The English translation is my own.

[5] Ibid.

[6] Pompeo Molmenti, *Venice, Its Individual Growth from the Earliest Beginnings to the Fall of the Republic*, Part II, *The Golden Age*, trans. Horatio F. Brown (Chicago: A.C. McClurg & Co., 1907), II, Pt. 2, pp. 66-68.

[7] Pietro Bembo, *Gli Asolani*, trans. with introduction by Rudolf B. Gottfried (Bloomington, Indiana: Indiana University Press, 1954), p. 122.

[8] Ibid., pp. 122, 126.

[9] Ibid., p. 148.

[10] Ibid., p. 150.

[11] Ibid., p. xv.

[12] Rudolf Wittkower, "L'Arcadia e il Giorgionismo," in *Umanesimo Europeo e Umanesimo Veneziano*, ed. Vittore Branca (Florence: Sansoni, 1963), p. 480.

[13] For information on the Aldine Press and its possible connections with the Corner family, see Heinrich Kretschmayr, *Geschichte von Venedig* (Gotha, 1920; rpt. Stuttgart: Scientia Verlag Aalen, 1964), II, 492; Carlo Dionisotti, "Aldo Manuzio Umanisto," in *Umanesimo Europeo e Umanesimo Veneziano,* ed. Vittore Branca (Florence: Sansoni, 1963), pp. 213-43; Richard Jebb, "The Classical Renaissance," in *Cambridge Modern History* (London and New York: The University Press, 1902), I, 561-63.

[14] W. Theodor Elwert, "Pietro Bembo e la Vita Letteraria," in *La Civiltà Veneziana del Rinascimento* (Florence: Sansoni, 1958), p. 137.

MARGUERITE DE NAVARRE AND HER CIRCLE
(1492–1549)

C.J. BLAISDELL

The important influence of aristocratic women on the political, intellectual, and religious life of the French royal court has been recognized for some time by historians.[1] Among their European contemporaries in the Renaissance there was a generally held belief that "the women of France were freer than elsewhere."[2] Whether this was, in fact, the case or whether it only appeared to be because some women took advantage of their favorable circumstances, it is evident that from the time of Anne de Beaujeau (1441-1522), until the death of Catherine de Medici (1519-1589), noblewomen played a unique and powerful role at the French court. Although it was the accident of noble birth and the policies of princes that made these women prominent at court in the first place, nevertheless it appears that through education, personal style, and conscious effort they made the most of their circumstances and became both independent and influential.

The tradition of feminine influence at court was advanced by Anne de Beaujeau, daughter of Louis XI, who ruled France as regent for her brother Charles VIII until he attained his majority.[3] An intelligent and ambitious woman, Anne did more than merely maintain the crown for her younger brother. She ruled conscientiously according to deliberate strategies she developed from experience. Later, in a little book she wrote for the instruction of her daughter Suzanne de Bourbon entitled *L'Enseignement des filles*, she emphasized how important it was for noblewomen to receive an education.[4] In reality Anne's legacy had less influence on Suzanne than on two other noblewomen who had been a part of her court: Anne de Bretagne (1477-1514), Duchess of Brittany, wife of Charles VIII and later of Louis XII; and Louise de Savoie (1476-1531), wife of the French nobleman Charles d'Angoulême and mother of Marguerite de Navarre and François I. Both of these women were politically powerful and patronesses of writers and artists; they wielded an important influence on the younger women in their entourages by supervising their education and encouraging intellectual independence.[5] A direct line of feminine influence on French political and cultural life can be traced from Anne de Beaujeau through these women to Catherine de Medici, the wife of Henri II, queen mother and regent for her son Charles IX. Educated and influenced by Marguerite de Navarre, Catherine continued the tradition of female influence and dominated the French court and politics in the second half of the sixteenth century.[6] The importance of what has been aptly labelled "the entourage factor" in producing these independent women who made a career of court life and patronage ought not to be underestimated.[7] Mature women at the French court had an extraordinary and powerful influence on the lives of the younger women in their circles.

Standing in the middle of the tradition and dominating court life as an inheritor and innovator in the first half of the sixteenth century was Marguerite de Navarre. Marguerite (1492-1549), often referred to as "the pearl of princesses," was by all contemporary accounts an extraordinary woman. Even in a period when a number of outstanding women figured significantly in court life, Marguerite engraved her name indelibly on the pages of French history because of her unique royal status, her unusual intellectual capacity, and her absolute devotion to her brother the king. It was, for example, Marguerite who encouraged the interest of François I in the "new learning" and the arts; it was she who brought writers and artists into the inner circle at court and invited critics of the medieval Church to preach to the royal entourage. Following the tradition established by generations of royal women before her, Marguerite directed the education of the royal children and of the women at court. In addition, she wrote poetry, plays, short stories, and devotional literature. A moving spirit of the French Renaissance, Marguerite's personality and learning stimulated the minds of those around her, preparing them to accept the new spiritual awakenings of the "reform from within," and her personal interest and patronage contributed to the acceptance of the new intellectual and spiritual stirrings of French humanism.

Fate and circumstance dictated Marguerite's royal position and controlled the events of her youth. The birth of princesses was accorded little notice compared to that of their brothers, and it is doubtful that Marguerite's birth in 1492 was greeted with any special joy by her ambitious and discontented mother

37

Louise de Savoie, wife of Charles d'Angoulême, a "prince of the blood" by virtue of being a great-grandson of Charles V. At best, her birth was living proof that Louise could bear healthy children: it boded well for the eventual birth of a son to help advance her dynastic ambitions. Louise's hopes for a son were fulfilled in 1494 with the birth of François whom she joyfully received and designated her "little Caesar," an epithet which already revealed her plans for his future.[8] The untimely death of her husband Charles d'Angoulême the following year left Louise a widow at nineteen and an unprotected poor relation of the royal family. Uncommonly ambitious to begin with, from that moment on Louise devoted her energies and talents to promoting the fortunes of her children, especially those of her beloved son; she watched with unbridled satisfaction as her dreams were gradually fulfilled through the premature deaths of Charles VIII in 1498 and Louis XII in 1515 without male heirs. According to Louise, that remarkable combination of events was the prophetic fulfillment of "the destiny of her Caesar," whom she absolutely adored.

Encouraged from the beginning to emulate her mother and to devote her life to serving her brother, Marguerite grew up as a poor relation in the royal court and as a sister subservient to François. Louise appears to have encouraged service and devotion to the young prince less as subordination for its own sake than for the purpose of creating a team, referred to as the "Trinity," which would work together to realize her ambition to see her son on the throne of France.[9]

The political ambition and intellectual interests of her mother meant that Marguerite was reared as a princess and educated to serve the crown. In accordance with the ideals of humanism and the "new learning," which had become fashionable at court, aristocratic women often received educations comparable or superior to those of their brothers and husbands.[10]

In the tradition of Anne de Beaujeau, Louise carefully supervised the education of her children. If her passion for books is any indication, she was well educated. Her personal library plus the books she inherited from her husband and father numbered over two hundred volumes, an impressive collection for the period, and included a variety of works such as Dante's *Paradisio*, Arthurian tales, French chronicles, and books of religious devotion.[11] In addition to her own library, Louise and her children had access to the fine collection of books at Amboise where they went to live after Louis XII ascended the throne in 1498. Louise personally gave the children lessons in French and Spanish. Marguerite learned Hebrew, Latin, some Italian and German, but she probably was not taught Greek, even though Greek studies were becoming the vogue in educated circles. Special tutors including Robert Hurault, the humanist and advocate of Church reform, taught her religious history, philosophy, and theology.[12]

She used her education to her advantage, and there is no doubt that her learning enhanced her position when, in 1508, as Marguerite d'Angoulême, she accompanied her mother and François, then heir apparent to the throne, to the court of Louis XII. As she entered the limelight with her brother, her intellectual accomplishments were widely acknowledged. According to Brantôme, a keen observer of life at the Valois court whose grandmother had been a member of Marguerite's entourage, the learned men of Louis XII's circle referred to her as their "Maecenas," and "foreign ambassadors reported her impressive learning when they had occasion to converse with her."[13]

Customarily, noblewomen were pawns to the dynastic ambitions of their overlords, and Marguerite fared no better. Although she was earnestly sought after in marriage by the future Holy Roman Emperor Charles V of the House of Hapsburg, in 1509 Louis gave her instead to Charles, Duc d'Alençon, a twenty-year-old insignificant member of the royal family. He held a claim to the county of Armagnac against the king, but he agreed to withdraw his claim in exchange for Marguerite's hand in marriage. Lacking intellectual aptitude and devoid of character, Charles could never hope to match the intelligence and spirit of his young wife; the marriage was never a happy one. Marguerite, who was now known also as the Duchesse d'Alençon, spent a significant amount of time in provincial obscurity during the early years of the marriage. However, when François inherited the throne in 1515, she happily left Charles for long periods of time to join her beloved brother. At court she served as his hostess, received foreign ambassadors, and with her mother performed official functions "as a sort of viceroy."

Women of lesser capacities and ambition than Marguerite might have accepted the subservient role which the society of the time demanded of them and for which they had been trained. The wife of her brother François, who was called "good Queen Claude," was a shy, retiring, sickly young woman who made little impression on the court except for her sweetness and patience with her husband's mistresses. Although she had been reared and educated at the courts of her mother, Anne de Bretagne, and her mother-in-law, Louise de Savoie, Claude's passive role as queen is proof that education did not necessarily permit women to overcome their training in subservience, or guarantee that they would develop independent spirits. Marguerite stood in brilliant contrast to Claude and to Eléonore of Austria, the second wife of François; she became an arbiter of intellectual tastes and a supporter of the new ideas and attitudes of humanism.

In 1517 François, who had already showered his sister and brother-in-law with honors and gifts, gave Marguerite the Duchy of Berry, a rich region south of the Paris basin, which provided her with revenues and financial independence from Charles. With the Duchy went the University of Bourges, in the ancient capital of the Duchy which, especially in classics and law, had become a renowned center for the new learning. With her patronage Marguerite attracted some of the best European scholars. In addition to managing the lands, revenues, and university in her Duchy, she continued to develop her own intellectual and spiritual interests.

In spite of his Renaissance education, François was not a scholar, preferring to focus his energies on planning and renovating royal residences to serve as a stage for his splendid Renaissance court. More than anyone else at court, Marguerite was responsible for cultivating the atmosphere of intellectual and artistic excitement which prevailed. Her encouragement helped Guillaume Budé, the distinguished French humanist, and Jean du Bellay, the liberal Bishop of Narbonne and later Paris, to persuade the king to support the "new learning" through the creation and patronage of royal lectureships in Greek, Hebrew, Oriental languages, and mathematics—subjects which the conservative doctors at the Sorbonne refused to permit to be taught. The popularity of the lectures was amazing and led ultimately to the establishment of the famed Collège de France in Paris.

Marguerite also turned her attention to spiritual concerns, and during this period used her privileged position as the king's sister to protect the humanist-reformers who were struggling to reform the Roman Church. This movement, usually referred to either as *pré-réforme*, because its advocates were intent on reforming the abuses of the Church without destroying the institution, or as *évangélisme*, because they took as their ideal the primitive Church outlined in the Gospels, was contemporary with Erasmus. In its earliest phase in France, one of the centers of the movement was the city of Meaux, where the Bishop Briçonnet gathered together individuals who wished to restore the Roman Church to its early simplicity and who were sympathetic to the Bishop's ideas of enforcing ecclesiastical discipline at the local level as a first step.[14]

Marguerite was the undisputed patroness of this religious movement. As one of the most distinguished prelates in France, the Bishop Briçonnet was a familiar figure at court and well-known to Marguerite even before discovery of their common religious interests created a unique bond between them. Through visits and letters Briçonnet became Marguerite's spiritual mentor; in turn she became the royal protector of the circle at Meaux which included Jacques Lefèvre d'Etaples, who translated the New Testament into French; Guillaume Farel, who with John Calvin established a reformed Church in Geneva; and Gérard Roussel, a priest who later became Marguerite's personal chaplain.[15]

The correspondence between Marguerite and Briçonnet, which extended over a period from 1521 to 1524, is important because it reveals the decisive influence Briçonnet had on the development of her religious thinking. It reveals the Bishop's respect for Marguerite's intellect and establishes a basis for Marguerite's keen interest in the *évangéliste* movement. No one else received the same kind of personal spiritual tutelage from Briçonnet.

There has been considerable controversy regarding Marguerite's religious beliefs, primarily because they are difficult to define according to sectarian criteria. They show a mystical bent involving a very personal fusion of medieval mysticism and renaissance Neoplatonism. In her spiritual writings she reveals a knowledge of Dante, Plato, Bernard of Clairvaux, St. Francis, and Nicholas of Cusa. More mystical than either Luther or Calvin, whose polemics distressed her, she nevertheless drew on their ideas and sometimes attempted to adapt them to her own position and outlook. She supported three particular tenets of the reform: justification by faith, the primacy of Scripture, and the doctrine of election. Although her protection of Briçonnet and his circle at Meaux contributed to the spread of their ideas, she did not personally participate in the popular movement for reform, realizing that a possible consequence of reform might be disruption of the unity of the Church.

As Marguerite studied Scripture with Briçonnet's guidance, she recognized her longing for a spiritual mentor closer to court. Briçonnet sent Michel d'Arande, an Augustinian preacher, who was so successful in his preaching to the royal family that at one time it was rumored in court circles that the king and Marguerite might convert to Protestantism.[16] Marguerite, however, never left the Church even though she supported the ideals of the reform and used her influence to protect accused heretics. Both sides in the religious controversies attacked her for weakness, and both sides courted her support.[17] In her later years, Marguerite turned increasingly inward for spiritual comfort and developed feelings of deep melancholy which are reflected in her writings.

Marguerite entered the political limelight in 1525, when, following her brother's ignominious capture at the Battle of Pavia, she went to Spain to negotiate his release with the Emperor Charles. Her courage and strength were noted in the courts and chanceries of Europe as she made the arduous three-week journey across France and the Pyrenees to Madrid. She nursed her dying brother back to life and tried to negotiate terms for a peace treaty more favorable than those under discussion before her arrival in Spain.

Prior to her departure for Spain, her husband, who had been accused of inept leadership at the Battle of Pavia, died of wounds received in battle. This event left Marguerite freer to spend time at court following her triumphant return from Spain. She was frequently present, acting as her brother's hostess or companion at court events, and, according to the reports of foreign ambassadors, her beauty and intelligence dazzled the court.

In 1527 Marguerite was married to the dashing young Henri d'Albret, King of Navarre. They were not well-suited, and the location of his kingdom meant that she was frequently far from the French court. The willingness of François to sacrifice the interests of Navarre to the larger interests of France in the Treaty of Cambrai (1529) created difficulties between Marguerite and Henri, and between François and Marguerite. At the same time that she turned her attention to helping her husband govern his lands, she wrote poignant, melancholy letters to her brother in which she poured out her love for him, her desire to please him, and her longing to be near him at court.[18] These letters and poems for François have fascinated scholars, prompting a variety of explanations. The love letters have sometimes been interpreted as evidence of an incestuous relationship between the royal pair, but a recent study suggests that the letters may be an expression of an unconscious need for male approval on the part of a woman reared without a father.[19] Even allowing for the conventional self-abnegation appropriate in addressing one's secular or spiritual overlord, François emerges from her letters and poems as Marguerite's reason for living. One suspects that this open expression of intense love is a result of her mother's insistence upon Marguerite's devotion to her younger brother, "the little Caesar" who might one day be a king.

In Béarn, the sovereign territory of the king of Navarre, Marguerite helped her husband bring about reforms to improve the economy and legal and judicial systems of the region. At the Château of Nérac she established her own court, which, given the distance from Paris, was ideally suited as a sanctuary for reformers who were coming under the close scrutiny of both civil and ecclesiastical authorities in Paris. In 1529 Lefèvre d'Etaples, whom Marguerite had always protected in Paris, fled to Nérac where he remained until his death in 1536. Others followed him there in the ensuing years, years which were marked by François' growing conservatism.

François probably cared very little personally about religion, an attitude common among many Renaissance princes, but the pressure on him to eradicate the Protestant threat was enormous. As François became more conservative on the issue of reform, the 1530's were marked by increased persecution throughout France and in Paris in particular. Marguerite continued to protect her reformist friends and to maintain her usual intimacy with her brother, a task which was not always easy. Religious uprisings in her lands in Alençon forced the king to send in authorities to bring about order, but at great embarrassment to Marguerite who felt obliged to direct her officials to submit peacefully.[20] At court Gérard Roussel, Briçonnet's successor as her personal chaplain and spiritual advisor, delivered with Marguerite's encouragement sermons attacking Catholic ritual and created a sensation. Out of respect for his sister, the king exiled the Catholic troublemakers who demanded Roussel's immediate trial for heresy. When Marguerite's little religious treatise *Le Miroir de l'âme pécheresse* was condemned in 1531 by the Sorbonne for containing heretical material and placed on a list of condemned books, François backed Marguerite and "graciously allowed" the theology faculty to back down.

In 1534 the reformers had grown impatient and more aggressive in their activities and had been so bold as to place posters attacking the Church and doctrine under the king's very nose at the Château at Amboise. François, who was angry and shocked at their audacity, ordered the instigators caught, arrested, and tried. Paris and the environs of the court were no longer safe for anyone suspected of reforming tendencies. Among others Clément Marot, a court poet and pensioner of Marguerite, was placed on the list of those officially outlawed and was forced to leave Paris. A well-known court poet who had been attached to the royal entourage since 1519, Marot fled to Marguerite's court. A royal edict published in January of 1535 which ordered all protectors of fugitive heretics to be punished made it dangerous even for the king's sister to protect Marot for long; so she sent him to her cousin Renée de France, Duchesse de Ferrara, who welcomed him at her court in northern Italy later that year.[21]

la feü reine de nauare
marguerite

44

John Calvin also visited briefly at Marguerite's court where he temporarily hid from the authorities. Because of the circumstances the details of his visit are understandably obscure, but he must have discussed the reform with Marguerite during his stay, since after he left France and established himself in Geneva, he inaugurated an exchange of letters in which he attempted to direct her spiritual thinking and to convince her to support the reform in France publicly. Calvin recognized Marguerite's powerful influence on her brother's thinking, and he hoped that by gaining her open support he could acquire influential backing in France. Marguerite, who remained intellectually independent even though she was attracted to some of Calvin's ideas, preferred to make selective use of his teaching. She withstood his attacks upon her for befriending people he did not approve of, men he called "libertines."[22] She refused to give in and maintained the tolerant stance of the *évangéliques* who still hoped for an institutional reform brought about within the Church.

As he saw his court increasingly become a refuge for religious fugitives, Marguerite's husband, Henri, grew less tolerant of her religious views and practices. Years after Marguerite's death, her daughter Jeanne related an incident which took place at Nérac in which her father ". . . when Marguerite was praying in her room with the ministers Roussel and Farel . . . slapped her on the cheek and forbade her to meddle in doctrinal affairs. . . ."[23] Nevertheless the independent Marguerite continued to participate in reformed worship and to protect reformers. Gérard Roussel remained her chaplain; Mass was said in French; there was no elevation of the host as in Catholic Mass; no mention was made of the Virgin Mary. Moreover, both the bread and the wine were offered to the congregation at communion, and it was said that Marguerite did not believe that priests should be celibate.

Many of the reform-minded people in Marguerite's circle were also artists and writers. Some, such as Antoine de Papillon, a scholar and friend of Erasmus and a translator of Luther's writings into French, came and went at her court. Others, such as Etienne Dolet, enjoyed her protection and patronage, but seldom, if ever, came to her court. A humanist printer in Lyon, who published works on both sides of the religious controversy, Dolet was her protégé, but she was powerless to save him from burning at the stake in 1546 for denying the soul's immortality. Bonaventura des Periers became her secretary in 1535. A reputed atheist who wrote an anti-Christian tract entitled *Cymbalum Mundi*, in which he ridiculed both Catholics and Protestants for their extreme positions, he committed suicide in 1544. Some writers who were never a part of her circle dedicated their works to her; a particularly famous example was

François Rabelais, who in his dedication of the *Tiers Livre* of *Gargantua and Pantagruel* referred to her "rapt, transported, ecstatic spirit." Erasmus wrote to her of his admiration for her "moderation, piety, and invincible strength of soul."[24] Her correspondence with the Italian aristocrat, Vittoria Colonna, whom Marguerite never met, reveals a strong bond between these two women who shared with each other their mystical insights.[25]

Marguerite's wider circle included several noblewomen who sympathized with the Reform: Louise de Montmorency, Michelle de Saubonne, Mademoiselle de la Roche, and Jacqueline Longwy. Whether Marguerite influenced their religious opinions or whether they were attracted to her because they shared her ideas is not known. Like her they had been educated at court. All of them exhibited remarkable independence, attributable to both their education and their noble position.

Louise de Montmorency (d. 1547) was the sister of the Constable Anne de Montmorency, the most powerful man in France after the king, and the ancestress of two generations of Huguenot leaders. Her early years at the court are obscure, but she seems to have grown up in the entourage of Louise de Savoie. Her brother Anne was among the close companions of the young François, and it is possible that Louise became a part of Marguerite's circle as a child. In 1530, she became *dame d'honneur* to Eléonore of Austria, the second wife of François. Louise provided her children with humanist tutors who had unorthodox religious attitudes, and she was reported to have been a crypto-Calvinist at the time of her death.[26]

Among the close friends of Louise de Montmorency was Michelle de Saubonne, also known as Madame de Soubise (d. 1549), ancestress of the famed Rohans who were Huguenot military leaders and heroes. Madame de Soubise began her career at court as *dame d'honneur* to Anne de Bretagne who thought so highly of her that at her deathbed she requested that Louise de Savoie appoint her as governess to Anne's younger daughter Renée de France. A woman of remarkable independence, and reputed to have a sharp tongue, Madame de Soubise served Renée only a short time before she was removed from her post and banished from court through the jealousy, some said, of Louise. She retired to her lands in Poitou which, as a widow, she controlled outright, and brought up her children "in the reformed religion." She later accompanied Renée to Ferrara where the combination of her forceful personality, unbridled tongue, and reformist sympathies earned her the hatred of Renée's husband and banishment from the d'Este court.[27]

When Madame de Soubise left Ferrara, she left behind a daughter Anne de Parthenay-Soubise, Madame de Pons (d. 1549), who was subsequently expelled for being a troublemaker at the d'Este court and who was an avowed Protestant and follower of John Calvin. Her replacement, Mademoiselle de la Roche, who was rumored to be a Protestant, was sent by Marguerite to replace Anne de Parthenay. We know nothing about the woman except that she was a part of Marguerite's circle and probably educated at the royal court.[28]

Jacqueline Longwy, Duchesse de Montpensier (d. 1561), was another independent and outspoken noblewoman. We know nothing of her early life, but she may have grown up at court in the company of the young Catherine de Medici under the eye of Marguerite, who was supervising the education of the royal children. Jacqueline married the Duc de Montpensier, a member of the high nobility and a man vehemently opposed to the Reform. As a member of Queen Catherine's entourage in 1560, Jacqueline used her influence to intervene on behalf of the Huguenots. Like Louise de Montmorency, she may have been a secret convert to the Huguenot faith. Contemporary narratives suggest that she refused to permit a priest to be present at her deathbed, a request often regarded as a certain sign of conversion to Protestantism.[29]

Two noblewomen in particular came under Marguerite's influence while they were growing up at court: Renée de France, Duchesse de Ferrara (1528-1575), and Marguerite de France, Duchesse de Savoie (1523-1574). Renée, the daughter of Louis XII and Anne de Bretagne, was orphaned at five but remained at court under the supervision of Madame de Soubise and Marguerite. Court chronicles noted Renée's presence at court functions in Marguerite's entourage until the time of her marriage in 1528 to the Duc de Ferrara. Renée and Marguerite maintained an intimate correspondence until Marguerite's death in 1549. In 1536 Marguerite intervened with the king to assure Renée's protection against the Inquisitor in Ferrara, and Renée welcomed fugitives from Marguerite's court on more than one occasion. Like Marguerite, Renée protected and financially supported known heretics who sought her help; she corresponded with John Calvin who may have visited her court in 1536 before going to Geneva, and she was suspected of worshiping according to reformed practices in her private apartments. Like Marguerite, she feared the divisiveness which the reform caused and resisted Calvin's persuasive letters. Although she refused to support publicly the Calvinist cause, after 1560 she was closely associated with the Huguenot movement in the minds of her contemporaries.[30]

Marguerite de France, her aunt's namesake and daughter of François I, married the Duc de Savoie in 1559 as part of the treaty agreements which ended the Hapsburg-Valois conflict. Educated under the care and supervision of Marguerite de Navarre, she was not only an acknowledged scholar, but also a patron of the early literary efforts of the poets of the Pléiade, especially of Ronsard. Sympathetic to the objectives of the Reform, she urged tolerance from the authorities and her husband for her Protestant subjects in Savoie, and, although like her aunt she was accused of heresy, she never openly accepted Protestantism or left the Roman Church. In her intellectual interests and her protection of heretics, the influence of her aunt seems obvious.[31]

There are some interesting parallels between Renée and Marguerite de Savoie: their childhood at the court of François, their close relationship with Marguerite de Navarre, their marriages across the Alps to husbands vehemently opposed to the Reform, and their rapport with Protestant leaders. Both Renée and Marguerite continued the tradition of the older Marguerite by tolerating and protecting reformers, but neither showed the strong spiritual inclinations of Marguerite de Navarre. The irenic or Erasmian stance of these younger women is all the more interesting when compared to the behavior of noblewomen of the next generation who were neither nurtured under Marguerite's care nor influenced by the moderate attitudes of the early reformers of her circle, such as Briçonnet and Lefèvre d'Etaples. The most obvious example is Marguerite's own daughter Jeanne d'Albret, who became a Huguenot leader in France and who instituted religious reform in the lands in Navarre which she inherited from her parents. In the cases of Renée and Marguerite de Savoie, the liberal atmosphere at court when they were growing up, Marguerite's influence as a second mother, and their marriages to husbands who vigorously persecuted heresy influenced their moderate stance toward the Reform. Jeanne, on the other hand, had an inherently rebellious spirit, the advantage of a husband who was ambivalent about the Reform, and a court which was remote from the authorities in Paris. Marguerite de Navarre influenced the learning and the religious attitudes of this circle of noblewomen, but in spite of their unusually high quality of education, they were surprisingly undistinguished as writers. They read, they collected books, they acted as patrons. Marguerite, in contrast, wrote in a variety of literary *métiers*, including plays, poetry, spiritual meditations, and prose fiction.

No one has ever advocated placing Marguerite among the foremost writers of sixteenth-century French literature; her critics, in fact, agree that "she did not know how to polish a piece of literature or to restrain herself."[32] She has been given a place in literary anthologies because she was a prolific author who captured the spirit of her period and because of her important influence on the cultural life of France. In 1547 she collected many of her poems and plays, publishing them together under the title *Les Marguerites de la Marguerite.* This volume contained her long spiritual work *Le Miroir de l'âme pécheresse* (condemned by the Sorbonne in 1531), two short meditations or prayers entitled *De l'âme fidèle* and *A notre Seigneur Jésus Christ,* and poems such as *La Coche,* in which three women debate which one has been made most unhappy by love, a genre reminiscent of the medieval *chanson de toile.* Many of her religious poems reflect the *évangéliste* ideas of faith as simple love of God and capture the spirit of protest against a Church which refused to dispense the simple, divine doctrine of the Gospels—themes which the Sorbonne censors easily identified as unorthodox and dangerous.

In her later years Marguerite began writing the *Heptaméron,* her most important prose work. In this collection of seventy-two tales, a group of court ladies and gentlemen are on a trip and isolated by bad weather; they decide to pass the time by telling stories. Each day is devoted to a theme which each story is required to follow. The story tellers or *devisants* comment to each other upon the story and the behavior of the characters and argue among themselves in an elegant style reminiscent of Castiglione's *Courtier.* Although the influence of Boccaccio's *Decameron* is unmistakable, Marguerite's characters are more fully developed than those of Boccaccio, and underlying the refined courtly discussion the reader is aware of Marguerite's spiritual and moral concerns. While the theme of the *Heptaméron* is love in all its forms from sacred to profane, we find elements of feminism (comments on the *Querelle des Femmes*), anticlericalism, and *évangélisme* (emphasis on the importance of Scripture for spiritual nurture). Marguerite, in spite of her knowledge of classical languages and Platonic philosophy, still seems closer to the piety and mysticism found in Lefèvre d'Etaples than to the secular spirit of Rabelais, Ronsard, and Montaigne.

Renaissance writers departed very little from the medieval tradition of extolling the passive virtues of the female sex; they, too, encouraged women to cultivate modesty, temperance, purity, and humility. As Ruth Kelso has observed, "suppression and negation of self were urged upon women . . . life was a lesson in submission to the will of another" (p. 36). For most women subservience and negation of self were realities to such a degree that one scholar has recently questioned whether, in fact, there was a Renaissance for women.[33] How, then, did Marguerite and her female contemporaries successfully ignore the conservative and traditional ideals of feminine virtue extolled by writers? There seem to be at least two explanations. First, it seems clear that the determining factor for the achievement of French noblewomen was not sex, but class. As aristocrats, their options were more numerous than those of men of even slightly lower rank. Their noble status permitted them access to the "new learning," the leisure to pursue their interest, and the proximity to power. Moreover, in spite of the ideology of subservience articulated by writers of handbooks and supported by the Church, the historical reality was that French noblewomen had always played a more important role than society officially sanctioned; they functioned as managers of the family lands and estates in the absence of their husbands, as abbesses and managers of monastic lands, and, sometimes, as widows who controlled their own wealth.

An additional explanation has been suggested by Nancy Roelker in her study of Huguenot noblewomen; according to Roelker, when some women successfully perform roles not sanctioned for their sex, the expectations of others are raised, and more options become available for all women.[34] Virtual overlord in her own lands and the inheritor of a tradition of female influence, Marguerite grasped, partially from Anne de Beaujeau and the other women who preceded her, a sense of the opportunities that her education and position afforded her. She supplied an example to an immediate circle of French noblewomen, but, more significantly, largely because of her literary and devotional writing, she also became famous throughout Europe as a model of female learning and piety. One of her works was later translated into English as *A godly medytacyon of the christen sowle* (1548) by the young princess who was to become Elizabeth I, Queen of England.

In spite of the impact her example undoubtedly had on European women, it would be a mistake to see this sister, wife, and grandmother of French kings as strongly feminist in her orientation. When she gave birth to her daughter Jeanne in 1528, she left her supervision and education to others. Jeanne was reared in the country until she was almost ten; during that time there are only two known references to the child in her mother's voluminous correspondence and records of only occasional visits to the château in Normandy where the little girl lived with her governess and tutor.[35]

Marguerite de Navarre is recognized historically as a significant cultural influence in her own time and in the generation which followed her. Ambassadors and courtiers realized that she was a powerful political force and courted her favor; Erasmus solicited her opinions on philosophical and religious questions;

reformers facing persecution sought her protection. Marguerite accepted the power and extended the responsibilities of her position; in so doing she enlarged the roles of women in learning, patronage, and public life.

NOTES

[1] Pierre de Bourdeille, Seigneur de Brantôme, *Oeuvres complètes, Société de l'histoire de France*, ed. Louis Lalanne (Paris: Jules Renouard, 1864-92), VII, 380-82, lists almost 150 noblewomen prominent at Catherine de Medici's court. See also Nancy L. Roelker, "The Role of Noblewomen in the French Reformation," *Archiv für Reformationsgeschichte*, 63 (1972), 168-95, and "The Appeal of Calvinism to French Noblewomen in the Sixteenth Century," *The Journal of Interdisciplinary History*, 2 (1972), 391-418.

[2] Ruth Kelso, *Doctrine for the Lady of the Renaissance* (Urbana: Univ. of Illinois Press, 1956), p. 267, lists over 800 treatises written about European noblewomen between 1400-1600.

[3] Hèdwig de Polignac (Chabannes), *Anne de Beaujeau* (Paris: Crépin-Leblond, 1955).

[4] References to the sixteenth-century editions of *L'Enseignement* are in Kelso, *Doctrine*, Bibliography, no. 33. Chabannes mentions a nineteenth-century edition that I have not located.

[5] Emile Gabory, *Anne de Bretagne* (Paris: Plon, 1941), and Paule H. Bordeaux, *Louise de Savoie* (Paris: Plon, 1954).

[6] See Irene Mahoney, *Madame Catherine* (New York: McCann and Geoghegan, 1975), for Catherine's significance.

[7] Roelker, "The Role of Noblewomen," p. 173.

[8] *Journal de Louise de Savoie*, in *Nouvelle Collection des mémoires pour servir à l'histoire de France*, ed. Joseph Michaud and Jean Poujoulat (Paris: chez l'editeur du Commentaire analytique du Code Civil, 1836-39), V, 87.

[9] Cardinal Bibbiena, Letter to Louise de Savoie, in Giuseppe Molini, *Documenti di storia italiana* (Florence: Tip. all' insegna di Dante, 1836-37), I, 75.

[10] There is no study of the education of women in Early Modern France, but see Eugenio Garin, *L'educazione in Europa, 1400-1600* (Bari: Laterza, 1957).

[11] For the libraries to which Louise and her children had access, see the definitive study by Pierre Jourda, *Marguerite d'Angoulême* (Paris: H. Champion, 1930), I, 20.

[12] Augustin Renaudet, "Marguerite de Navarre à propos d'un ouvrage récent," *Revue du seizième siècle*, 18 (1931), 272-308, questions her knowledge of Greek. She knew enough German to read some of Luther in the original. See also Jourda, *Marguerite d'Angoulême*, I, 3-28.

[13] Brantôme, VIII, 115, 118.

[14] The literature on the movement is enormous, and while the role of Marguerite and other artistocratic women is important, the sources are scattered. See, especially, Roland Bainton, *Women of the Reformation in France and England* (Minneapolis: Augsburg Publishing House, 1973); Augustine Renaudet, *Pré-réforme et humanisme* (Paris: Librairie d'Argences, 1953); and Michael Screech, *Marot évangélique* (Geneva: Droz, 1967).

[15] Henry Heller, "Marguerite of Navarre and the Reformers of Meaux," *Bibliothèque d'humanisme et renaissance*, 33 (1971), 271-310.

[16] Jourda, *Marguerite d'Angoulême*, I, 80-82.

[17] Aimé-Louis Herminjard, *Correspondance des réformateurs dans les pays de langue française* (Geneva: H. Georg, 1886-87), IV, 71 (no. 566); VI, 119 (no. 833).

[18] *Nouvelles lettres de Marguerite d'Angoulême*, ed. François Génin. (Paris: J. Renouard, 1842), II, 148-50 (no. 90); see, also, Pierre Jourda, *Répertoire analytique et chronologique de la correspondance de Marguerite d'Angoulême* (Paris: H. Champion, 1930), p. 160 (no. 700), and p. 162 (no. 709).

[19] For the suggestion of incest, see Génin, Introduction, *Nouvelles lettres*, but see also Nancy L. Roelker, *Queen of Navarre, Jeanne d'Albret* (Cambridge Mass.: Harvard Univ. Press, 1968), p. 37.

[20] *Bulletin de la société de l'histoire du protestantisme francais*, 33 (1844), 113, contains documents relating to this crisis; hereafter cited as *BSHPF*. See, also, Jourda, *Répertoire*, p. 128 (nos. 572-73).

[21] See my "Renée de France between Reform and Counter-Reform," *Archiv für Reformationsgeschichte*, 63 (1972), 204-07, for a discussion of Marot in relation to Marguerite and Renée de France, Duchess of Ferrara.

[22] Calvin to Marguerite, 28 April 1545; this letter seems to have marked the end of their friendly correspondence. *Johannis Calvini Opera quae supersunt omnia*, ed. Johann Baum et al. (Brunswick: C.A. Schwetschke et filium, 1863-1900), XII, col. 64-68 (no. 634).

[23] Roelker, *Queen of Navarre*, p. 15.

[24] Erasmus to Marguerite, 28 September 1525, in Jourda, *Répertoire*, p. 55 (no. 255).

[25] Jourda, *Marguerite d'Angoulême*, I, 247-51; *Répertoire*, p. 182 (no. 806); p. 219 (nos. 983-84).

[26] Jules Delaborde, *Gaspard de Coligny* (Paris: Sandoz et Fischbacher, 1879-82), I, 26-31, 54; François Génin, *Lettres de Marguerite d'Angoulême* (Paris: J. Renouard, 1841), pp. 265-66, 303.

[27] Blaisdell, "Renée de France between Reform and Counter-Reform," pp. 202-07.

[28] Jules Bonnet, "Disgrace de Monsieur et Madame de Pons à la cour de Ferrare," *BSHPF*, 29 (1880), 3-71; "Madame de la Roche à la cour de Ferrare," *BSHPF*, 32 (1883), 3-10.

[29] Little is known of Jacqueline; her support of the Huguenots is acknowledged by historians who base their account on Jeanne d'Albret, *Mémoires et poésies*, ed. Alphonse du Ruble (Paris: Paul Huart et Guillemin, 1893), pp. 7-12.

[30] See my "Heretics and Politics in Ferrara," *The Sixteenth Century Journal*, 6 (1975), 67-93.

[31] Henri Parry, "Le Protestantisme de Marguerite de France," *BSHPF*, 53 (1904), 7-27; Roger Peyre, *Une Princesse de la renaissance, Marguerite de France* (Paris: Paul, 1902).

[32] Heller, p. 279. See Donald Stone, *France in the Sixteenth Century* (Englewood Cliffs, New Jersey: Prentice Hall, 1969), and Marcel Tetel, *Marguerite de Navarre's Heptaméron* (Durham: Duke Univ. Press, 1973).

[33] Joan Kelly-Gadol, "Did Women Have a Renaissance?" in *Becoming Visible: Women in European History*, ed. Ranata Bridenthal and Claudia Koonz (Boston: Houghton Mifflin, 1977), pp. 137-64, and Sherrin M. Wyntjes, "Women in the Reformation Era," ibid., pp. 165-91.

[34] Roelker, "The Appeal of Calvinism," pp. 394, 404-05.

[35] Roelker, *Queen of Navarre*, pp. 9-34.

MARIA DE ZAYAS Y SOTOMAYOR:
SIBYL OF MADRID (1590?—1661?)

SANDRA M. FOA

> Who doubts, dear reader, that it will amaze you that a
> woman has the confidence, not only to write a book, but to
> send it to press. . . . Who doubts, I repeat, that there will be
> many who will attribute to madness this virtuoso audacity
> to give to the world my scribblings, being a woman, which in
> the opinion of some fools is the same as a useless object. . . .[1]

With these words Maria de Zayas y Sotomayor introduces her first collection of
short stories and shows her awareness of entering a new realm for women by
writing and publishing a book. Her introduction displays as well the conviction that women have the same potential as men, a potential that has not been
allowed to develop. To defend her entrance into the literary world, she cites
examples of famous women from antiquity: Argentaria, wife of the poet
Lucan, who, according to him, helped correct three books of the *Pharsalia*, and
even wrote many verses which passed as his own; Themistoclea, sister of
Pythagoras, who wrote a very learned book of maxims; Diotima, revered for
her eminence by Socrates; Eudoxa, author of a book on political counsel, and
others (I, 22).

Maria de Zayas remains a stranger to the English-speaking world because there
has been no complete translation of her stories.[2] Yet she should be known, not
only because her stories are entertaining and interesting historically, but also
because she is a female writer in an age and in a country in which women
writers are conspicuously absent. The names of only four women have survived
to our day from the Spanish Golden Age: Santa Teresa de Jesus, Sor Maria de
Agreda (who carried on a lengthy epistolary correspondence with Philip II),

Mariana de Carvajal y Saavedra (a later and inferior short story writer), and María de Zayas.[3]

The desire to vaunt her own intellect and ability is, in part, what impelled Zayas to write first verses and then novellas (I, 23). Although she also wrote a play, she is known exclusively for her two narrative collections. The first collection, published in 1637, is entitled *Novelas amorosas y ejemplares* [Amorous and Exemplary Novels]. The second, published ten years later and entitled *Parte segunda del sarao y entretenimiento honesto* [Part Two of the Honest Entertainment and Festivity], is also known as the *Desengaños amorosos*. Each novella in this second collection is called a *desengaño*[4] and its purpose is to point out to women the treachery and cruelty of men. Each of the two collections consists of ten stories narrated over a period of several days by a group of storytellers—five men and five women in the first one, ten women in the second.

The works of Zayas were very popular both in her own time and in the following century. The first collection was published twice in 1637 and again in 1638, the second in 1647, and the two together in eleven editions between 1648 and 1786. She was also influential abroad, especially in France, where some of her stories were translated, along with those of Cervantes, by Paul Scarron and Antoine de Methel. Moreover, Zayas was praised by various contemporaries, including Lope de Vega and Castillo Solórzano. The latter writes the following in *La garduña de Sevilla:*

> . . . it is very daring to write in these times when I see that such brilliant people give birth to creations as admirable as they are witty, and not only men who profess to know humanity; but in these times the wit of Doña María de Zayas y Sotomayor sparkles and shines with happy laurels. She has justly deserved the name of Sibyl of Madrid, acquired thanks to her admirable verses, her felicitous mind, and great prudence, having published a book of ten novellas which are ten wonders for those who write in this genre, since the meditated prose, the artifice, and the verses that she interpolates are all so admirable that they intimidate the most valiant pens of our Spain.[5]

Both of her collections of stories use narrative frames which present a society of storytellers with individual personalities and personal conflicts. At times the narrative frames are merely a literary pretext used to link the stories together, but for the most part they are coherently integrated into the narratives and closely related to the individual novellas and to the moral purpose that inspires them. On occasion, however, the identity of the individual narrator fuses with that of the author, and the storytellers give long feminist discourses that may not be consistent with their own personalities.[6] These seeming contradictions do not concern Zayas, whose principal purpose is didactic and whose storytellers are clearly the voices for her own ideas.

The frame story of the *Novelas amorosas* begins conventionally in the style of Boccaccio's *Decameron* and Marguerite de Navarre's *Heptaméron*: a woman is ill, four of her friends arrange a party to entertain her, and they invite five men. They are joined by the mother of the sick woman, and it is decided that for five nights they will sing, dance, and tell each other stories. The author's feminist preoccupations surface immediately in the amorous intrigue involving several members of the frame story: Lisis, who loves Don Juan; Don Juan, who loves and is loved by Lisarda; Don Diego, who, having noted Don Juan's indifference to Lisis, resolves to court her himself, thereby causing Don Juan to become jealous. The complications in the frame story introduce the themes of deceit and disillusionment and of the inconstancy and cruelty of men, themes which reappear in most of the individual stories. At the end of this first collection of novellas María de Zayas promises the conclusion of the amorous intrigue in a second part, "and in this the punishment of Don Juan's ingratitude, Lisarda's change of heart, and Lisis' wedding" (I, 423).

Don Juan's punishment and Lisarda's change of heart occur in the *Desengaños*, but Lisis' wedding does not take place. In this second collection, in which the frame story is more integrated into the individual stories, both structurally and thematically, the storytellers, who are all women this time, have been required to relate only true stories. The introductions that they make to their stories are therefore more personal. The first storyteller, for example, recounts her own life and relates the events of her story to the fact that she is now a slave in Lisis' house.

More important, perhaps, is the conclusion of the *Desengaños*. The pretext for the telling of the tales in the second collection has been the festivities that will culminate in the marriage of Lisis to Don Diego. Having enumerated all of the heroines of the *Desengaños* who suffered at the hands of husbands, fathers, or brothers, Lisis asks: "If a sad little life has so many enemies, and the greatest of them is a husband, who can force me to enter into a battle from which so many women have emerged defeated?"[7] For this reason, she concludes, "like one who has committed some crime, I am taking shelter in a place of safety, and I am taking for my refuge the retreat of a convent, from where (as from a tower) I intend to see what happens to the rest. Thus . . . I am going to save myself from the deceits of men" (II, 459). Because of this conclusion it is possible to view the frame story of the *Desengaños* as an eleventh exemplary novella ending with overt disillusionment when Lisis renounces marriage and decides to enter a convent.

It is clear that Zayas' purpose in writing these two collections of short stories is to defend women, to affirm their intellectual capacity, and to offer them advice. At the same time she wishes to entertain and to amuse. Consequently, she alternately stresses the aesthetic and the didactic aspects of her work:

> If by chance it should appear that the *desengaños* that have been related here, and those still to come, you have already heard elsewhere, it will be because they have been told by someone who, like me and the other *desengañadoras*, has heard them wholesale, but not with the circumstances with which they have been beautified here. . . . It is one thing to compose only with the imagination a story that neither was nor could be, and quite another thing to tell a true story that serves not only to entertain, but to advise women . . . and also to defend them . . . (II, 143-44).

First we have the reaction of the creative writer who defends her personal artistic contribution to these "true stories," then that of the moralizing writer who is emphasizing the veracity of the tales and their didactic intention.

In her opinion, an essential prerequisite for a novella to be truly exemplary is that it be authentic. Zayas' overwhelming desire to authenticate her stories is such that at times she even goes to the extreme of belittling her own inventive capacity in order to stress the importance of the truth:

> So many martyrs, so many virgins, so many widowed and chaste, so many that have died and suffered by the cruelty of men, that if this had not been so, our lady *desengañado-ras* would have had little cloth from which to cut their

desengaños, all as true as truth itself, so much so that they owe very little to fiction (II, 454).

At the same time, Zayas is clearly proud of her achievement and rushes to defend her purely artistic contribution to these "true stories": "and I say this, because if anyone has heard anything about this person, it will be as I say, *but not published or handled by other talented persons*. And since it has been proposed that these *Desengaños* be based on true stories, it is inevitable that some will have heard them elsewhere, *but not as they are told here*" (II, 409).[8]

María de Zayas feels that her works are even more worthy of praise than those of men because she has not been aided by art (i.e., training and education), but by her own natural ability, the gift of heaven (II, 413). This is an idea repeatedly expressed in both collections of novellas:

> But believe me that even if women are not Homers with skirts and petticoats or Virgils with chignons, at least they have the same soul, abilities, and feelings as men. I do not wish to say intellect, because although many could compete with men in this, they lack the art to which men have recourse through study, and since what women do is only natural, it is inevitable that it should not be as refined (II, 104).

In spite of her obvious interest in education for women, there is very little that can be said about the education Zayas herself received. Indeed, very little is known about her life. It is believed that she was born in Madrid about 1590, that she belonged to an aristocratic family, and that she died in 1661. Although she spent most of her life in the city of her birth, she may also have actually traveled to those cities which are the settings of some of her stories. But whether she married and when exactly she died we do not know.

It is tempting to identify María de Zayas with Lisis, the principal character of the frame story, for, by explicitly renouncing marriage and all its inherent dangers in favor of life in a convent, Lisis seems to play an exemplary role within the context of the frame story. The author's last words, addressed to an unknown person, Fabio, suggest, furthermore, that perhaps Lisis' decision was Zayas' own:

And so, illustrious Fabio, in order to carry out your request that I not give a tragic ending to this story, the beautiful Lisis remains in a cloister . . . not disillusioned through her own misfortunes. It is not a tragic end, but the happiest that could be, since coveted and desired by many, she subjected herself to none. If you still desire to see her, look for her with a chaste intention, and you will find her as ever yours, and with her will as firm and honest as she has promised, and as much at your service as ever, and as you deserve . . . (II, 461).

This is signed "Doña María de Zayas y Sotomayor." If indeed, like Lisis, Zayas did enter a convent, this could help to explain why nothing is known about her following the publication of the *Desengaños*.

For lack of concrete evidence, we can only approach María de Zayas through her works, either from what she says directly or from what we can surmise. Zayas does inform us of her overwhelming interest in reading: "What reason is there why we [women] should not have promptitude for books? Especially if they all have my inclination, that whenever I see one, old or new, I put down the sewing cushion and do not rest until I've read it all" (I, 22-23). It is also clear from the variety of her sources that she has read a great deal: *Les cent nouvelles nouvelles*, Boccaccio, Timoneda, Bandello, Marguerite de Navarre, Lope de Vega, Cervantes.[9] Though the sources of many of her novellas have been identified, the reader is struck by the very personal style she has developed; while she makes use of earlier works, she generally subordinates what she borrows to her own didactic feminist purposes.

Although Zayas claims that she writes without art and that she has not "sought rhetorical or cultured arguments," but rather has "endeavored to speak in the language that nature has taught [her]" (II, 412), we find various examples of rhetorical ornaments in her prose: rhetorical questions, antithesis, anaphora, litotes, polysyndeton, oxymoron, hyperbole, apostrophe. The use of these embellishments suggests that while Zayas may have learned these tropes and figures from her reading, it is more likely that she received an elementary education in the art of rhetoric, or at least that she knew some of the many manuals of rhetoric circulating in Spain in the seventeenth century.

Zayas' theme, the battle of the sexes, is also related to a tradition, the *Querelle des Femmes*, which dates from the early fifteenth century when Christine de Pisan actively and consciously assumed the defense of women. We find in Christine's works some of the themes which were to recur two centuries later in the work of María de Zayas. Like Zayas, Christine advocates the education of women:

> If it were the custom to put little girls in school, and to teach them sciences, they would learn as perfectly and would understand the subtleties of all the arts and sciences as boys do.[10]

Zayas, however, goes beyond defending women and advocating that they be given an education: she attacks the customs which have kept women ignorant. One of her storytellers goes so far as to suggest that it is out of fear and envy that men deprive women of the opportunity to study the arts of arms and letters:

> Therefore they accuse them [women] of being of easy virtue and of little value so that they will not usurp their power. And so, as soon as the little girls can talk, they put them to do needlework and to do hemstitch, and if they teach them to read, it is a miracle. For there are fathers who consider it of little value that their daughters should know how to read and write, contending that knowledge makes them bad, as though there were not many who do not know how to read and write and are still bad, and this is natural envy and fear. . . . It would be strange indeed if a woman who armed herself with a sword allowed a man to wrong her at any time; it would indeed be a wonder if a woman who professed letters did not compete with men . . . for official positions. Consequently, women are oppressed and obliged to exercise domestic chores (II, 176-77).

Although concern for the position of women in society is frequently reiterated in the writings of sixteenth-century Spain, by the seventeenth century the theme of the *Querelle des Femmes* survives only in the theater where it invariably ends with the defeat of feminist ideas in favor of a more traditional view of women as subservient to men. The seventeenth-century Spanish woman was to be content with her home and not make herself ridiculous by trying to rival men in learning or achievements.[11] Zayas' defense of women and of their right to education derives from a tradition extending back to Christine de Pisan, but her treatment of this theme departs sharply from contemporary practice. Her vigorous support of the feminist position is unconventional and thus seems to be a response to a social situation as well as to a literary tradition.

The seventeenth century was a time of crisis in Spain. In the first place, it was a century of almost continual warfare. Although Spain had already been at war for many years, it was around the middle of the seventeenth century that battles took place not only in the colonies and in neighboring countries, but also within Spain itself. The situation changed radically with the uprisings of Catalonia and Portugal in June and December of 1640, respectively. As a consequence, Spain was for many years constrained to fight simultaneously in France, Italy, Flanders, Catalonia, and Portugal. It is natural that all these wars, the majority of which ended in defeat after the year 1640, should have negatively affected the Spaniards who thought they were still living in the Golden Age of the Spanish Empire.

The economic problems of the period intensified this unrest. We see in the writings of the time numerous allusions to the scarcity of food, to the decline of the currency, and to the lack of money.[12] The glory of the sixteenth century gave way to unemployment, hunger, sickness, and depopulation in the following century. The Spaniards of the 1600's were thus living in an unstable condition, "supported by a net-work of tensions, by internal oppositions," with evidence of the progressive political and economic decadence of their country.[13]

It is natural that the resulting pessimism and *desengaño* in the political and social sphere should have been reflected in the literature of the seventeenth century. We see, for example, the importance of the theme of *desengaño* applied to a number of different motifs: *desengaño* with the world, with love, with men, with life. As a result, we note an enormous preoccupation with death and with physical decay, a new emphasis on the evil of the world and of human beings, and the cultivation of violence and the grotesque. Nothing is what it appears to be: all is illusion and deceit. Men are frequently compared to beasts, with the latter appearing in the more favorable light. Life is represented as constant warfare, or as dream, shadow, theater. This is the world view that characterizes the major writers of the seventeenth century: Mateo Alemán, Francisco de Quevedo, Baltasar Gracián, Pedro Calderón de la Barca. Like them María de Zayas presents a world of cruelty, of lasciviousness, of betrayal, of hatred, of war, and, above all, of *desengaño*.

61

The fictional occurrences of the second collection, the *Desengaños amorosos*, are more bitter and more clearly associated with historical events than those in the *Novelas amorosas*. This is not surprising in view of the worsening political and economic situation in the decade that separates the two collections. This decade saw the uprisings of Catalonia and Portugal as well as the continuation of wars in Flanders and in Italy. Zayas' novellas recall these events, emphasizing the enmity between the Spanish and the Portuguese.[14]

In the last story of the *Desengaños amorosos*, in a lengthy interpolation which merits attention, Zayas bitterly criticizes the effeminacy of the Spaniards, linking their unwillingness to fight to their low opinion of women:

> What human or divine law do you find, noble gentlemen, that justifies your condemnation of women, so much so that one can barely find one [man] to defend them, when one sees so many that attack them? . . . Where do you think the little valor that you have nowadays comes from, that you suffer the enemy to be inside Spain, and our king in the field, while you are at the Paseo del Prado and the river, covered in ornaments and in feminine garb, while the few who accompany him are sighing for their pampered life of the good old days? It comes from the little that you esteem women, for I vow that if you esteemed women, and loved them as once was done, in order not to see them in the hands of your enemies, you would offer yourselves, not just to go to war and fight but to die . . . as used to happen . . . at the time of the Catholic King Ferdinand, when it was not necessary to take men by force or handcuffed, as they do now. . . . But since you consider women the most contemptible and worthless jewels in your houses, you do not care if they become the slaves of others in other kingdoms.
> Is it possible that you can see us almost in the hands of the enemy . . . and that you are not ashamed to be in the Court, wearing out your fine clothes, preening your hair, lolling about in carriages, and strolling through the gardens, and that instead of defending us you take away our reputation and our honor, telling tales of what has happened to you with ladies . . . ? That Spanish breasts should do this! That Spanish spirits should suffer this! A wise man said that the French have stolen your valor, and you have appropriated their dress (II, 454-56).

Thus, María de Zayas reflects her concern for the condition of her country; the world she presents in her novellas is a world torn by hatred and betrayal. In the majority of her narratives we witness the breakdown of affective ties: love and friendship have disappeared; fathers turn against daughters; husbands against wives; brothers against sisters.

During the reign of Philip IV in the second third of the seventeenth century the relationship between the sexes was seen in a new light because the Catholic Church began increasingly to emphasize purity and chastity. Antonio Domínguez Ortiz has described this new religion as "hostile to the world and its pleasures," observing that the relations between women and men were now "hemmed in by an incredible series of taboos."[15] Although the relationship between the sexes is a common theme in the *desengaño* writers, Zayas is unique in having made it the central theme of her narratives and in having blamed men for the tensions between the sexes. She denies quite explicitly the possibility of true love, and, by extension, of happiness in marriage. Her rejection of an idealized view of marriage represents a significant deviation from the more traditional approach of Cervantes and Lope de Vega.

At no time does Zayas attack the sacrament of marriage per se, but in story after story her protagonists reject married life, either before or after marriage, and decide to enter a convent. While stressing the vanity of the world and the need to withdraw from it, the seventeenth-century ascetic Juan Eusebio Nieremberg does not permit married women to take such a step. He recognizes the difficulties inherent in the matrimonial state, but declares that "this is her state, and in it she must remain, following the advice of St. Paul that everyone persevere in his vocation and calling."[16] Zayas, on the other hand, advocates withdrawal into a convent even for married women. One woman refuses to return to her husband, although he pleads with her to do so, because

> she had become disillusioned with the world and with men, and so no longer wanted to do battle with them. . . . For this reason she wanted to enter a convent, a powerful haven from which to protect herself against the miseries to which women are subject (I, 246).

Although the retreat from the world, typical of her heroines, is backed by a lengthy tradition of renunciation, the motivation of her women is different. Instead of renouncing the world to escape vice and temptation, they are motivated by a longing to escape the deceits, cruelties, and betrayals of men.

The only work closely approaching that of María de Zayas in both tone and theme is the French novel *La Princesse de Clèves* by Madame de Lafayette, which appeared in 1678. A member of the fashionable French world, friend of Madame de Sévigné and La Rochefoucauld, Madame de Lafayette belonged to the kind of cultivated literary circle in which the works of Zayas might well have been known and read. In any event the two authors share a disillusionment with love and marriage. Madame de Lafayette depicts a court characterized by amorous intrigue, deceit, and betrayal. In such an atmosphere it is to be expected that love should be regarded with a certain suspicion, but to this general distrust is added a particular distrust of men:

> Madame de Chartres . . . faisait souvent à sa fille des peintures de l'amour. . . . Elle lui connait le peu de sincérité des hommes, leurs tromperies et leur infidélité.
> [Madame de Chartres often described love affairs to her daughter. . . . She told her of men's inability to be sincere, of their deceits, of their infidelities.] [17]

In this world love cannot be preserved once possession has been achieved. For this reason the princess rejects the proposal of the Duke of Nemours; she is convinced that obstacles alone have caused him to remain constant. When a long illness causes her to view the things of this world with other eyes, she renounces the court and withdraws into a convent. The ending of *La Princesse de Clèves* is reminiscent of that of the *Desengaños amorosos* where Lisis, also in the wake of a lengthy illness, and in order not to be deceived, rejects marriage in favor of the convent.

The picture that Zayas paints, however, is bleaker. Few of her male protagonists are, like the Prince of Clèves, good husbands; on the contrary, most are exaggeratedly presented as violent, lascivious, deceitful, inconstant, and cruel. One husband believes a false accusation and treats his wife like a dog: she is locked in a small room and only allowed out at meal times, at which time she crawls under the table, and her husband feeds her bones and crumbs. Another husband walls up his wife for six years for a sin that she has committed involuntarily; a third beheads his wife because she is poor; the examples could be multiplied indefinitely. [18]

In six stories from the second collection Zayas presents a series of women who are, she tells us, martyrs, victimized by men. Calling love "war and pitched battle" (I, 71), she uses military images to underscore the stratagems and artifices by which men lay siege to women's honesty. In the second collection the storytellers, or *desengañadoras*, are described as having declared war on men, "armed with comparisons and prodigious cases" (II, 102). One of the male members of the audience is forced to recognize men's culpability and yield: "We declare ourselves defeated and confess that there are men who with their cruelties and deceits condemn themselves and exonerate women" (II, 292). In a witty suggestion of role reversal, Zayas ends the *Desengaños amorosos* with an allusion to the Spanish wars, an allusion suggesting that women will have to defend themselves in both a figurative and a literal sense:

> If my written defense is not sufficient, it will be necessary
> for all of us to take up arms to defend ourselves against
> their [men's] ill intentions, and to defend them against
> our enemies (II, 460).

For the heroines of Zayas' stories the battle between the sexes reaches a triumphant conclusion only when they leave the social battlefield, ascetically renouncing marriage.

More insistently a feminist in her point of view than many of her female predecessors and more critical of the treatment of women than most of her contemporaries, Zayas deserves a place in the tradition of learned women by virtue of her own intense awareness of herself as a woman writer, espousing the cause of women. Her awareness of herself as a woman causes her to reverse the *topos* of modesty. She is certain that she has creative skill and that she is not a "useless object" because of her sex. On the contrary, she asks, "if souls are neither male nor female, why should men be learned and yet assume that women cannot be?" (I, 21). With fierce conviction she answers her own question: men are tyrants who lock women up and deprive them of teachers. "Thus," she writes, "the true reason that women are not learned is lack of opportunity, not lack of ability" (I, 22). In the work of María de Zayas there is not only a commitment to education for women, but also a passionate conviction that, granted an education, women might enter public life and engage in those professions traditionally regarded as the province of men: "If in their education they were given books and preceptors rather than fine linen, working cases, and sketches for embroidery frames, then they would be as capable as men of filling official posts and university chairs" (I, 22).

NOTES

[1] María de Zayas y Sotomayor, *Novelas amorosas y ejemplares* (Madrid: Biblioteca Selecta de Clásicos Españoles, 1948), p. 21. All references will be to this edition; page numbers will appear in parentheses in the text, preceded by "I," indicating the first collection. All translations are mine.

[2] There has only been one translation of María de Zayas in recent years and this only in a partial and limited edition. See John Sturrock, *A Shameful Revenge and Other Stories* (London: The Folio Society, 1963).

[3] Melveena McKendrick, *Woman and Society in the Spanish Drama of the Golden Age* (London: Cambridge University Press, 1974), pp. 22-23.

[4] *Desengaño* translates variously as "realization of the truth," "disillusionment," "lessons learned from experience," "undeception," "warning." Since the Spanish contains all these nuances, I have used the Spanish word throughout this study.

[5] Alonso de Castillo Solórzano, *La garduña de Sevilla* (Madrid: Clásicos Castellanos, 1957), p. 66. The translation is mine.

[6] Since I am not as concerned here with literary form as I am with Zayas' ideas, I have made no attempt to distinguish between the voices of the individual storytellers and the voice of the author of the written text. For a full-length study of the literary form, see my *Feminismo y forma narrativa: un estudio del tema y las técnicas de María de Zayas y Sotomayor* (Chapel Hill: Estudios de Hispanófila, forthcoming).

[7] María de Zayas y Sotomayor, *Parte segunda del sarao y entretenimiento honesto* (Madrid: Biblioteca Selecta de Clásicos Españoles, 1950), p. 459. All quotations will be from this edition; page numbers will appear in parentheses in the text, preceded by "II," indicating the second collection. All translations are mine.

[8] The emphasis is mine.

[9] Some of the Italian works she might have read in Spanish include the *Decameron*, which had been translated into Spanish several times, and several of Bandello's works (through a French translation), but I know of no Spanish translation of the *Heptaméron* available to her.

[10] Christine de Pisan, *La Cité des Dames*, cited by Emile Telle, *L'Oeuvre de Marguerite d'Angoulême, Reine de Navarre, et la Querelle des Femmes* (Toulouse, 1937; rpt. Geneva: Slatkine Reprints, 1969), p. 35. The translation is mine.

[11] Barbara Matulka, "The Feminist Theme in the Drama of the Siglo de Oro," *Romanic Review*, 26 (1935), 230.

[12] José Pellicer, *Avisos históricos* (Madrid: Taurus, 1965), pp. 150, 182, 215, 250.

[13] José Antonio Maravall, "Los españoles del 1600," *Triunfo*, 532 Extra (9 December 1972), 15. The translation is mine.

[14] One of her narrators states: "At this time the uprising of Catalonia took place as a punishment for our sins, or only for mine . . . since those who died on this occasion gained eternal fame, whereas I, who remained alive, gained ignominious infamy" (II, 19). In another story the narrator says the following: "Since he was Spanish, he did not find in them [the Portuguese] what he was hoping for, on account of the feeling that this nation has toward ours that, although they live among us, they are our enemies" (II, 420).

[15] Antonio Domínguez Ortiz, *The Golden Age of Spain, 1516-1650*, trans. James Casey (London: Weidenfield and Nicolson, 1971), p. 201.

[16] Juan Eusebio Nieremberg, *Epistolario* (Madrid: Clásicos Castellanos, 1915), p. 121. The translation is mine.

[17] Madame de Lafayette, *La Princesse de Clèves* (Paris: Gallimard, 1958), p. 27. Translation is by Mildred S. Greene, who has prepared a new translation of *La Princesse de Clèves* for Romance Monographs, forthcoming from the University of Mississippi Press.

[18] See stories V, III, and VIII of the *Desengaños amorosos*.

ANNA MARIA VAN SCHURMAN:
THE STAR OF UTRECHT* (1607–1678)

JOYCE L. IRWIN

The Tower of London, the Arc de Triomphe, the Roman Coliseum—these are the European traveler's sightseeing "musts" in our day. For the mid-seventeenth-century traveler, one essential of a complete tour was a visit to the Star of Utrecht, Anna Maria van Schurman. Queens and princes, poets and philosophers all sought an audience with this extraordinarily learned young woman. "To have been in Utrecht without having seen Mademoiselle de Schurman," wrote her friend and biographer Pierre Yvon, "was like having been to Paris without having seen the king."[1] Indeed, claiming lack of time for her studies, she was perhaps as selective in her choice of visitors as was the king. Had not her friends the Dutch theologians Andreas Rivet, Frederic Spanheim, and Gisbertus Voetius prevailed upon her to receive noted personages, she might have cloistered herself with her books. Both a temperamental modesty and a conservative view of women's roles in society prevented her from actively seeking to extend her own reputation.

Yet in spite of her wishes, her fame spread through the European scholarly world, partially because of the prominence of her close friends. Not only the above-mentioned Dutch theologians, but also prominent Dutch poets Jacob Cats and Constantin Huygens were in close contact with her. They, and many less talented writers, were inspired to express their admiration of her in verse. Dutch physician Johan van Beverwijck went beyond poetry to write a lengthy volume in praise of women, in which Anna Maria van Schurman was declared the marvel who outshone all previous remarkable women of learning. From

*Portions reprinted with permission from *Church History*, 46 (March, 1977), 48-61.

beyond the borders of the Netherlands came letters from Cardinal Richelieu and philosophers Pierre Gassendi and Marin Mersenne. The most noted of French philosophers, René Descartes, paid a visit to her, although his doubts about the value of learning Hebrew brought the visit to an unfriendly end.[2] Her circle of admirers also included many of the educated women of the time, including Queen Christine of Sweden, Princess Elizabeth of Bohemia, and the Englishwomen Bathsua Makin and Dorothea Moor.

Holland in its Golden Age was, to be sure, a better place than most for a woman to carry on a life of scholarship. Economic prosperity provided the advantages of leisure, and a tradition of religious and intellectual tolerance created a relatively open-minded atmosphere. It is also significant that even before the Reformation girls were given an elementary education in Holland.

Anna van Schurman's exceptional education, however, could hardly have taken place in an elementary school. Descended from Protestant grandparents who had fled the Duke of Alva's persecution, she was born in Cologne in 1607 to staunchly Reformed parents Eva van Harf and Frederic van Schurman. When Reformed services were banned in Cologne, they retreated for a few years to the van Harf family castle in Dreiborn and later to Utrecht, but since the Remonstrants had gained prominence in the churches of Utrecht, religious controversy pursued them even there. The strength of the parents' orthodox convictions was transmitted to their daughter at an early age. It was reported by Yvon that once when she was sent to church at age seven or eight, "she could scarcely remain until the end, feeling such repugnance toward all she had heard preached against the truths of predestination and grace. There was no way to make her go again, although her parents, who did not attend, had believed she was not capable of deciding what evils or errors were being preached."[3]

Serious about their religion, Frederic and Eva van Schurman were also serious about their daughter's education. After sending her to school for two months, they withdrew her, convinced that she would get more thorough instruction at home with her brothers. At first her brothers, who were two and four years older than she, were given more advanced lessons, but when she started prompting them in their lessons, she was allowed to study at their level. Under the tutelage and encouragement of her father, she learned quickly and eagerly, soon mastering Greek and Latin and reading selections from the classics. In addition to languages, she studied arithmetic, geography, astronomy, and music, traditional components of a Renaissance education. Remarkable as were her accomplishments in these areas, the most lasting achievements from this period of her life were in the visual arts. Her paintings, engravings, and intricate paper-cuttings are still on display in the Dutch town of Franeker, where the family moved when she was sixteen. Franeker at the time had a leading university—the university in Utrecht was yet to be founded—and the Schurman sons were to pursue their education there. Soon after the move their father died, and Anna and her mother returned to Utrecht. Nevertheless, the paternal influence was to persist with Anna long after his death in his admonition to flee the secular world and beware of marrige as a distraction from the love of God.

The guiding influences of Schurman's next few years are unclear because not much is known of her life between the ages of sixteen and twenty-five. Biographer Una Birch calls this the "frivolous time of her life" when she delighted in depicting herself in engravings as a fashionably dressed young woman.[4] These elaborate portraits seem the product of someone absorbed in enjoyment of the good things with which her relative wealth had provided her.

In her late twenties she turned more wholeheartedly toward the intellectual pursuits for which she was to become so famous. Her knowledge of Latin had already at the age of thirteen or fourteen attracted the attention of the poet Jacob Cats who, it was said, subsequently wished to marry her.[5] Now more than a decade later she, as the foremost Latinist in town, was chosen to write a festive Latin poem for the opening of the new university in Utrecht. The man who made the request, Rector Gisbertus Voetius, was to be her mentor at the university for the next several years. As theologian and professor of oriental languages, he arranged a special cubicle opening into his lecture room where she could attend lectures without attracting the attention of those who had never seen a woman in a lecture hall. Under Voetius' guidance, Schurman engrossed herself in the study not only of Hebrew, but also of such exotic languages as Arabic, Chaldee, Syriac, and Ethiopian.[6] She wrote occasional letters in Hebrew (to Dorothea Moor, for instance), but her most unusual accomplishment was an Ethiopian grammar which she composed for her own use. Through Voetius, Schurman was brought into contact with other orientalists, such as Job Ludolf, who marvelled at her knowledge of Ethiopian.

As the leading Dutch Reformed theologian of the day, Voetius' influence quite naturally extended beyond instruction in languages. Although much foreign language study was undoubtedly motivated by curiosity, the primary expressed motivation was a better understanding of Holy Scripture. In the scholastic mode, theology remained for Voetius the queen of the sciences. His inaugural oration on the opening of the academy at Utrecht was entitled "On Joining Piety with Knowledge,"[7] and a later sermon on a similar topic expressed the view that the aim of all education should be the knowledge of God.[8] The Bible, he claimed, is the most reliable source of information on everything from physics to music.

Anna van Schurman became very much a disciple of Voetius in this respect. Though her religious convictions were always strong, it was only during the mid-1630's that she began to devote herself to theology. One of her earliest published works was a theological treatise, "On the End of Life."[9] While not particularly noteworthy in its own right, the discussion revealed her breadth of familiarity with both classical and Christian authors, whom she invoked as witnesses to the power of God or of fate. The essay was dedicated to the physician and Deputy to the States-General Johan van Beverwijck, who had it published with suitable introductory praise by Cats and others. From another philosophical camp, however, enthusiasm for her theological pursuits was not so strong. Descartes, whose philosophy was out of favor in Utrecht, bemoaned the hold which Voetius had gained over her:

> This Voetius has also ruined Mademoiselle Schurman, for she used to have an excellent spirit for poetry, painting, and other pleasantries; but for the last five or six years he has possessed her completely. She occupies herself solely with theological controversy, which has caused her to lose contact with all polite company.[10]

If Descartes and "polite company" regarded her as "ruined," this loss of admirers was offset by the immense respect she gained in other circles. Her impressive credentials became a testimony to the power of women's intellect. Her close friend Beverwijck took up the praise of women, cataloging all the notable women known to him throughout history; heading the list of "learned ladies" was "the incomparable young lady Anna Maria van Schurman."[11] As far away as the American colonies, Cotton Mather made reference to the "most renowned Anna Maria Schurman" as background for adding his own nominee, poet Anne Bradstreet, for the disputed title "Tenth Muse."[12]

Not only Schurman's own educational accomplishments but also her treatise in defense of women's education contributed to the emerging feminist cause. Voetius, in raising the question whether women ought to be educated,[13]

deferred entirely to the arguments Schurman set forth in her *Amica dissertatio
. . . de capacitate ingenii muliebris ad scientias.* This work, written in 1638 in
scholastic format, debated the question "whether the study of letters is fitting
to a Christian woman." First published in Paris, it was republished in Leiden
with a slightly altered title in 1641, then translated into French (1646)[14] and
English (1659).[15] In *Opuscula*, the 1648 collection of her writings, the *Dissertatio* was printed along with her correspondence on female scholarship with
Andreas Rivet, an influential Calvinist theologian in Leiden and The Hague.[16]
Although Schurman's assertions were not radical even by seventeenth-century
standards, the objections raised by Rivet indicate that she had probably reached
the limits of what would be acceptable in orthodox Calvinist circles.

The very definition of terms with which she prefaces her treatise narrows the
scope of possible conclusions. The woman whose education is being debated
must possess at least average mental ability, means of instruction, freedom
from domestic cares, and a desire to glorify God through study. Education of
girls, as she conceives it, remains a private matter dependent on the parents'
ability to provide tutors and to free their daughters from housework. Advanced
learning is consequently possible only for single women supported by their
families or for the well-to-do. In contrast to the English Puritan ideal of the
same time, Schurman's primary reason for educating girls is not to make them
better wives and mothers. Should this be their lot, their learning would indeed
be beneficial for teaching the family, but the main goal should be "the glory
of God and the salvation of one's soul" (p. 31).

A conviction of the close relationship between devotion and knowledge is
apparent throughout both the treatise and her letters to Rivet. Reminiscent
of Voetius, natural knowledge is believed to supplement and reinforce revealed
knowledge: "Arts and science allow us to observe and recognize God and
divine works at a higher level" (p. 212). Confident that acquaintance with the
harmony and complexity of the natural world could only lead to praise of
God, she exclaimed to Rivet:

> Certainly we would be tree trunks, not men; strangers, not
> inhabitants of this world, if we did not bring an excited
> mind, as if fired by divine love, to such beautiful, august
> things in which the majesty of the eternal divinity shines
> forth (p. 72).

Rivet's objection at this point has nothing to do with the desirability of educating women in the sciences, but instead he questions Schurman's grounds for confidence in the complementary relationship between faith and science.

Whatever the theoretical relationship, Rivet maintains, in practice increased knowledge more often undermines than enhances devotion. In actuality it is more often the less educated who are drawn to the praise of God through observation of the stars and planets:

> It often happens that those who are considered greatly versed in such things are seen turning from God in order to attribute all things to nature; and, on the other hand, those who possess a simple range of vision may be inspired to sing the praises of God's wondrous works. They may find comfort wholeheartedly in their author, while the most learned weary their minds in vain and after long disquisitions feast upon the wind (pp. 89-90).

Even Voetius, in those writings which sound so similar to Schurman's, had been attempting to ward off the threat of secularism and atheism which he perceived as plaguing scholarship. But Schurman, in her unworldliness, seemed at this point oblivious to the danger.

A second major theme in her defense of education was its contribution to morality. Ignorance and idleness, she notes, are sources of error and vice. The study of letters provides a basis for proper action and occupies the mind with a "solid and enduring occupation" (p. 36). It leads to "true greatness of soul" (p. 45). This line of argument lay at the basis of such sixteenth-century defenses of women's education as that of the Spanish humanist Juan Luis Vives, *De Institutione foeminae Christianae*.[17] Vives, brought to the English court by Catherine of Aragon, believed education was valuable for females in that it gave them a worthy alternative to idleness; yet censorship must be exercised in the choice of reading material, for all female learning must have moral value. Rivet, in his response to Schurman, also pointed out a qualification in Vives' praise of study: the practical arts of homemaking are equally worthy, even for the leisured classes. Schurman, professing enthusiasm for Vives' treatment of the issue, nevertheless gives the distinct impression that household activities are a lesser calling—compelling indeed for the married woman without servants, but lacking the moral value of intellectual activity. Vives and Schurman were agreed on the close relationship between ignorance and vice. Human nature, as they viewed it, inclines toward the bad and can be expected to do good only if instructed therein. But Schurman again in this respect seems unduly sanguine about the positive effects of knowledge. For her there is no question of censorship. It is as if all knowledge were uplifting to some extent, no matter what the subject matter.[18]

This trend of thought merges with the third main argument of her treatise: pursuit of knowledge is valuable for its own sake. Those who have the capacity or the desire to study should be allowed to do so. As she states in three of her theses:

> Arts and sciences are fitting for those who by nature desire them (p. 35).
> Whatever perfects and adorns human understanding is fitting to a Christian woman (p. 41).
> Whatever fills the human mind with uncommon and honest delight is fitting for a Christian woman (p. 45).

Such a teleological approach to the human mind is reminiscent of scholastic-Aristotelian assertions of a natural yearning for the Highest Good or of a natural knowledge of God as the ultimate object of human desire. Yet Schurman stops short of making such a claim, arguing in effect that happiness may be attained merely by using the mind, not by using it as a means to either a divine or a human end.

Here again Rivet saw grounds for criticism. Many fields of knowledge, he argued, are not ends in themselves but only aids in preparing for positions in church or state. Yet neither Rivet nor Schurman thought it appropriate for women in ordinary circumstances to assume such positions of leadership. The Bible, after all, enjoins women to silence in the church. To what end, then, should women learn the art of rhetoric or politics? Knowledge, in Rivet's view, does not justify itself; learning must be directed toward some more concrete goal. Rivet called for such a goal to be established for women's education, following which "those things might be chosen which were suitable or necessary to that end" (p. 84).

To Schurman's way of thinking even the goal of practically-oriented studies need not involve public practice: "even if [women] do not follow the primary or public goal, nevertheless the secondary or private goal is greater" (p. 54). Scholarship is to be defended for women only as a leisure-time activity, yet this is not to belittle it. The tranquility of a life freed from practical concerns is the proper setting for the pursuit of wisdom: "For, [Seneca] says, of all men only those are at leisure (that is, they best use their leisure) who have time for wisdom; they alone live, for they do not only look after their age well, they apply all eternity to themselves. For one must not seek leisure from the best things but seek the best things in leisure" (pp. 67-68).

Although only a small portion of women are blessed with this leisure, Schurman rejected the notion that learning was only for the few. Wisdom for her was so valuable, such a beautiful adornment of the human race, that "it ought by right to be extended to one and all" (p. 65). Hence what she found most objectionable in Rivet's letters was the assertion, "it may not even be expedient for many to choose this kind of life, and it may suffice if a few, called to it by a special instinct, sometimes stand out" (p. 60). Fearing a disturbance of the social order, Rivet doubted that it would be in the public interest for more than a few to devote themselves to intellectual achievement (p. 87). Schurman, on the other hand, saw no basis for such fears; widespread education among women, far from upsetting the social order, would strengthen it:

> Nor is there any reason why the Republic should fear such a change of this kind for itself, since the glory of the literary order in no way obstructs the light of the rulers. On the contrary, all agree that state at length will flourish most which is inhabited by many subjects obedient not so much to laws as to wisdom (pp. 65-66).

Again at this point we might wish to credit Rivet with greater insight into the ultimate ramifications of Schurman's proposals. Extensive education of women could not help but lead to changes in society. Underlying Rivet's criticisms of Schurman's optimism is, nevertheless, a basic agreement: as valuable as learning may be for women, it should never become the basis for claiming women's superiority or for leading women into positions of public leadership. Both feminine modesty and the Biblical injunctions to remain subordinate to men should prevent any such assertiveness.

These assumptions cause Schurman to be one of the more conservative defenders of the feminist cause in the early seventeenth century. At the beginning of the century a more radical writer, Lucretia Marinella, a Venetian widow, had attempted to demonstrate the superiority of women over men. In *Le Nobiltà et Eccellènza delle Donne* (1600), she argued that women's greater physical beauty reflects their greater spiritual beauty and greater likeness to God. Because of their more beautiful souls, women are superior to men in all virtues and capable of equalling any masculine accomplishment. As prescribed in Plato's *Republic*, they should share equally in educational, political, and military endeavors. After exhorting women to emulate great women of the past, Marinella proceeds in the second half of her book to examine the defects of males. Such an approach was an affront to Anna van Schurman's feminine modesty:

> If the hypothesis [that women are more fitted for study than men] is put forward, then the arguments I should introduce for my thesis could not only seem weakened and foolish but could also be accused of a new and haughty vanity. It is so far from me to think this fitting with maidenly modesty or at least with the bashfulness inborn in me that it caused disgust to read that otherwise outstanding treatment of Lucretia Marinella . . . (p. 92).

She preferred the more moderate essay of Marie le Jars de Gournay, disciple and close friend of the essayist Montaigne. At the outset of *L'Egalité des Hommes et des Femmes* (1622), Marie de Gournay remarked, perhaps with indirect reference to Marinella, that she was content to plead for equality rather than superiority.[19] Her treatise was for this reason more acceptable to Anna van Schurman, who praised Marie de Gournay both in prose and in verse. Yet it is difficult to imagine staunchly Calvinist Schurman sharing the Biblical interpretation of Gournay, who set out to demonstrate that the Bible could support the equality of the sexes.[20] Male and female, says Gournay, were created together, and therefore share the same nature, the same honor, the same virtues. If Paul demanded the silence of women in the church, it is not because of any disdain for them but for fear that, given their greater charm and beauty, they might not be able to resist the temptations of a public ministry. The fact that Jesus was incarnated as a man does not indicate that divinity is masculine, only that, needing to mingle with crowds at all hours of the day and night, he was better able to avoid scandal as a man.

Such thoughts surely must have seemed irreverent to the pious and demure young woman from Utrecht. Yet if they did, she recognized her common cause with Gournay whatever their differences. Although Gournay defended sexual equality on a much broader scale than did Schurman, the letters which the two exchanged give no indication of their differing approaches to

ANNA VAN SCHURMAN
AT THE AGE OF 33
(*Etched by herself*)

feminism. The source of expressed disagreement was more specific: Schurman's preoccupation with exotic languages bothered Marie de Gournay, who felt that any ideas worthy of consideration could be found in Greek, Latin, Spanish, French, or Italian. A mind as noble as that of Mademoiselle Schurman should not be wasted on the trivialities of grammar.[21] In her response Schurman distinguished sacred from profane languages, claiming to study the latter only in leisure hours. Sacred languages, on the other hand, seemed almost to have redemptive power. Knowledge of Hebrew "will remain with us to the heavens" and "its use will endure in the next life" (p. 320).

As in this instance, Anna van Schurman's exchanges with learned women had more to do with questions of scholarship than of feminism. The network of learned women in Europe was already so large that Schurman's defense of women's education strikes one as almost superfluous. To the extent that she restricted her advocacy of education to those without other pressing concerns, Schurman appears merely to have confirmed the status quo. While Anna van Schurman may have been particularly outstanding, many women in many parts of seventeenth-century Europe had amassed impressive educational credentials. A large number of them were in contact with Schurman at one time or another.[22]

Her friendship with Princess Elizabeth of Bohemia was to prove the most enduring. Princess Elizabeth, daughter of Elizabeth Stuart, herself a learned woman, and of Elector Palatine Frederick V, the "Winter King" of Bohemia,[23] was one of the women with plenty of leisure to develop her intellect. Her interest in philosophy brought her into close contact with Descartes, who dedicated his *Principiae Philosophiae* to her in 1643. Living at the Dutch court during the uncertainties of the Thirty Years' War, Princess Elizabeth belonged to the same intellectual environment as Anna van Schurman. In spite of their widely divergent opinions on the value of Descartes' philosophy, their common interests caused the friendship to survive. Their lives followed a parallel course, ending in even greater comradeship in their search for a deeper spiritual life.

Anna van Schurman's search began in the middle years of life when familial responsibilities provided her with a very different perspective on the purpose of life. Her mother had died in 1637, leaving her for the next twenty years with the care of two elderly aunts. For the first ten years she was able to remain involved in her studies, but from the age of about forty the aunts demanded her full attention. Having fled Germany during the Thirty Years' War, they wanted, in spite of blindness, to return to Cologne when the war ended in 1648. This trip had the effect of loosening Anna's attachment to Utrecht and to scholarship. When she returned to Utrecht, an ecclesiastical dispute arose which led Anna Maria, her brother, maids, and aunts, to retreat to the country until the deaths of the aunts at the respective ages of eighty-nine and ninety-one.

In her autobiography, *Eukleria seu melioris partis electio* [Choice of the Better Part] (1673), she reports that she learned the satisfaction of devoting herself to the care of others. At the same time, her naive optimism concerning human nature was replaced by a critical realism: she found the Reformed Church less reformed than she had previously thought. As Yvon explained:

> She had previously been as if shut up in her closet and had not seen the world except in passing; but viewing it now more closely and beholding the lives of men in general and of those who bore the name Reformed, she was extremely surprised to find there so little fear of God and so little practice of True Christianity.[24]

But if she became less trusting of many nominal Christians, her ties to those she considered true Christians grew all the stronger. Within the "little Christian community" of her family, she felt such a "tight and sweet bond of love" that the several years seemed only a few days.[25] This experience predisposed her afterwards to seek the fellowship of devoted believers in a tightly knit community. Such a community would necessarily be more exclusive than the State Church to which she had previously belonged. It is for such sectarianism, as much as for any theological shift, that her adherence to the pietistic preacher Jean de Labadie was so severely criticized.

Labadie, a former Jesuit turned Reformed, had found both Catholicism and Calvinism in need of reformation. Inclined to both mysticism and asceticism, Labadie settled for a time in Geneva, where he seemed to renew the spirit of Calvin in his attempts to impose moral discipline. There Anna's brother Gottschalck, who had journeyed to Switzerland on a religious quest, was inspired by the power of Labadie's charismatic preaching and by his exemplary life. Through Gottschalck, who died soon after, praising Labadie with his last words, Anna Maria grew eager to meet this saintly man, whose reputation was spreading to the Netherlands by other routes as well. Her persuasive efforts, coupled with a call to the pastorate of a church in Middelburg, succeeded in bringing him to her country in 1666. After three years of attempting to impose stricter discipline in matters of communion and pastoral leadership, he was suspended from his duties by the synod. His strongest followers, however, remained with him and formed the basis of a religious community in Amsterdam in which his standards of behavior and belief could be more readily imposed. Schurman was to join this community and follow it throughout its stormy course to Herford and Altona in Germany and back to Wieuwerd in the Netherlands, where she died in 1678. Princess Elizabeth, now Abbess of Herford, attempted to provide sanctuary for them; but the setting was, even with her sympathetic support, too inhospitable for the religious fanaticism of which the community was accused. Altona offered the advantage of official religious toleration, if not necessarily the full approval of local neighbors. After two years there, some members of the community offered an estate in Friesland, which proved the most hospitable surroundings.

Whatever the rest of the world may have thought of Labadie and his community, they represented the fulfillment of Anna van Schurman's life. Her devotion to God and to learning, which had motivated her from childhood, could in this setting be combined with her devotion to a family of Christians, something which she had grown to appreciate in adulthood. Yet the intensity which had characterized her earlier studies was incompatible with complete commitment to the love of fellow Christians. The latter, she now realized, was more important, the former far less valuable than she had previously believed. Embarrassed by her earlier claims for the worth of study, she set forth in her autobiography to acknowledge publicly the scholarly follies of her youth. Of the major justifications for study presented in her *Dissertatio* and correspondence with Rivet, none was any longer compelling.

First, natural philosophy and science, she now admits, do not complement revealed knowledge, nor are they the preliminary steps to fuller knowledge of God. In the long tradition identified with Tertullian, she concludes that pagan philosophy has nothing to contribute to Christianity. Even Platonists, who have the most to offer, commit the basic error of aiming at self-perfection rather than union with the Highest Good. Christians should be motivated by the love of God rather than love of self. They reach God not through any virtuous actions of their own, but by being "sunk in the Ocean of divinity, immersed, penetrated, and filled by the goodness and happiness of the same" (pp. 46-47), for "the Christian religion has completely other and much higher means of coming to true union with the Highest Good" (p. 48).

80

The orthodox scholasticism, then, in which grace builds on nature, was replaced in Schurman's later life by a pietistic demand for the regeneration of corrupt nature. This applies to the moral as well as the intellectual realm. Her second reason for defending education is also found to be without basis: learning bears no necessary connection to morality. Moral philosophy cannot teach, much less instill, virtue because it lies within the realm of nature, "which can bring forth no true virtue in us" (p. 50). Secular studies can only give an intellectual understanding of morality; Christian morality not only gives knowledge of virtue but also, through the Holy Spirit, inculcates that virtue in the believer.

Even theological sophistication, if it brings mere knowledge without its fruits, is useless. Whereas, in her *Dissertatio*, theology was highly valued because of its assumed significance for all Christians, she now admits that even the study of theology can become a merely academic exercise. Her earlier efforts to arrange in charts all distinctions, subdivisions, and definitions of philosophical, dogmatic, and practical theology are now viewed as misguided. Much more conducive to a moral life than the study of theology is a "total reversal, conversion, and rectification of the mind and heart" (p. 52).

In her retraction of the third and last of her earlier arguments for study, Schurman in effect admits the validity of those criticisms levelled against her for being undiscriminating in her intellectual pursuits. Knowledge for its own sake does not provide happiness. Only those studies which lead to glorification of God and service of neighbor contribute to true satisfaction. Study of oriental languages is indeed most likely a waste of time and energy. To seek to understand Scripture better by recognizing derivatives from Syriac, Arabic, or Ethiopian is like "setting up torches before the sun, or like making an elephant from a fly" (p. 31). The inner meaning of Scripture is understood only through the illumination of the Holy Spirit. If this is lacking, "it is useless to bring forth the grammatical explanation of one or another little word in order to find the most inward and spiritual meaning of the same" (pp. 31-32).

None of this was meant to imply that Christianity and learning are antithetical or that the Christian should eschew scholarship altogether. She tried to assure her readers of this early in her autobiography, *Eukleria*: "But we do not say these things in order to throw out all sure sciences and advantageous or necessary arts at once without distinction; or that we should fail to recognize that the purified may be able to use some of these in purity and with advantage" (p. 34). Nor, when speaking of an inward illumination of the Spirit, did she mean to refer to a revelation apart from Scripture. Hers was not a religion of mystical visions. Yet her words were too similar to those of visionaries and spiritualists who had been proclaimed heretical. Too much emphasis on the Spirit always seemed to the orthodox to undermine the ordinary means of revelation through Word and Sacrament. So it was that, in confessing the excesses of her youthful views, she was charged with excesses of another sort. Among her many critics, a German Lutheran theologian, representing an orthodoxy closely related to Schurman's earlier Calvinist orthodoxy, wrote a lengthy response to her *Eukleria*. Johann Gabriel Drechssler of Halle, in *Eukleria Eukeatos* (1675), charged her with detracting from the authority of Scripture by demanding internal illumination and with condemning not merely the abuse of natural knowledge but the pursuit of human sciences altogether. In spite of some distortions of Schurman's position by Drechssler, the interchange, continued in her *Eukleria Part II*, exhibits a significant difference of opinion on the value of education for religion. Drechssler's was an intellectual approach to religion in which natural philosophy figured prominently: "Philosophical knowledge concerning creation, even if drawn from the books of the pagans, bestows the prelude, as it were, of a saving knowledge of God."[26] By observing creation one can know that there is a "provident, omnipotent, good eternal creator."[27] Schurman, who had earlier espoused similar views, now subordinated the intellectual to the moral element. The two were by no means as closely related as she had thought: it was perfectly possible to know about God without serving Him or His creatures. And to do so has little or no religious value.

In certain respects, then, Anna van Schurman's system of values had shifted. Her circle of friends was no longer the best-known thinkers of the literary and philosophical world. Although piety had always been one criterion for choosing her friends, it was now the sole criterion. Few of her former admirers approved of the course she had chosen, but she clearly considered it the better part, as the Greek title of her autobiography signifies. The happiness she had sought in knowledge had been found in friendship: "So I too in this sense must be considered happy in the judgment of all, since in our house or church Christian friendship, which alone is true friendship, illumines and quickens all like the sun" (pp. 205-06).

Is this a betrayal of her earlier ideals? If one views her as a feminist, perhaps so. But her form of feminism had been so restricted as to be virtually a dead end. It led to no change in society or in the lives of those who might espouse it. It provided no outlet for the knowledge which took so much effort to acquire.

There were insufficient rewards to offset the sacrifice of companionship and the immersion in solitude. As preparatory neither for educating children nor for pursuing a vocation, it had no pragmatic purpose. Precisely because her view of women was moderate enough to be inoffensive, it was ultimately unsatisfying. From a personal standpoint—apart from any theological convictions—her choice of a community in which she could feel the companionship of home and the purposefulness of a religious vocation is perfectly comprehensible.

The transition was not solely a personal one, however. The intellectual climate of the late seventeenth century was quite different from that of the first half of the century. The general mood was expressed in the search for greater emotional depth under the intellectual structures of Calvinist or Lutheran orthodoxy. As pietism began to replace orthodoxy, Schurman's scholastically modelled defense of education was likely to find fewer sympathetic readers—either female or male—among her contemporaries.

Nevertheless, in spite of fluctuations in educational styles and attitudes, Anna van Schurman can be said to have made a permanent contribution to the cause of women's education.When in 1709 Elizabeth Elstob, the first female Anglo-Saxon scholar, set out to justify female learning, she referred her opposition to the Latin treatise on female scholarship written by Schurman in 1638. Though largely forgotten in our own century, her fame in her own time served to create an atmosphere favorable to learned women. If some, such as Rivet, objected that Schurman was so exceptional as to have little significance for the vast majority of women, her example in any case could only make the way easier for those women who were to follow. Her direct influence on other women is impossible to measure, but the mutual support of these female scholars must have provided encouragement in the face of opposition or indifference. Together they formed a powerful testimony against the many who feared for women's brains lest they be too delicate to absorb the heavy burdens of much learning.

[1] Pierre Yvon, "Abrégé sincere de la vie et de la Conduite et des vrais sentimens de feu Mr. De Labadie," *Gottfrid Arnolds Unparteyische Kirchen— und Ketzerhistorie* (Frankfurt am Main, 1715), II, 1264f. Yvon was a member of the pietist circle led by Jean de Labadie which Anna van Schurman joined in later life. All translations mine.

[2] Yvon, II, 1263.

[3] Yvon, II, 1262.

[4] Una Birch, *Anna Van Schurman: Artist, Scholar, Saint* (London: Longmans, Green and Co., 1909), p. 24.

[5] Yvon, II, 1263.

[6] Claims that she also studied Persian, Turkish, and Samaritan have not been substantiated. See Anna Margaretha Hendrika Douma, *Anna Maria van Schurman en de Studie der Vrouw* (Amsterdam: H.J. Paris, 1924), pp. 29-30.

[7] Gisbertus Voetius, "Oratio Inauguralis de Pietate cum Scientia conjungenda," *Illustris Gymnasii Ultraiectini Inauguratio una cum Orationibus Inauguralibus* (Utrecht, 1634).

[8] *Sermoen van de nuttigheytt der academien en scholen* (Utrecht, 1636).

[9] Dutch version: *Paelsteen van den tijt onzes levens* (Dordrecht, 1639); Latin: *De Vitae Termino* (Leiden, 1639).

[10] Descartes, Letter to Mersenne, 11 November 1640, *Oeuvres*, publ. by Victor Cousin (Paris: F.G. Levrault, 1842), VIII, 388.

[11] Johan Van Beverwijck, *Van de Uitnementheyt des Vrouwelichen Geslachts* (Dordrecht, 1639), p. 171.

[12] Cotton Mather, *Magnalia Christi Americana: or, The Ecclesiastical History of New-England* (Hartford, 1852 [original: London, 1702]), I, 134f.

[13] Gisbertus Voetius, *Politicae Ecclesiasticae* (Amsterdam, 1663-1676), Pars 2, Lib. 1, Tract 4, Cap. 2, q. 7.

[14] *Question célèbre, s'il est necessaire ou non que les filles soivent scavantes?* (Paris, 1646).

[15] *The Learned Maid; or, Whether a Maid may be a Scholar?* (London: 1659).

[16] Anna Maria van Schurman, *Opuscula* (Leiden, 1648; 2nd ed., 1650), pp. 28-95. All further references to the *Opuscula* will be to the 1650 edition; page numbers will be cited in the text in parentheses.

[17] Joannes Ludovicus Vives, *De Institutione foeminae Christianae* (Antwerp, 1524) [*Instruction of a Christian Woman*].

[18] This is not the principle which guided her own education. As she later remarked with gratitude toward her parents, she was directed away from any

writings which might impair her "maidenly purity," reading of the classics little but Homer and Virgil. Anna Maria van Schurman, *Eukleria seu melioris partis electio* (Altona, 1673), p. 16.

[19] Text for *The Equality of Men and Women* (1622) is in Mario Schiff, *La Fille d'Alliance de Montaigne: Marie de Gournay* (Paris: H. Champion, 1910).

[20] Calvin, emphasizing woman's creation as helpmeet for man, had viewed women as companions but not equals and had taken seriously the Pauline statements on the subordination of women. See, for instance, John Calvin, *Commentaries on the First Book of Moses Called Genesis*, trans. John King (Edinburgh: Calvin Translation Society, 1847).

[21] Unpublished letter of Marie de Gournay to Schurman, 20 October 1639, in Koninklijke Bibliotheek, The Hague.

[22] On Bathsua Makin, see the following essay. On the relationship between Schurman and Queen Christine of Sweden, evidence is fragmentary. It is doubtful that they corresponded directly. Yvon reports that, urged by her friends, Schurman sent a poem and a gift of artistry to Christine, but that, hearing of some of the blasphemous goings-on in Christine's court, Schurman took care never to have anything more to do with her (Yvon, II, 1264). Birch reports, however, that after her abdication Christine paid a friendly visit to Schurman, at the end of which Anna presented a portrait "with a charming compliment to the royal stranger" (Birch, p. 99).

[23] When the Bohemian estates revolted against Hapsburg rule, leading to the Thirty Years' War, they elected Frederick in 1619 to be king of Bohemia. Defeated by Catholic forces the following year, Frederick received the title the "Winter King" because of his short reign.

[24] Yvon, II, 1266.

[25] *Eukleria*, p. 134. See n. 18 above. All further quotations from Schurman's works are taken from her *Eukleria* (1673): page numbers will be cited in parentheses.

[26] Johann Gabriel Drechssler, *Eukleria Eukeatos seu Melioris Partis Electio rescissa* (Leipzig, 1675), p. 85.

[27] Drechssler, p. 87.

BATHSUA MAKIN: EDUCATOR AND LINGUIST
(1608?—1675?)

J.R. BRINK

Perhaps because of the glamour of the late sixteenth century, when a brilliant and learned Queen ruled England, the period after the death of Elizabeth in 1603 has seemed to observers, both ancient and modern, to represent a decline in female learning.[1] William Wotton, when he wrote his *Reflections upon Ancient and Modern Learning* in 1694, looked back with admiration at the Tudor period, describing it as a time when knowledge of the classics was fashionable for women as well as men:

> It was so very modish, that the fair Sex seemed to believe that *Greek* and *Latin* added to their Charms; and *Plato* and *Aristotle* untranslated, were frequent Ornaments of their Closets.[2]

Wotton's comments cannot be dismissed as mere nostalgia for a golden age in English history; William Harrison, more than a hundred years earlier, had remarked upon the impressive accomplishments of sixteenth-century English-women. In his *Description of England* (1587) Harrison praises the linguistic talents of both gentlemen and ladies, attributing to the average courtier a knowledge not only of Greek and Latin, but also of Spanish, Italian, and French; he concludes that the ladies "come very little or nothing at all behind [the gentlemen] for their parts."[3] Even that inveterate gossip John Aubrey, after repeating the slanderous tidbits he relished, acknowledged that the talented Mary Sidney Herbert, Countess of Pembroke, had turned Wilton House into a center of learning which could be described as a college.[4]

By 1694 William Wotton believed that there had been a general decline of enthusiasm for learning which had affected both sexes, but he seems to have felt that the changed atmosphere was especially unfortunate for women. Regarding the education of Tudor women, he says:

> One would think by the Effect, that it was a proper Way of Educating them, since there are no Accounts in History of so many very great Women in any one Age, as are to be found between the Years 15[00] and 1600.[5]

There is ample evidence to support William Wotton's view that female learning was not always encouraged in the seventeenth century. When Sir Ralph Verney's goddaughter told him that she planned to learn Hebrew, Greek, and Latin, he urged her to be content with the Bible and catechism in English because it was more suitable to her sex.[6] Even Lady Anne Clifford, of whom John Donne said, "she knew well how to Discourse of all things from Predestination to Slea Silk," was not allowed to study Latin.[7] By her own report, her father George Clifford, Earl of Cumberland, decided that she should not be allowed to learn languages.[8] Even so, there are indications that a circle of learned women flourished in the seventeenth century and that they were part of a continuing tradition extending back to the educated daughters of Sir Thomas More and Sir Anthony Cooke and forward to Elizabeth Elstob, the Anglo-Saxon scholar, and Elizabeth Robinson Montagu, "Queen of the Blues."[9] An important, and possibly central, figure in this tradition was Bathsua Pell Makin, tutor to the daughters of Charles I.

Although she was one of the most learned women of her time, we have only tantalizing hints concerning Bathsua Makin's acquaintances and activities. In the preface to his *Memoirs of Several Ladies of Great Britain, who have been Celebrated for their Writings or Skill in the Learned Languages, Arts, and Sciences* (1752), George Ballard mentions her linguistic skill, but includes her in a list of learned ladies about whom little is known. She was born in Southwick, Sussex, the daughter of the rector John Pell and of Mary Holland; her father died in 1616, and her mother died a year later. The older of her two brothers, Thomas Pell, became a gentleman of the bedchamber to Charles I and then went to America in 1635. Her other brother John Pell (1611-1685) was educated at Stenning, a free grammar school in Sussex. Since both parents were dead, Bathsua probably tutored John at home, enabling him to enter Trinity College, Cambridge, at the age of thirteen. According to Anthony à

Wood he was "as good a scholar as some master of arts" when he entered the university.[10] John became an ambassador and an eminent mathematician, occupying the mathematics chair first at Amsterdam and then at Breda; an account of his life is included in Aubrey's *Brief Lives*.[11] Little is known of how or when Bathsua Makin received an education, or of her childhood or married life, but she seems to have supported herself after her husband died as a private tutor and later as a school teacher at Tottenham High Cross, a few miles from London.[12]

Since her parents were dead and her older brother had emigrated to America, she seems, not too surprisingly, to have had financial difficulties. In a pamphlet dated 24 September 1646 and entitled *The Malady and Remedy of Vexations and Unjust Arrests and Actions*, she pleaded with Parliament to repeal the statutes allowing imprisonment for debt upon very little evidence; she also asked them to pass laws imposing heavy penalties upon those who abused the statutes by bringing false charges.[13] The passion with which she argues suggests that she had personal knowledge of these fraudulent practices. Her brother John was later twice imprisoned for debt, but he seems not to have experienced serious financial problems until the 1670's and 1680's.

Her relationship with her brother John Pell appears to have been at times unpleasant. While serving under Cromwell as resident ambassador to the Swiss cantons, Pell wrote letters to his wife Ithumaria in which he alludes to his sister with hostility:

> I thought I had reason to expect more money from you the last time; but I perceive I have a receiver that uses me at pleasure. You will constrain me to warn everybody to deliver no money to you for me. I perceive Mrs. Mack. hath found the way to you again. Her counsel, added to your own inclinations, will make you altogether unfit to meddle with any money of mine; so that I shall be forced to seek some other, who will dispose of it punctually, according to my order.[14]

His letters to his wife are nearly always concerned with money; their harsh tone suggests that, although they had eight children, he regarded her with contempt rather than affection. In response to his wife's questions about when he will return, he admonishes her "to order our affairs so that, when I do come, I may not have occasion to wish that I had always tarried abroad."[15]

He also warns her that he will allow her no money whatsoever if she "abate anything, upon what pretence so ever."[16] Since he expected to receive 150 of his 200-pound quarterly allowance, it is to be hoped that his wife had another source of income. Whether because of his own or his wife's improvidence, John Pell always seems to have been short of money. It is unlikely that he ever contributed substantially to his sister's support. Ironically, he may have owed to her the early linguistic training which furthered his career as a diplomat.

From Bathsua's Makin's *An Essay to Revive the Antient Education of Gentle-women* (1673), a work written to advertise her school for young women, we can gain some information regarding her career as a tutor. She mentions with understandable pride the linguistic achievements of her pupil, the Princess Elizabeth, daughter of Charles I. At nine the Princess could read and write Greek, Latin, Hebrew, French, and Italian.[17] Since Princess Elizabeth was born in 1635 and died in 1650 at the age of fifteen, we can date Bathsua Makin's duties as a royal tutor during these years. Charles I awarded her an annual pension of forty pounds a year, but she may have had difficulty collecting it during the Civil War. Her petition for payment of arrears to the Council of State under Cromwell was dismissed on 16 August 1655.[18] Records of Bathsua Makin's marriage might throw light on her circumstances in 1646, when she wrote her pamphlet about imprisonment for debt, but so far little is known of her life other than that she may have had a son and that she was definitely a widow in 1664.[19]

Among her acquaintances Bathsua Makin numbered Sir Simonds D'Ewes, the barrister and antiquarian collector of parliamentary records. D'Ewes also knew Anna Maria van Schurman, probably the most famous woman scholar of her time in Europe, and in a letter to Schurman dated 1645 he mentions that he has been eager to make her acquaintance because "her industry in the sublimer studies has been so highly praised by that learned matron, Madame Bathsua Makin."[20] Makin may have become aware of Anna Maria van Schurman's scholarship through her brother John who spent nine years in Holland, or she may have met Schurman's brother when he visited England; we know that she herself corresponded with Schurman. Two of her Greek letters to the learned Dutch woman were published in Schurman's *Opuscula*.[21]

In her essay on female education Makin also alludes to her connection with Lady Lucy Hastings, the Dowager Countess of Huntingdon. Somewhat obliquely she says:

I am forbidden to mention the Countess Dowager of Huntingdon (instructed sometimes by Mrs. Makin) how well she
understands *Latin*, *Greek*, *Hebrew*, *French*, and *Spanish*;
or what a proficient she is in Arts, subservient to Divinity,
in which (if I durst I would tell you) she excels (p. 10).

Among the unpublished papers in the Hastings Collection at the Henry E.
Huntington Library, there are two poems and a letter which Makin sent
to the Countess. The first poem, a Latin elegy, was written on the occasion of
the death of Henry, Lord Hastings, the oldest son of the Countess, and so can
be dated around 24 June 1649.[22] Her elegy, like much of the polite, occasional verse of the seventeenth century, is undistinguished, but it does show
that her knowledge of Latin was excellent. Bathsua Makin also wrote a letter
and poem on 2 May 1664 when her former pupil, the Lady Elizabeth [Hast-
ings] Langham died. The poem was printed in a collection entitled *A Christian's Acquiescence in all the Products of Divine Providence*, which included the
sermon preached at the young woman's funeral and a selection of commemora-
tive verse.[23] In her poem Makin mentions Lady Elizabeth's linguistic achievements in Latin, French, and Italian; Lady Elizabeth appears to have been less
skilled than the Countess, who knew these languages and Greek, Hebrew, and
Spanish.

Even so, it is worthwhile to observe that this learned noblewoman insisted
upon having her daughters as well as her sons educated in the classical and
modern languages. Female learning became a tradition in the Huntingdon
family. Lady Elizabeth Hastings, the granddaughter of the Countess, was
regarded in the early eighteenth century as a paragon of learning, piety, and
beauty. Congreve eulogized her in No. 42 of the *Tatler*, followed by Steele in
No. 49; Steele was responsible for the famous sentence, "To love her is a
liberal education."[24] A patron of female learning, Lady Elizabeth was one of
the subscribers to Elizabeth Elstob's *Homily on the Birthday of St. Gregory*,
and she appears also to have attempted to relieve the poverty of the great
Anglo-Saxon scholar by offering her a position as mistress of one of her charity
schools. Like Lady Mary Wortley Montagu, she contributed liberally to Mary
Astell's design for a female college.

The best source of information concerning Bathsua Makin's own views of
education is her *An Essay to Revive the Antient Education of Gentlewomen*.
The *Essay* was published in 1673 and dedicated to "all Ingenious and Virtuous
Ladies" and especially to the Lady Mary, daughter of the Duke of York (p. 3);

Forma nihil, si Pulchra perit: sed pectoris alma
Divini species, non moritura viget.
W. M. sculpsit

MRS. BATHSUA MAKIN

"Facsimile copy from an almost unique print by Marshall." From an engraving in
Woodburn's *Gallery of Rare Portraits*, 1816, Vol. II, page 39.

at the back there is specific information about Makin's school at Totten-ham High Cross. Two letters are included as a preface to the body of the essay, the first written by a man sympathetic to female education and the second, dated 29 May 1673, purportedly written by a friend of his who regards the idea of educating women as preposterous. He explains his position as follows:

> Women do not much desire Knowledge; they are of low parts, soft fickle natures. . . . And that which is worst of all they are of such ill natures, they will abuse their Education, and be so intolerably Proud, there will be no living with them (p. 6).

In her summary of her opponent's arguments, Bathsua Makin identifies the major points she will consider: first, is the education of women a new and revolutionary idea? Second, can women be improved by a liberal education? Third, if women can be improved by such an education, will it benefit them? Fourth, where can women obtain such an education without experiencing the dangers of coeducation?

To demonstrate that educating women is not a new and dangerous idea, Makin provides a catalog of learned women gleaned from anecdotes related by biblical and classical authors. Some of her examples are forced and many are based on inferences. Her discussion of the Muses illustrates the tenuous nature of her historical proof:

> We may infer from the Stories of the Muses, that this way of Education was very ancient. All conclude the *Heroes* were men famous in their Generation, therefore canonized after their Deaths. We may with like Reason conclude, *Minerva* and the nine Muses were Women famous for Learning whilst they lived, and therefore thus adored when dead (p. 9).

After she concludes her list of women outstanding in linguistics, oratory, logic, philosophy, mathematics, and poetry, she points out that the Muses, the Christian virtues, Faith, Hope, and Charity, and even the seven Liberal Arts are depicted as women. Makin interprets this phenomenon as evidence that women "were the inventors of many of these Arts, and the promoters of them" (p. 21). Although inventive and resourceful, Makin's historical demonstration of the ancient practice of educating women is not very convincing.

Her arguments improve when she begins to argue that seventeenth-century women should be educated. Even though she, like Anna Maria van Schurman, qualifies her position by advocating education only for those who are intelligent and whose social circumstances allow them leisure time, she unequivocally censures contemporary treatment of women:

> Meerly to teach Gentlewomen to Frisk and Dance, to paint their Faces, to curl their Hair . . . is not truly to adorn, but to adulterate their Bodies; yea (what is worse) to defile their Souls. This (like Circes Cup) turns them to Beasts . . . (p. 22).

Her historical explanation of the origin of these practices is quite vague; she remarks that, "[d]oubtless this underbreeding of Women began amongst Heathen and Barbarous People" (p. 22). She is convinced, however, that those of her contemporaries who oppose female education do so in order to keep women subservient:

> We cannot be so stupid as to imagine, that God gives Ladies great Estates, meerly that they may Eat, Drink, Sleep, and rise up to Play. . . . Poor Women will make but a lame excuse at the last day for their vain lives; it will be something to say, that they were educated no better. But what Answer Men will make, that do industriously deny them better improvement, lest they should be wiser than themselves, I cannot imagine (p. 28).

Later, she even more pointedly attacks the motivation of her opposition: "Let Women be Fools, and then you may easily make them Slaves" (p. 34).

In response to the frequently cited argument, based on scriptural authority, that women must keep silent in church, Makin replies that she pleads for private instruction, not public employment: "There are other ends of Learning, besides pleading in the Hall, and appearing in the Pulpit" (p. 33). Her *Essay* is a reasoned argument for female education, but Makin's own love of scholarship and unmistakable sincerity give her writing emotional impact. With considerable poignance she says:

> Men are very cruel that give them leave to look at a distance, only to know they do not know; to make any thus to tantalize, is a great torment (p. 25)

Although at times indignant about seventeenth-century views of women, Bathsua Makin is not so much a feminist as an educator concerned about the waste of potential which occurs when gentlewomen spend their youth, "in making Points for Bravery, in dressing and trimming themselves like Bartholomew-Babies, . . . in making Flowers of Coloured Straw, and building Houses of Stained Paper, and such like vanities" (p. 30).

Of the issues raised by those opposing female education, Makin takes most seriously the question of time. She acknowledges that boys, even though they begin their early education at seven and continue until sixteen or seventeen, rarely become skilled linguists before they enter universities; her program would involve teaching girls twice as much in half the time. She resolves this dilemma by proposing a new approach to language study, which obviates the necessity of spending years learning formal grammar. In this respect, she is echoing the pedagogical theories of John Milton, whose views were also based on practical experience as a tutor.

Milton's *Of Education* first appeared in 1644 as an informal and anonymous eight-page pamphlet; it was reissued in 1673, the date that Makin's *Essay* was published. Milton addressed his tract to Samuel Hartlib, who was a close friend of Makin's brother John Pell. When Hartlib proposed "Commissioners for the Act of the Council for Schooling," he included both Milton and John Pell. Although there is no evidence that they were acquainted, Bathsua Makin and John Milton were both in touch with the circle of educational reformers which included Hartlib, Pell, Robert Boyle, John Hall, and Theodore Haak.[25] In *Of Education* Milton deplores the waste of seven or eight years spent in "scraping together so much miserable Latin and Greek as might be learned otherwise easily and delightfully in one year."[26] Makin is concerned with Latin and French rather than Latin and Greek, but she, like Milton, thinks that the basics can be learned in a year. She plans to start her students at nine years old and concludes that if they spend six hours a day studying for nine months, they will learn Latin so well that only three months will be required for French.

Both educators are critical of contemporary practices. Milton waxes indignant at the idea of "forcing the empty wits of children to compose themes, verses, and orations, which are the acts of ripest judgment" and concludes that "these are not matters to be wrung from poor striplings, like blood out of the nose, or the plucking of untimely fruit . . ." (p. 631). Bathsua Makin is equally impatient with the ordering of priorities in language instruction:

94

> [I] t's the universal process of Nature to rise by degrees, to proceed from Seeds to Leaves, from Leaves to Flowers; from plain things to things ornamental. One would think those learned Men mad, that go quite contrary to this Process; that propose to season with Rhetorick . . . before Children understand any thing of the plain signification of words (p. 37).

Instead of expecting her pupils to spend three or four years memorizing *Lilly's Grammar*, Makin plans to teach them English grammar to use as a foundation for Latin and then to allow Latin to serve as a foundation for French and Greek. In addition, she proposes to use distributional criteria for the definitions of the parts of speech and so anticipates the analytical approach of modern structuralists like Charles Fries.[27] Instead of defining a noun as "the name of a thing which may be seen, felt, heard, or understood," as Lilly does, she selects criteria specifically related to English. A noun can be preceded by a, an, or the; unlike an adjective, it varies in number, as in good book and good books (p. 39).

Both Milton and Bathsua Makin also regard the learning of languages as a means to an end rather than an end in itself. Milton describes languages as "the instrument conveying to us things useful to be known" (p. 631), and Makin, likewise, regards learning "Tongues" as subservient to learning the "Principles of Arts and Sciences" (p. 34). In spite of her obvious interest in languages and language study she concludes:

> My opinion is, in the Educating of Gentlewomen, greater care ought to be had to know things, than to get words. If one must be neglected, it's better to neglect Tongues than Arts; though it is best where both may be had (p. 35).

With a remarkable lack of chauvinism, she says that if "all learning [were] in *English*, as it is now in *French*, I think those dead Languages would be of little use, only in reference to the scriptures" (p. 35).

Appreciative as Makin frequently is of domestic arts, such as how to buy flax and wool or dye various fabrics, she rejects the notion that women should be educated in fashionable and ornamental accomplishments. Like Milton she is convinced that practical knowledge is worthwhile. To teach natural science and mathematics Milton, for example, suggests bringing shepherds, gardeners,

95

apothecaries, mariners, and engineers into the classroom so that students will have a "real tincture of natural knowledge" (p. 635). His insistence that students must study agriculture and acquire "applied" as well as "theoretical" knowledge is ahead of his time, but no more so than Makin's rejection of the "finishing school" approach to female education. Both writers advocate a solid education in the arts and sciences and yet acknowledge the value of practical skills; although acceptable today, in the seventeenth century Makin's views were the more radical.

In addition to its interest as an educational treatise, the *Essay* supplies a useful record of the social and intellectual relationships among female seventeenth-century writers. She lists some familiar English names including the daughters of Sir Anthony Cooke; Lady Mary, Countess of Pembroke; and the "Lord Burglies three daughters" of whose occasional Latin verse she quotes a sample (p. 20). It is interesting, however, that she also mentions "how excellent a Poet Mrs. Broadstreet is," a poet better known to us as the American Anne Bradstreet (p. 20). She is also aware of Christine of Sweden, the famous seventeenth-century queen who attempted to surround herself with scholars; the Italian Olympia Fulvia Morata, who, according to Makin, tutored the Empress of Germany (?); Isola Navarula (Isotta Nogarola), author of a dialogue between Adam and Eve which attempted to prove that Adam was the greater sinner; Elizabeth of Schonaugia, author of *A Path to Direct Us the Way to God*; and several other learned European women.

Of her contemporaries, she seems most impressed with the learning and accomplishments of Anna Maria van Schurman. She mentions that Schurman understands Arabic and has printed works in Latin, Greek, French, and Persian. In addition to her linguistic achievements, Makin singles her out for praise as a poet (p. 12), philosopher (p. 13), and logician (p. 13). It may have been the example of Anna Maria van Schurman that caused Makin to suggest that English women should use Dutch women as models:

> One great Reason why our Neighbours the *Dutch* have thriven to admiration, is the great care they take in the Education of their Women, from whence they are to be accounted more vertuous, and to be sure more useful than any Women in the World (p. 28).

Later, she compares Solomon's "vertuous Woman" in Proverbs 31 to an "honest, well-bred, ingenious, industrious Dutch-woman" (p. 35).

In assessing the significance of Makin's *An Essay to Revive the Antient Education of Gentlewomen* it is important to realize that in the seventeenth century it was difficult to justify educating women who were not likely to occupy a throne. Makin, however, is less concerned with gentle birth than she is with the leisure and aptitude essential for scholarship. She divides women according to wealth (rich and poor) and aptitude (good and low natural parts) and limits the relevance of her proposals to wealthy intelligent women. Presumably, a middle-class woman with aptitude would be as eligible for an education as a member of the nobility. She regards wealthy parents who deny their daughters an education with disdain:

> If there be any persons so vain, and yet pleased with this Apish kind of Breeding now in use, that desire their Daughters should be outwardly dressed like Puppets, rather than inwardly adorned with Knowledge, let them enjoy their humour; but never wonder if such Marmosets married to Buffoons, bring forth and breed up a generation of Baboons, that have little more wit than Apes and Hobby-Horses (pp. 31-32).

To the objection that learned women will disobey their husbands, she replies scornfully: "[L]et silly Men let wise Women alone" (p. 33).

When Milton wrote his *Of Education* he succinctly summarized the traditional Christian humanist rationale for education: "The end of learning," he said, "is to repair the ruins of our first parents by learning to know God aright" (p. 631). He adds that a complete and general education will fit a man "to perform justly, skillfully, and magnanimously all the offices both private and public, of peace and war" (p. 632). On religious grounds it was impossible to justify educating women in the classics and Hebrew when the Bible and an abundance of devotional materials were available in English. Latin, of course, was still the language of diplomacy and essential for those interested in mastering European learning or in entering public life. Since women could neither attend universities nor enter public life, there was no practical reason to instruct them in ancient or modern languages.

To justify a solid education for women it was in a sense necessary to justify learning for the sake of learning, a challenge to which Bathsua Makin admirably responded. In a tribute to scholarship upon which it would be difficult to improve she says:

. . . there is no pleasure greater, nor more sutable to an
ingenious mind, than what is founded in Knowledge; it is the
first Fruits of Heaven, and a glymps of that Glory we afterwards expect. There is in all an innate desire of knowing,
and the satisfying this is the greatest pleasure (p. 25).

NOTES

[1] For recent studies suggesting that enthusiasm for classical learning and
for any kind of liberal education for women declined at the end of the sixteenth century, and continued to wane during the seventeenth century, see
Pearl Hogrefe, *Tudor Women: Commoners and Queens* (Ames: The Iowa State
University Press, 1975), p. 115; Josephine Kamm, *Hope Deferred: Girls'
Education in English History* (London: Methuen & Co., 1965), p. 51. See also
an earlier study, Myra Reynolds, *The Learned Lady in England, 1650-1760*
(1920; rpt. Gloucester, Mass.: Peter Smith, 1964), pp. 427-28.

[2] William Wotton, *Reflections upon Ancient and Modern Learning*
(1694; rpt. Hildesheim: Georg Olms Verlag, 1968), pp. 349-50.

[3] William Harrison, *The Description of England*, ed. Georges Edelen
(Ithaca: Cornell University Press, 1968), p. 228.

[4] See *Aubrey's Brief Lives*, ed. Oliver Lawson Dick (1949; rpt. London:
Secker and Warburg, 1960), pp. 138-40: according to Aubrey, she was "very
salacious" and would watch the "Stallions leape the Mares" in the spring and
then "would act the like Sport herselfe with *her* stallions" (p. 138). He adds
that "[i]n her time, Wilton House was like a College, there were so many
learned and ingeniose persons. . . . She was a great Chymist, and spent yearly
a great deale in that study" (p. 139).

[5] Wotton, p. 350.

[6] Margaret M. Verney, *Memoirs of the Verney Family* (London: Longmans, Green & Co., 1899), III, 72-74.

[7] *Diary of Lady Margaret Hoby, 1599-1605*, ed. Dorothy M. Meads
(London: Routledge & Sons, 1930), p. 60.

[8] Wallace Notestein, *Four Worthies* (New Haven: Yale University Press,
1957), p. 128.

[9] Elizabeth Drake, the mother of Elizabeth Robinson Montagu, the famous bluestocking hostess, is reported to have attended the school established by Bathsua Makin at Tottenham High Cross. See Dr. Doran, *A Lady of the Last Century (Mrs. Montagu), illustrated by her unpublished letters* (London: Bentley, 1873), p. 5.

[10] *Biographia Britannica: or, the Lives of the Most Eminent Persons Who Have Flourished in Great Britain and Ireland* (1670; rpt. Hildesheim: Georg Olms Verlag, 1969), V, 3312; see also Aubrey's *Brief Lives*, p. 229.

[11] Aubrey, pp. 229-33.

[12] The *D.N.B.* article on Bathsua Makin errs in placing her at Putney in 1649. As the modern editor of John Evelyn's *Diary* acknowledges, there is no reason to connect his very general reference to a school for gentlewomen with Bathsua Makin.

[13] Bathsua Makin, *The Malady and Remedy of Vexations and Unjust Arrests and Actions* (London: n.p., 24 September 1646). This tract has been reprinted with a short biographical introduction in *The Female Spectator: English Women Writers Before 1800*, ed. Mary R. Mahl and Helene Koon (Old Westbury, New York: The Feminist Press, 1977), pp. 115-24.

[14] *The Protectorate of Oliver Cromwell and the State of Europe during the Early Part of the Reign of Louis XIV, Illustrated in a Series of Letters between Dr. John Pell, Resident Ambassador with the Swiss Cantons, Sir Samuel Morland, and Sir William Lockhart, Mr. Secretary Thurloe, and other Distinguished Men of the Time*, ed. Robert Vaughan (London: Henry Colburn, 1839), II, 406. See also the letter from Pell to Ithumaria in 1657 which is reprinted in *The Female Spectator*, p. 116: "I could wish that you had made an end with your sister Makin. You know that she is a woman of great acquaintance and no small impatience. She will not strike to rail at me and you, where ever she comes. . . ."

[15] *The Protectorate of Oliver Cromwell*, II, 393.

[16] Ibid., II, 410.

[17] Bathsua Makin, *An Essay To Revive the Antient Education of Gentlewomen, in Religion, Manners, Arts & Tongues With An Answer to the Objections against this Way of Education* (London: J.D., 1673), p. 10. All further references will be to this edition; page numbers will be cited in parentheses.

[18] *Calendar of State Papers, Domestic Series*, ed. Mary Anne Everett Green (London: Longmans & Co., 1875-1886), VIII, 290.

[19] See Huntington MS. HA 8799 for a letter which Makin wrote to the Countess of Huntingdon on 2 May 1664 in which she describes herself as a widow. The editors of *The Female Spectator* (p. 116) suggest that she may have had a son.

[20] Anna Maria van Schurman, *The Learned Maid; or, Whether a Maid may be a Scholar?* (London: Redmayne, 1659), p. 48.

[21] Anna Maria van Schurman, *Opuscula hebraea, latina, graeca, gallica, prosaica et metrica* . . . (Lipsiae: M.C.F. Mulleri, 1749), pp. 126-27.

[22] Huntington Library, Hastings Collection, Uncatalogued Papers, Miscellaneous Literature, L5A6. Her elegy was not included in *Lachrymae Musarum: The Tears of the Muses*, a collection which did include the first published poem of John Dryden. Lucy, Countess of Huntingdon, wrote her own elegy on the flyleaf of the 1650 issue which is now located at the Henry E. Huntington Library. Dryden's editors have obligingly printed the poem; see *Works of John Dryden*, ed. E.N. Hooker and H.T. Swedenberg, Jr. (Berkeley: Univ. of California Press, 1956), I, 172-73.

[23] The poem, Huntington MS. HA 8799, has been reprinted in *The Female Spectator*, pp. 124-25.

[24] For further information, see Thomas Barnard, *An Historical Character, relating to the holy and exemplary Life of the Lady Elizabeth Hastings* (London, 1742).

[25] Hartlib translated and edited the works of Comenius (1592-1670), an important Czechoslovakian educator and reformer, whose *Orbis Sensualium Pictus [The World of Sense Objects Pictured]* , published in 1658, was the first illustrated textbook. For the influence of Comenius on Hartlib and his circle, see Christopher Hill, *Milton and the English Revolution* (New York: Viking Press, 1977), pp. 146-49.

[26] *John Milton: Complete Poems and Major Prose*, ed. Merritt Y. Hughes (Indianapolis: Odyssey Press, 1957), p. 631. All further references will be to this edition; page numbers will be cited in parentheses.

[27] See Makin, *An Essay*, pp. 38-41, and cf. Charles Fries, *The Structure of English* (New York: Harcourt, 1952), pp. 65-86.

MADAME DE SEVIGNE: CHRONICLER OF AN AGE
(1626—1696)

JEANNE A. OJALA

Marie de Rabutin-Chantal, the Marquise de Sévigné, was the annalist of an entire period in French history, the glorious and terrible reign of Louis XIV. The bulk of her correspondence began in 1671 when her daughter, the Countess de Grignan, married and moved to Provence.[1] From the more than fifteen hundred letters which have survived, one learns a myriad of details about life among a class of people who set the cultural standards in Europe for decades. Mme de Sévigné's lively, vivid prose recounts battles won or lost, describes the enchanting and at the same time shallow and effete court life at Versailles, mentions the fashions, the literature, the health remedies, and the perils and joys of travelling by water and coach. Although her aristocratic background dictated her life-style and many of her attitudes, the reader of the letters is always aware of her independent personality, her love of nature, her critical and perceptive intelligence, and her charm. Journalist, historian, and social commentator for this classical age, Mme de Sévigné saw clearly and described faithfully the values and views of her society, supplying a unique and valuable record of people and events.

Little is known of the early years of Marie de Rabutin-Chantal. She was born on 5 February 1626 in Paris at the residence of her grandfather, Philippe de Coulanges, in the Place Royale (now the Place de Vosges). Her most noted ancestor was her grandmother, Jeanne de Chantal, who left her family to enter the religious life under the spiritual guidance of Saint Francis de Sales; she was canonized in 1767 by Pope Clement XIII. The father of Marie de Rabutin-Chantal, Baron de Chantal, was descended from the old illustrious Burgundian family of Rabutin. Her mother's family was bourgeois but had grown rich and titled from collecting salt taxes. When Marie was a year old, her father was killed in a duel; her mother died six years later. After a lengthy family conference, the young orphan was made the ward of her maternal uncle, the Abbé Christophe de Coulanges. Her twenty-nine-year-old guardian brought her to the Abbaye de Livry in Brittany to be educated. It was here that she developed her lifelong love of nature. The abbey was surrounded by woods where nightingales sang and where Marie delighted in observing the change of seasons. Mme de Sévigné returned often to her beloved Livry after she grew older. The Abbé, whom she styled *Le Bien Bon*, remained her friend for over forty years.

The education of Marie de Rabutin was unusual for a girl in seventeenth-century France. The Abbé selected two learned tutors for his niece, the Abbé Gilles Ménage, well-known for his erudition, and Jean Chapelain, the literary advisor to Cardinal Richelieu.[2] Chapelain was responsible for drawing up the regulations governing the French Academy established by Richelieu. Perhaps because the Abbé lacked experience in educating young females, his niece received a thorough and practical education which included the study of Latin and other subjects usually regarded as appropriate only for men. To this instruction Mme de Sévigné may have owed some of her independence of mind and rationality. From her poet-tutors she unquestionably learned to love literature and acquired a solid knowledge of Italian and Spanish.

All her life Mme de Sévigné read voraciously. Perhaps because they both appreciated nature, she especially admired La Fontaine. She preferred Corneille to Racine who seemed to her too sentimental[3] and read Montaigne rather than Descartes whom her daughter favored.[4] The *Pensées* and *Lettres Provinciales* by Blaise Pascal were among her favorite works. She wrote, "Where could you find a style more perfect, more sincere, more delicate."[5] Her assessment of the purity and clarity of Pascal's writings indicates an ability to appreciate and recognize the best in literature. Pierre Nicole's *Essais de Morale* also impressed her, more for the content than the style. Even though she preferred Jansenist writers and thinkers to the Jesuits, Mme de Sévigné also lauded the popular Jesuit preacher, Louis Bourdaloue. In addition to French histories and plays, she read *Don Quixote* in Spanish, and Tasso and Ariosto in Italian.[6] She frequently quoted Molière whom she found amusing and Rabelais who made her "die of laughter."[7] Her eclectic literary taste included romances which her daughter thought frivolous and frothy. But Mme de Sévigné defended her delight in different kinds of literature: "There is more good than bad in this adaptable taste, which can do honor to what is best and can also appreciate what is suitable for lighter moments."[8]

The Abbé, *Le Bien Bon*, also arranged the marriage of his niece at the age of eighteen. After consultation with the family, the Abbé chose a young Breton nobleman, Henri, Marquis de Sévigné. He had good family connections and the Coulanges family knew his mother. The young couple exchanged vows at 2:00 a.m. on 4 August 1644. They were both handsome and had secure positions in Parisian and provincial society, but the young Marquis soon returned to the trivial pleasures of his bachelor existence, leaving his wife at his château of Les Rochers in Brittany. Henri de Sévigné, his son Charles, and his grandson, the Marquis de Grignan, all shared a common experience in Paris as young men —they each had a liaison with the most famous courtesan of their day, Ninon de Lenclos. Interestingly, Mme de Sévigné knew about all three affairs. In 1651 Henri was killed in a duel over a woman, leaving his wife with two children to rear, a tarnished reputation to overcome, and a greatly diminished fortune. She remained at Les Rochers for two years with her daughter Françoise-Marguerite (born 1646) and her son Charles (born 1647). Mme de Sévigné then reentered Paris society and never mentioned her husband again.

The young widow neither remarried nor engaged in a love affair. To remain chaste during a time of arranged marriages and casual amours was rare indeed. She was accused by her cousin, the Count de Bussy de Rabutin, and others of being frigid, but Mme de Sévigné cherished her freedom. In a letter to the Count de Bussy in 1690 after the battle of Fleurus she wrote, "I pity the bereaved mothers . . . not so the young widows who, doubtless, will appreciate their liberty, or still more a change of lord and master."[9] But the pragmatic and self-reliant young widow of twenty-five chose liberty rather than a new lord and master.

In Paris an intimate circle of friends surrounded Mme de Sévigné. Mme de Lafayette was closer than any other, and her friend and companion, the Duke de La Rochefoucauld, shared the interests of the two women. Even the infamous Cardinal de Retz (related to the Sévignés) received her loyalty and remained a lifelong friend. These friends met to discuss literature, religion, and the writings of Mme de Lafayette and de La Rochefoucauld.[10] Witty, cultured, and intelligent, these companions complemented the serious side of Mme de Sévigné. The morose La Rochefoucauld read aloud his maxims which reflected his belief that self-interest was the mainspring of man's behavior, while Mme de Lafayette analyzed the underlying motivation for behavior. The two women also shared a need for periodic solitude. For Mme. de Sévigné this meant an escape to her château of Les Rochers: "I live here that pleasant and quiet life . . . perfect freedom—good company—plenty of reading—still more walks alone."[11]

103

Mme. de Sévigné, however, is most often associated with the coterie of *précieuses* who flourished in Paris during the reign of Louis XIV. The establishment of the salon by Mme de Rambouillet in the time of Louis XIII opened up new prospects for society women. The salons were the neutral ground on which the nobility, leading writers, and famous wits met on equal terms.[12] Conversation dealt with subjects ranging from language and literature to the varied nuances of love. Anyone who spoke well and was entertaining found entrance into the aristocratic salon society. Music was a favorite amusement, and Mme de Sévigné loved to sing passionate Italian arias among her friends or in the solitude of her woods at Les Rochers.[13] But literary discussions were the most common activity and were of particular interest to Mme de Sévigné. A typical gathering took place on 3 February 1665 to celebrate the return of several of the Marquise's friends from exile. Boileau, the famous French critic, read one of his satires, and Racine recited a part from his yet unpublished tragedy *Alexandre*.[14]

Because of her association with the salon society it is customary to describe Mme de Sévigné as a *précieuse*; this term later degenerated into a shibboleth for all that was shallow and glib in *haute société*. *Précieuse* is an umbrella word used to refer to all women who frequented salons, but it is possible to identify several strata. At the crest one finds the *véritables précieuses*.[15] They represent the educated, cultured women who sought intellectual stimulation among their peers. The supreme *précieuse* would "know about books, speak several languages and . . . write in prose and verse."[16] The illustrious *bleu chambre* at the Hotel Rambouillet on the rue St. Thomas du Louvre was the archetype of the salon. After 1660, one finds numerous petty imitations of the original salons; their "ludicrous and trivial" refinements evoked ridicule from contemporaries. Molière satirized dim-witted salon women in his "Précieuses ridicules," not the cultured women of the Hotel Rambouillet, but their imitators. Mme de Sévigné disliked the constraint and artificiality of style and manners that evolved out of the salons. She had an aversion to "the daintiness of the poor *ruelles*."[17] La Fontaine too mocked the "mauvaises ruelles." He thought highly of Mme de Sévigné, however, for he used one of her letters as the basis of his work, "Le Curé et le Mort," and her account of the death of Louvois is reworked in his fable "La Mort et le Mourant."[18] The definition of the *véritable précieuse* as the "ultimate in self-possessed womanhood"[19] could serve as an epitaph for Mme de Sévigné. She cannot be likened to the frail, frivolous, lisping *précieuses* who were "groupy" and found "no self-definition in solitude or seclusion."[20]

Mme de Sévigné is what the French call a *primaire* personality: one who lives in the present. In her letters she mentions her mother only once, her father a few times; her husband, too, is singularly absent. She was expansive, perhaps too expansive for the "decorous salon circles."[21] Hers was a lively imagination, an avid curiosity and a robust nature. She liked change—in residences, in seasons, and in reading matter. To Mme de Sévigné ennui and inactivity were "deux villaines bêtes."[22] Her *primaire* personality compelled her to accept life as it came: "Life is too short for us to dwell long upon the same sentiment; one must take time as it comes; I feel myself of this happy humour."[23] Simple pleasures delighted her. Reading, writing letters, walking, traveling and managing her affairs filled her life. It is through the eyes of this active, intelligent, observant woman that we perceive the Age of Louis XIV. Everything is described with verve and excitement, rather hyperbolically at times, but nevertheless she captures the flavor, the mood, and the ambiance of this dazzling period.

It is important not to judge Mme de Sévigné or her social environment by modern standards; she was a creature both of her time and of her social milieu. Her relations with her daughter, the Countess de Grignan, may seem overly emotional to the modern reader. Tears and advice flow in equal proportions to a daughter who was cold, haughty, and at times insensitive to the feelings of others; the love of this doting mother was, in a word, excessive. Moreover, it was lavished unequally between the arrogant Countess and her charming younger brother Charles. The foibles of the young Marquis were faithfully detailed in his mother's letters. Even his failure as a lover was bluntly recorded. When Charles broke off his love affair with Ninon de Lenclos, a raucous scene ensued with his mother. Mme de Sévigné describes it: "Ninon has dismissed him. . . . I told him I was overjoyed to find him punished in the sinful part. . . . It was a scene worthy of Molière. . . . In vain I assured him that the empire of love abounds in tragic stories; he is deaf to all reasoning. . . . Ninon told him that he was a *mere pumpkin fricasseed in snow*. See what it is to keep such good company! One learns such pretty expressions!"[24] His indiscreet amours, his extravagances, and military adventures were also duly discussed. The family fortune was as unjustly divided as was Mme de Sévigné's affection, but Charles was good-natured, and the issue of money affected his relations with neither his mother nor his sister. Mme de Sévigné scolded Charles for his profligacy, but they enjoyed one another's company and shared a mutual love of books.

Mademoiselle de Sévigné was married at the advanced age of twenty-three to one of the great noblemen of France. The Count de Grignan was forty years

old and twice a widower in 1669 when he married Françoise-Marguerite de Sévigné. Madame de Sévigné heartily approved of this alliance and remained on excellent terms with her son-in-law. In 1671 Mme de Grignan finally left Paris to join her husband in Provence where he was Lieutenant-Governor. Her infant daughter, Marie-Blanche, remained at her mother's house in Paris, and the famous correspondence began. Mme de Sévigné kept her daughter constantly informed of the fêtes, liaisons, fashions, scandals, and amusing incidents at court. Unlike Saint-Simon, who was anything but objective in his memoirs of the court, Mme de Sévigné chronicled a quarter of a century with veracity. This complex woman, who was loved and admired by all who knew her, worshiped her austere, beautiful daughter to the extreme: "Your love is the very breath of my existence," she wrote in 1671 shortly after her daughter left Paris.[25] This passion is difficult to explain. Perhaps her disastrous marriage caused her to transfer all her love to her daughter. Mme de Sévigné fretted and bombarded the Countess with advice—she was to be less extravagant with money, gamble less, take care of her health, space her pregnancies, love her mother, love her children. To this concern the Countess responded with reserve and at times insolence.

The unfortunate Mme de Grignan may have contracted venereal disease from her husband, for she was often ill. Several children born to her were sickly and died. Three children survived, a boy and two girls. In contrast to what is generally regarded as a period of loose family ties among the aristocracy we discover in the letters firm, loving relationships among many of this class. The coldness of Mme de Grignan for her own daughters caused Mme de Sévigné to suffer at times, but she and her friends and relatives displayed a genuine concern for their children, legitimate and otherwise. The Duchesse de Longueville grieved over the death of her brilliant son in battle. La Rochefoucauld, who was probably his father, also mourned his untimely death.

The life of a female was difficult in the seventeenth century. Among the nobility a woman had only two alternatives, to accept an arranged marriage or to enter a convent. Most girls received a convent education at some time in their childhood. Those whose parents could not afford a dowry or those who were unmarriageable for other reasons, physical or mental, were relegated to a nunnery. Mme de Sévigné escaped this unfortunate fate because of the concern of her uncle, *Le Bien Bon*. In turn her own daughter was spared because of Mme de Sévigné's love for her. Mme de Sévigné's granddaughter, Marie-Blanche, however, was packed off without ceremony at the age of five and a half years, destined to spend her life in a convent in Aix.[26] The Count de Grignan already had daughters from his previous marriages, and one more girl would only add to the burden of providing dowries. In vain, Mme de Sévigné pleaded with her daughter not to confine the child: "We cannot have too many things to love, real or imaginary, it doesn't matter which," she penned, trying to convince Mme de Grignan to save little Marie-Blanche from confinement.[27] "My heart is broken," she wrote when her pleas were not heeded.[28] In 1690 Mme de Sévigné was still sorrowing for her eldest grandchild: "Poor dear child! How good it will be if, in lieu of happiness, she finds contentment. This, of course, goes without saying, but you will not fail to observe the innuendo in my remark."[29] The sharp barb was very likely observed by her daughter, but ignored.

Mme de Sévigné was more successful in saving her younger granddaughter, Pauline, from a similar fate. She counselled her daughter, "Don't deprive yourselves of the pleasure she can give you. Alas! We have not always such pleasures at our command."[30] Eleven years later the devoted grandmother was writing in the same vein: "Ah, my child, keep her with you! She will never get a good education in a convent, neither in religion (of which the nuns know very little) nor in anything else. . . . At home she could read good books . . . for her taste lies that way; you could discuss them with her. . . . I am sure that would be much better than a convent."[31] A poignant entreaty, "aimez, aimez, Pauline," speaks volumes for the solicitude of the loving grandmother.[32] Pauline avoided the fate of her older sister; her marriage was a love-match which turned out well.

Mme de Sévigné's concern for her grandson, the Marquis de Grignan, was no less sincere. The young man was brave, chivalrous, and handsome, but he lacked one attribute Mme de Sévigné considered vital for a full life—he had no interest in reading: "To be ignorant is a gross blunder," she stated.[33] A few days later she again returned to the importance of learning: "The Marquis [her grandson] would be a happy man if, like Pauline, he could acquire a taste for books and learning. Most blest and happy state, which puts us out of reach of two formidable enemies—boredom and sloth."[34]

In addition to reading, Mme de Sévigné travelled frequently. She resided for months at a time at her château of Les Rochers in Brittany where she was free from social commitments.[35] Over the door of her château was inscribed "Sainte Liberté, ou fais ce que voudras"[36] ["Sacred Liberty, or Do As You Wish"; this was the rule of the Abbey of Thélème of Rabelais]. The Marquise's description of her estate, the life of her peasants, and her relations with them reveal much about this period. She dismissed one of her servants, Picard, because he would not degrade himself to make hay on her estate.[37] On the other hand, she praised Pilois, her gardener, repeatedly for his compliance with her desires and for his loyalty.

When Mme de Sévigné inherited Les Rochers from her husband, she and her uncle immediately set about putting its business affairs in order. Les Rochers and her own family estate of Bourbilly in Burgundy provided her with the means to live well, but not lavishly. Bourbilly was an ancient estate that needed renovation, and Les Rochers suffered from the immense taxes Louis XIV demanded to conduct his numerous wars. Not surprisingly, in 1675-76 the oppressed peasants of Brittany revolted. Mme de Sévigné describes the horrors of hangings and quarterings of the desperate rebels. The thousands of troops sent by the king to pacify the province only added to the already miserable lot of the people. Again in 1689, repressive taxation led to another uprising: "the grief and astonishment of the inhabitants of Brittany are deplorable . . . nothing but tears and lamentations are to be seen and heard on every side."[38] During these events Mme de Sévigné, who was living at Les Rochers, criticized the harsh measures employed by the king. It was a brave, perhaps foolish, thing to do, for the mails were not safe from governmental scrutiny. Both Brittany and Provence, where her son-in-law was Lieutenant-Governor, had ancient privileges which Louis XIV was slowly diminishing. Mme de Sévigné felt the king was overstepping his traditional rights. Replacing the provincial governors with Intendants, agents of the the king, was part of Louis' plan for centralization begun by Richelieu. But how could Mme de Sévigné passively accept this new system when it affected her good friend, the Duc de Chaulnes, governor of Brittany, and especially her family in Provence? The enormous taxes demanded by the king also decreased the revenue of the nobility in the provinces. The king must be paid before the nobles could collect income from their tenants.

Mme de Sévigné was at Les Rochers during two terrible periods of upheaval, 1675-76 and 1689. Her descriptions of the misfortunes of the poor Breton peasants reflect her attitude toward the lower classes: peasants are of inferior stock, assigned their station in life by God in order to serve their superiors. In a letter to her daughter in November, 1675, Mme de Sévigné wrote: "The other day the Queen missed going to mass, and lost twenty thousand crowns in one morning. . . . And M de Montausier [a courtier and acquaintance of Mme de Sévigné] asked her the next day if she intended staying away from mass for the *boca* [card game] again; upon which she went into a great passion." In the paragraph following the news of the court, Mme de Sévigné describes the terrible affairs of Brittany: "You are very humorous upon our misfortunes; but we have no more breaking on the wheel now, except one in a week or ten days, just to keep the executioner's hand in; in short, hanging seems to be a kind of deliverance here from greater miseries."[39] The three million francs demanded by the king bled Brittany dry, but of more concern to the nobles and to the Marquise was the decreasing power of the governors.

In describing Mme de Sévigné both her admirers and detractors note a certain toughness and self-sufficiency. One cannot quarrel with this. Her strength served her well. She not only managed her own affairs, but aided and advanced the careers and fortunes of her children, which often meant pleading their cases at court.[40] Though she was not always successful, her failures did not discourage her. A commission in the army for her son had to be purchased, a pension for her daughter's family had to be obtained. In these affairs her efforts were rewarded, but Mme de Sévigné was never able to secure a position at court for her son-in-law, an appointment which would have brought her beloved daughter permanently to Paris.

Unlike many of her female contemporaries, Mme de Sévigné was not sedentary. She was almost constantly traveling to Brittany, Normandy, Picardy, Burgundy, Provence, Vichy, and Bourbon.[41] The means of conveyance, the condition of the roads, river transportation, and accommodations at inns along the way are described in her lively, gay manner. Her equipage gives a good idea of her importance: a large retinue assured the noble lady of a warm reception from local notables along her route. The frightful inconveniences and hazards of travel did not deter this active woman.

That Mme de Sévigné had a strong constitution cannot be doubted when we read of the cures she underwent at Vichy and Bourbon.[42] An attack of rheumatism caused her to seek relief from the waters at Vichy. The regimen at Vichy was only for the very hearty:

> We all assemble and drink and make wry faces; for only figure to yourself that they are boiling hot and have a very nauseous taste of sulfur. We walk to and fro, we chat, we go to mass, we work off the waters, and everyone speaks without hesitation of the effect they produce.[43]

In addition to drinking the waters, the patient had to be "pumped" and bathed in them. After reading the Marquise's account of her ordeal, one suspects that cures at this time were worse than the diseases. She tells her daughter:

> I began the operation of the pump today; it is no bad re-
> hearsal of purgatory. The patient is naked in a little subter-
> raneous apartment, where there is a tube of hot water which
> a woman directs wherever you choose . . . think of a spout
> of boiling water pouring upon one or other of your poor
> limbs. . . . It is necessary to suffer, and we do suffer; we are
> not quite scalded to death, and are then put into a warm
> bed where we sweat profusely, and this is the cure.[44]

Somehow this fifty-year-old woman survived her "cure," as she did numerous bleedings, potions, and powders; except for her bout with rheumatism in 1676 she was remarkably healthy until she succumbed to a virulent form of small-pox in 1696. Unfortunately those about her were not as vigorous as she was, and from constant references in her letters we know that this caused her great concern. Mme de Lafayette suffered from the "vapours," M de La Roche-foucauld was debilitated by gout, and Mme de Grignan was chronically ill. When Mme de Sévigné acquaints us with the remedies for the boils, the va-pours, the humours, and other ailments, it seems even more remarkable that she lived for seventy years.

Life was threatened not only by disease, but also by the almost incessant wars of Louis XIV. From the 1660's each decade saw a new war commence. Mme de Sévigné records the success and notes the toll taken by the wars among her friends and their relatives. Not only did she have to worry about her son, but also about her grandson. In both instances she was fortunate to have them survive with only minor wounds. Others close to her mourned their dead, and Mme de Sévigné has left us an impression of the gloom and anxiety that gripped Paris during the king's numerous campaigns. The effect on the French of the death of a great military commander is graphically described by the Marquise in July, 1675: the great Turenne was killed during the war against the Dutch. One passage in the letter of 31 July 1675 to her daughter reveals as much about Mme de Sévigné's views of life and belief in Providence or Destiny as it does about the death of Turenne: "Can we refuse to believe in Providence? Can we doubt that the cannon ball which sought M de Turenne among the ten people who were beside him had its course fixed from the beginning of the world?"[45] At the same time the recurring wars and their victims made the Marquise acutely aware of the precarious nature of life: "What vexes me," she wrote to her cousin the Count de Bussy, "is that the days pass away even when we do nothing, and that we grow old and die. I find great fault with this. Life is too short: scarcely is our youth passed before we find ourselves in old age. I could wish to have a hundred years certain, and to leave the rest to chance."[46] Wars, however, became an increasingly common occurrence as Louis XIV sought to enlarge his glory in the eyes of Europe—the French paid dearly. One unmistakably realizes that the losses among friends and acquaintances reminded Mme de Sévigné of her own end. True to her ideas of class distinction, only those men who ranked as nobles warranted a eulogy. After the siege of Condé in 1676, Mme de Sévigné wrote, "I feared the victory had cost us dear, but it does not prove so; we have lost some men, but none of any note; this may be reckoned a complete happiness."[47]

The almost continuous wars did not prevent the king from engaging in a display of elegant and sumptuous living on a scale never seen before in France. Balles, fêtes, theatricals, and innumerable ceremonies impressed those in attendance at court. In July, 1676, Mme de Sévigné paid one of her visits to the court at Versailles.[48] She did not often go in person, and the descriptions of the celebrations, and intrigues are often secondhand. At Versailles, Mme de Sévigné could not indulge in "Sainte Liberté." However, when she was in the king's presence, she was impressed with the magnificence, as was all of Europe. The trivialities and studied gestures of the courtiers still seem vivid and alive after three hundred years as one reads her detailed accounts. Nothing is ignored—gambling, food, dress, furtive glances, marks of favoritism, and the rise and fall of ministers and mistresses—all give us an intimate view of the most famous court in Europe.

The lavish entertainments provided for the king by his fawning aristocracy suggest the grandeur surrounding the Sun King. An elaborate affair given by the Great Condé for Louis XIV at his château of Chantilly is the scene of a tragicomedy which Mme de Sévigné recounts in detail to her daughter.[49] Vatel, the major-domo of Condé, committed suicide because he felt his honor had been stained; he had not provided enough roast meat for all the tables at supper. The next morning when the fish Vatel had ordered failed to arrive, he was so distressed that he "went to his apartment, and setting the hilt of his sword against the door, after two ineffectual attempts, succeeded in the third, in forcing the sword through his heart. At that instant the carriers arrived with the fish."[50] This letter illustrates the way Mme de Sévigné used the conversations of others to enliven her correspondence. At other times she would write an entire letter to her daughter on the latest fashionable coiffure, describing how to achieve the proper look through precise cutting and curling.[51]

The affairs of interest to the French in this period ranged from scandal and public execution to religious processions. In 1676 Mme de Brinvilliers was accused of poisoning several members of her family to acquire their fortunes. She plotted as well to rid herself of her husband, ostensibly to marry her lover who was also implicated. "Medea was a saint compared to her," wrote Mme de Sévigné.[52]

In like manner she regarded a religious procession as worth recounting. The great St. Geneviève procession in July, 1675 was a desperate attempt to make the rains cease so that there would not be famine in the country. Mme de Sévigné was present and was touched by the solemnity of the occasion. The reverent attitude shown to the clergy and the number of lay people involved suggest the still fervent religious sentiments of the French, feelings which in a little more than one hundred years would turn to scorn and skepticism. St. Geneviève was a patron saint of Paris, and during the procession her shrine, "which glitters with precious stones . . . is carried by twenty men clad in white and barefoot."[53] All the religious orders, the Archbishop of Paris, the canons of Notre Dame, and the Abbot of St. Geneviève participated in the prayer for warm and dry weather "which happened at the very time they were making preparations for the procession."[54] Mme de Sévigné had no doubt as to why the two-month-long rains ceased: "I am convinced that our shrine has affected this change."[55]

Mme de Sévigné was a sincere Catholic, or at least she thought she was. "You [her daughter] ask me if I am religious: alas! . . . I am not sufficiently so, for which I am very sorry; but yet I think I am somewhat detached from what is called the world."[56] This accurate description of her views is verified by her entire life. That she sympathized with the Jansenists and befriended its leading exponents, the Arnauld family, says a great deal about her independence of mind. Louis XIV, most of his court, and the powerful Jesuits were enemies of the Jansenists of Port Royal, but Mme de Sévigné does not spare the Jesuits from an occasional satirical slap.[57] The clergy in general are criticized for what she felt was neglect of their duties. Absentee bishops were special targets for censure. Mme de Sévigné regretted the death of a "pious prelate who was so much afraid of dying out of his diocese that to avoid this misfortune, he never quitted it," but, she continues, "there are some whom nothing but death could bring into theirs."[58] The worldliness of some of the church hierarchy served to debase them in the eyes of people like Mme de Sévigné. The Bishop of Alet was harshly denounced as "a supple courtier, a parasite, a gamester, a frequenter of operas and all places of gaiety, a stranger to his diocese."[59] False piety also came under fire. An acquaintance of Mme de Sévigné's became a *dévote* and consequently ceased wearing rouge: "Rouge is the law and the prophets; it is on rouge that rests the very foundation of Christianity," the Marquise caustically commented.[60] There were those, however, who quietly and sincerely withdrew from the world. Mme de Sévigné repeatedly praised the Duchesse de la Vallière, former mistress of Louis XIV, for retiring from the court at the age of thirty to enter religious life.

As she grew older, Mme de Sévigné's Jansenist leanings became more apparent. She read St. Augustine, Pascal, Nicole, and numerous Jansenist tracts which she discussed at some length with her correspondents.[61] Her lack of prejudice toward Jews was remarkable. In 1675, after reading a history of the Jews, she remarked, "As to the religion of the Jews . . . I should have liked it better than any other except the true religion. I admire its magnificence."[62] Again, in 1689, when commenting on a Jewish festival held in Avignon, she exclaimed: "The hatred which we bear for them is extraordinary."[63]

On the subject of the Huguenots [French Calvinists] Mme de Sévigné was not as tolerant. Louis XIV revoked the Edict of Nantes in 1685. This document had been promulgated in 1598 by Henri IV, Louis's grandfather, granting religious freedom to the Protestants of France. Louis XIV was determined to rule a state that had one king and one religion; after forced conversions and outrageous persecutions of his Huguenot subjects, he was convinced by 1685 that there were no longer any "heretics" living in his realm. The king had quartered his dragoons in the houses of those he meant to convert. Jesuits were sent out to the provinces to instruct and preach to the new converts. Among them was Mme de Sévigné's favorite preacher, Father Bourdaloue: "He is going, by the King's command, to preach at Montpellier [a Protestant stronghold] and in the Provinces where so many have been converted without knowing why. . . . The dragoons have hitherto been excellent missionaries; the preachers that are now sent will render the work complete." Mme de Sévigné was undoubtedly critical of the "booted and spurred missionaries," for as a Jansenist sympathizer she disliked forcing anyone to adhere to a strict faith. Nevertheless, she goes on to praise the king for the revocation of the Edict: "Nothing can be more noble than its contents, and no king has ever performed or ever will perform a more memorable action."[64] The Count de Bussy, to whom she had written the above, was also laudatory of the king's actions: "I admire the method the king has taken to ruin the Huguenots . . . and the edict he has just published, supported by the dragoons and the Bourdaloues, has been their death stroke."[65] Mme de Sévigné refers to the missionary activities a few days later in another letter, again extolling the actions against the Huguenots.[66]

Unlike memoirs written at leisure, usually later in one's life, those of Mme de Sévigné depict the contemporary scene without imaginative embroidery or softened recollections. Her literary style is what the French call *primesautier* —spontaneous, quick-witted, sprightly. Nowhere does one find the ridiculous use of phrases such as "children of the air," invented by the *précieuses* to mean "sighs." On the other hand, she could describe twilight as the period "à l'entre chien et loup,"[67] when one could not distinguish between a dog and a wolf because of the fading light. Her use of idiom and local color is of major literary and linguistic importance, because she is one of our few seventeenth-century sources for informal writing.[68]

From this active, engaging woman came a realistic and comprehensive picture of her age. Mme de Sévigné played a role similar to that of her English contemporary Samuel Pepys whose diary presents such a lively view of London. It can be said of both that they had "the instinct to live for the moment lyrically and at the same time prudently."[69] They delighted in pleasure, but were aware of the precarious nature of life. In 1672 Mme de Sévigné wrote to her daughter:

> You ask me, my dear child, if I am still as enamoured of life.
> I must confess I find it full of poignant grief, but the thought
> of death is even more repugnant. To think the inevitable end
> leads through those dread portals induces such sadness in
> me that I would willingly turn back and retrace my steps.[70]

Mme de Sévigné lived to be seventy years old, dying of smallpox in April, 1696 at her daughter's château in Grignan. She inadvertently became the social historian of an age; as a French commentator has put it, "Mme de Sévigné marche avec son siècle."[71]

Perhaps she best described the decline of the classical age in France in her comment on the death of the son of the great Colbert: "It seems to me that splendor is dead."[72] She was correct. The Splendid Century closed in war and misery, but Mme de Sévigné had preserved for posterity the grandeur and pageantry of an age.

NOTES

[1] The most complete edition of the letters of Mme de Sévigné is *Lettres de Madame de Sévigné, de sa famille et de ses amis: les grands écrivains de la France*, ed. Louis Jean Nicolas Monmerque, 14 vols. (Paris: Hachette et Cie, 1862-68).

[2] Arthur Stanley, *Madame de Sévigné: Her Letters and Her World* (London: Eyre and Spottiswoode, 1946), pp. 14-15.

[3] Violet Hammersley, *Letters from Madame La Marquise de Sévigné* (New York: Harcourt, Brace and Co., 1956), p. 86.

[4] Stanley, p. 239.

[5] Ibid., p. 180.

[6] *The Letters of Madame de Sévigné*, with Introduction by A. Edward Newton, 7 vols. (Philadelphia: J.P. Horn and Co., 1927), IV, 64, to Mme de Grignan, Livry, Friday, 23 July 1677. Hereafter referred to as *Letters*. All letters are written to Mme de Grignan unless otherwise indicated. To assist the reader who may not have the standard edition at hand, I have supplied the date and location for each quotation from Mme de Sévigné's letters.

[7] Stanley, p. 239.

[8] *Letters*, VII, 165, Les Rochers, Ash Wednesday, 8 February 1690.

[9] *Letters*, VII, 185, to Count de Bussy, Les Rochers, 12 July 1690.

[10] Mme de Lafayette's novel, *The Princess of Clèves*, trans. Mildred Greene, will appear in Romance Monographs, forthcoming, University of Mississippi Press. La Rochefoucauld's *Maxims* were widely read by his contemporaries.

[11] *Letters*, VI, 317, Les Rochers, Wednesday, 22 June 1689.

[12] Stanley, p. 81.

[13] Harriet Ray Allentuch, *Madame de Sévigné: A Portrait in Letters* (Baltimore: Johns Hopkins Press, 1963), p. 34.

[14] Stanley, p. 81.

[15] Dorothy Anne Lot Backer, *Precious Women* (New York: Basic Books, Inc., 1974), p. 17.

[16] Ibid.

[17] Allentuch, p. 123. A *ruelle* was the space on each side of a bed in the center of a room. Guests would gather in this area around the bed.

[18] Anne Isabella (Thackeray) Richie, *Madame de Sévigné* (Philadelphia: J.P. Lippincott and Co., 1881), pp. 58-59.

[19] Backer, p. 17.

[20] Ibid., p. 18.

[21] Allentuch, p. 21.

[22] *Letters*, VII, 104, 14 December 1689.

[23] *Letters*, V, 364-65, to de Bussy, Paris, 14 May 1686.

[24] *Letters*, I, 145-46, Paris, Wednesday, 8 April 1671.

[25] *Letters*, I, 157, Paris, Friday, 17 April 1671.

[26] Hammersley, p. 362.

[27] *Letters*, II, 4, Paris, Wednesday, 20 January 1672.

[28] *Letters*, III, 205, Paris, Wednesday, 6 May 1676.

[29] *Letters*, VII, 157, Les Rochers, Wednesday, 1 February 1690.

[30] *Letters*, IV, 65, Livry, Friday, 23 July 1677.

[31] *Letters*, VI, 195-96, Paris, Monday, 23 January 1689.

[32] *Letters*, IV, 65, as above, n. 30.

[33] *Letters*, VII, 102, Les Rochers, Sunday, 11 December 1689.

[34] *Letters*, VII, 104, Les Rochers, 14 December 1689. Voltaire echoes this sentiment in *Candide*: "Work keeps at bay three great evils: boredom, vice, and need."

[35] *Letters*, I, 190-92, Les Rochers, Sunday, 31 May 1671.

[36] *Letters*, VII, 20, Les Rochers, Sunday, 18 September 1689.

[37] Comtesse de Puliga, *Madame de Sévigné: Her Correspondents and Contemporaries* (London: Tinsley Brothers, 1873), I, 240-41.

[38] *Letters*, VI, 294, Dol, Monday, 9 May 1689.

[39] *Letters*, III, 90-91, Les Rochers, Sunday, 24 November 1675.

[40] *Letters*, II, 189-91, Bourbilly, Saturday, 21 October 1673, and VI, 251-52, to de Bussy, Paris, 16 March 1689.

[41] Allentuch, pp. 49-51.

[42] *Letters*, III, 220-42, Vichy, from 19 May 1676 to 12 June 1676.

[43] *Letters*, III, 220, Vichy, Wednesday, 20 May 1676.

[44] *Letters*, III, 227, Vichy, Thursday, 28 May 1676.

[45] *Letters*, II, 333, Paris, Wednesday, 31 July 1675.

[46] *Letters*, II, 342, to de Bussy, Paris, 6 August 1675.

[47] *Letters*, III, 198-99, Paris, Wednesday, 29 April 1676.

[48] *Letters*, III, 281-86, Paris, Wednesday, 29 July 1676.

[49] *Letters*, I, 165-66, Paris, Sunday, 26 April 1671.

[50] Ibid., p. 166.

[51] *Letters*, I, 144, Paris, Saturday, 4 April 1671.

[52] *Letters*, III, 199, Paris, Wednesday, 29 April 1676. See also III, 271-72, Paris, Friday, 17 July 1676.

[53] *Letters*, II, 322, Paris, Friday, 19 July 1675.

[54] Ibid.

[55] *Letters*, II, 325, Paris, Wednesday, 24 July 1675.

[56] *Letters*, III, 238, Vichy, Monday, 8 June 1676.

[57] *Letters*, V, 121, Les Rochers, Wednesday, 31 July 1680.

[58] *Letters*, VI, 294, Dol, Monday, 9 May 1689.

[59] *Letters*, V, 125, Les Rochers, Sunday, 4 August 1680.

[60] Puliga, I, 294.

[61] *Letters*, V, 72-73, Les Rochers, Friday, 21 June 1680.

[62] *Letters*, III, 108, Les Rochers, Wednesday, 11 December 1675.

[63] *Letters*, VI, 319, Les Rochers, Sunday, 26 June 1689.

[64] *Letters*, V, 355, to de Bussy, Livry, 28 October 1685.

[65] *Letters*, V, 357, de Bussy to Mme de Sévigné, Chaseu, 14 November 1685.

[66] *Letters*, V, 359, to President de Moulceau, Paris, 24 November 1685.

[67] *Letters*, V, 251, Les Rochers, Wednesday, 27 September 1684.

[68] Geoffrey Treasure, *Seventeenth-Century France* (New York: Doubleday and Co., Inc., 1967), p. 517.

[69] Albert C. Baugh, *A Literary History of England* (New York: Appleton-Century-Crofts, Inc., 1948), p. 780.

[70] *Letters*, II, 47-48, Paris, Wednesday, 16 March 1672.

[71] Allentuch, p. 3, quoting Daniel Mornet's review of *Portraits d'âmes* by Victor Giraud in *Revue d'histoire littéraire de la France*, 36 (1929), 600: "Mme de Sévigné marches in time with her age."

[72] *Letters*, VII, 191, to de Bussy, Grignan, 13 November 1690.

SOR JUANA INES DE LA CRUZ:
MEXICO'S TENTH MUSE* (1651—1695)

GERARD FLYNN

No other writer of colonial Latin America has received more praise than the Mexican nun Sor Juana Inés de la Cruz (1651-1695). Almost entirely self-educated, Sor Juana has earned recognition for both her learning and her literary achievement. Her contemporaries called her "the tenth muse from Mexico," a nineteenth-century Spaniard said that her love poems are some of "the softest and most delicate a woman ever penned," twentieth-century writers from three continents have compared her to Calderón, to the mystics, to the angels, and a German author has recently revived the adulation of the seventeenth century by titling his book on Sor Juana *Die zehnte Muse von Mexico.* [1]

Sor Juana's works derive from a Spanish rather than a Mexican tradition. Her sacramental plays and her comedies belong to the school of Pedro Calderón de la Barca (1600-1681),[2] Spain's renowned Baroque dramatist; her poetry finds its inspiration in the *liras* (poems of five heptasyllabic verses) and sonnets of the Peninsula, and also in the work of Gaspar Gil Polo (?-1585), author of *Diana*, a famous pastoral novel.[3] Her prose is concerned with the ecclesiastical society in which she lived, a society which mirrored Spanish culture. The works of Sor Juana thus support the commonly held opinion that until the nineteenth century Latin American literature was a part of Spanish literature and European culture.

---

*Portions reprinted with the permission of Twayne Publishers, A Division of G.K. Hall & Co., Boston.

It is remarkable that in spite of the attention paid to Sor Juana there was no satisfactory edition of her works until 1951-1957, when they appeared in four volumes. It is equally remarkable that the articles and books on Sor Juana have not demonstrated what one Hispanist has called "textual control of the imagination." Most "sorjuanists" have written a series of impressions that tell us more about themselves than about the Mexican nun, with the result that a kaleidoscopic range of opinions exists describing Sor Juana as pantheistic, Catholic, Cartesian, Scholastic, mystical, irreligious, generous, selfish, candid, or hypocritical. Sor Juana is apt to become whatever her critics want her to be.

From 1940 to 1952, a series of books appeared questioning the loyalty and religious persuasion of Sor Juana Inés de la Cruz.[4] The general image of Sor Juana presented by these books is that of a cunning woman who entered the convent in order to have a private study. She dissembled because as a clever intellectual she had to be careful of the Inquisition and the Jesuits. She fooled both Church and State. Disdaining religion, she acted hypocritically; she was a modern heretic. This series of books has created a *Leyenda negra sorjuanista*, a black legend of Sister Juana, which like all enthralling legends requires critical examination. The picture of a rebellious Sor Juana is indeed a romantic one; it appeals to the imagination, but it is supported neither by the facts of Sor Juana's life, nor by the internal evidence of her work.

Doña Juana de Asbaje y Ramírez de Santillana, the future Mexican nun, Sor Juana Inés de la Cruz, was born in November, 1651, and baptized on December 2 of the same year.[5] She was registered on the rolls as "a daughter of the Church," since her parents had only a common-law marriage. Her father was a Basque and her mother a Spaniard born in the new world; she was apparently one of six children. Sor Juana was reared in the country at the home of her maternal grandfather, whose library was her favorite entertainment. Neither punishments nor scoldings could keep her away from his books. She had learned to read when she was three years old, and when she was eight years old, she wrote a dramatic poem to the Eucharist. She was so eager to learn that she inflicted punishments on herself, showing a self-discipline unusual in a child her age. She refrained from eating cheese, which she liked, because she had heard that it made men stupid. She also cut her hair whenever she failed to learn her Latin grammar:

> I began to study Latin, in which I believe I took less than
> twenty lessons, and my concern was so strong that even
> though the natural adornment of hair is very important to

women, especially in the flower of their youth, I would cut off two or three inches of mine after first measuring its original length. And I made a rule for myself that if my hair grew back that far without my knowing such and such a point, which I had set out to learn while the hair was growing, I was to cut off the hair again as a punishment for my ignorance. It turned out that the hair grew back and I hadn't learned what I proposed to, because the hair grew quickly and I learned slowly. As a result, I cut off the hair in punishment for my head's ignorance, for it didn't seem right to me that a head so naked of knowledge should be dressed up with hair. For knowledge is a more desirable adornment *(Reply to Sor Filotea).*[6]

Sor Juana knew enough Latin after twenty lessons to learn the rest of the language. During her later life in the convent she continued to be in the position of educating herself. Her teacher, she once said, was always a mute book, her classmate an inkwell without feeling.

When she was fourteen, Sor Juana went to the Viceroy's palace as a lady of the Marquesa de Mancera. Favorite topics of discussion at the Court that year, 1665, were the arrival of the ship from the Philippines, the death of the Archbishop, the execution of certain Indian and *mestizo* highwaymen, the arrival of the flotilla from Spain, the magician who could take things out of his mouth, the burning of a village in Holland, the expulsion of a Carmelite priest, some big hailstorms, the arrival of the Capuchins, the earthquake that lasted "more than three credos," and the tightrope walker who came to Mexico at the end of December.[7] Sor Juana watched and learned the habits of the court. She was soon charming the other persons "with her genteel spirit."[8] The most charmed of all was the Viceroy's wife, the Marquesa, who urged her husband to have the professors come from the university to question Sor Juana on her knowledge. They came, some forty of them, and she defended herself "as a Royal Galley would against a few canoes."[9]

In spite of her success at the court, Sor Juana was attracted to the religious life. On the vigil of the Feast of the Assumption, 1667, at the age of sixteen, she entered the Convent of the Discalced Carmelites, but she became ill there and left three months later. A year after that she entered the Order of St. Jerome (the Hieronymites). This was a trying year for Sor Juana who, even as a young woman, had clear ideas concerning her religion and her own disposition. A person with a religious calling must distinguish between the substantial truth of her religion and the accidents surrounding it. She must, moreover, take into account her own likes and dislikes. Sometimes a person who takes religious vows will have to put up with inconveniences, but other states in life, such as marriage, also have their inconveniences. Reflecting on this period of her life, Sor Juana was to write:

> I became a nun because although I knew the religious state in life had many things (I mean the accessory things, not the formal ones) that were repugnant to my nature, nevertheless, owing to my total disinclination to marriage, it was the most fitting and suitable state I could elect, anxious as I was to assure my salvation (*Reply to Sor Filotea*, p. 446).

Because Sor Juana mentions her "total disinclination to marriage," these rather strong words have led zealous critics to look for autobiographical information in her poetry—even to the point of discovering an unknown lover who disappointed her.

Since she was young and not of great family background, her position at the court was probably at times difficult. That she was aware of the dangers of her position seems clear from her poem entitled "Sátira Filosófica." In it she argues that the appetites and censures of men are illogical because they cause in women the very infidelity and unchastity they criticize. For the Spanish text and my English translation of this well-known poem ["Hombres necios que acusáis a la mujer sin razón"], see Appendix A. Although not necessarily her best work from an artistic point of view, the poem analyzes the hypocrisy of the double standard and supplies a powerful argument against it. The last stanza is particularly striking:

> Bien con muchas armas fundo
> que lidia vuestra arrogancia,
> pues en promesa e instancia
> juntáis diablo, carne y mundo.

> [I seek a goodness with many defenses
> to fight your arrogance
> since in promising and pressing
> you join the devil, the flesh,
> and the world.]

Her conclusion seems to epitomize one of the paradoxes of her time—the combination of excessive license on the one hand and extreme purity on the other.

Sor Juana stayed with the Hieronymites from 1669 until her death in 1695. Mexico City during these years was a provincial capital on the periphery of events in Europe. The soldiers in New Mexico were engaged in civil war, the water drainage was causing serious aggravation, pirates were harassing the coast from Vera Cruz to Tampico, mercury shipments from Peru were not arriving in time for the silver mines, highwaymen were on every road, paper was in short supply because of hoarding, and the Indians were mutinous owing to the corn shortage: these notices were the major news of the day. The public was also concerned about the flotilla, the fleet of vessels that came once or twice a year from Seville, and the wonderful news it brought from Europe—there was a miraculous rain of blood in Naples; the Queen was bearing another child; James II, the new king of England, was going to favor his Catholic Christian vassals. With respect to Europe, Mexico was a borderland state, on the outside looking in.

As for Sor Juana, her life was bound to the ecclesiastical calendar and to the rituals of the convent. She rose early in the morning to recite the first of the Canonical Hours with the other sisters. She looked forward to the great feasts of the Church and sometimes she was commissioned to write *villancicos* (church carols) for them. She cooked with the other sisters, settled arguments among the convent's many servants (there were more servants than nuns),[10] consoled the other sisters even though they interrupted her studies, accepted the counsel of her prioress, occasionally attended theological discussions, served as archivist of the convent, refused an election to the office of prioress,[11] and studied whenever she had a chance. She noticed a certain tightening of the reins in convent life when the Archbishop ordered the nuns to get rid of their pet dogs. He also forbade the faithful to visit "the vestibules and railings of the convent."

From 1669 to 1690, Sor Juana studied as much as she could within the routine of her convent. She reportedly built up a library of over four thousand volumes. If the estimate of four thousand volumes is correct, then she had the best library in all of Spanish America.[12] Sor Juana had an extraordinary intellect and an even more extraordinary commitment to learning. In 1690 the so-called "incident of the letters" radically changed her way of life, so much so that when she died just five years later, she possessed no books and had been living an extremely ascetic life.

The "incident of the letters" began on Holy Thursday of 1650, when the Portuguese Jesuit Antonio de Vieyra gave a sermon in the Royal Chapel of Lisbon on the greatest gifts or favors (*finezas*) of Christ. In his sermon Vieyra rejected certain views of SS. John Chrysostom, Augustine, and Thomas Aquinas. Since Vieyra was the most famous orator of his day, his speech made a lasting impression and its influence extended to colonial Latin America. Some forty years later, Sor Juana was engaged in a casual conversation in the reception room of her convent when she praised parts of Vieyra's speech, but disagreed with some of his arguments.[13] The person she was talking to asked her to put her thoughts on paper, with the result that she sent him a letter passing judgment on the sermon of Vieyra. She did not name the recipient of the letter, whom she merely addressed as "My dear sir," but directly or indirectly the letter came into the hands of the Bishop of Puebla, Don Manuel Fernández de Santa Cruz.

Don Manuel had the letter published with the title *Carta atenagórica [The Athenagoric Letter, or, The Letter Worthy of Minerva]*, and he wrote a brief letter of his own as a prologue to Sor Juana's letter and signed it with a fictitious name, Sor Filotea de la Cruz. Although the bishop wrote as if he were one nun addressing another, in her *Reply to Sor Filotea*, Sor Juana knows that she is in reality writing to the august Bishop of Puebla.

In his pseudonymous *Letter from Sor Filotea de la Cruz*, Don Manuel reproved Sor Juana:

> I have seen your letter and admired your proofs and the clarity of your argument. Consequently I have had your letter printed. Now I should like to make some suggestions. You have a great talent and although I do not suggest that you stop reading books, I do suggest that you read more about Christ Our Lord. I do not agree with those who say that women should not be learned. St. Jerome certainly approved of their learning, and in spite of the fact that St. Paul said women should not preach, he did not say they should not learn. I suggest you continue your studies, but you ought to better the books you read, for knowledge should enlighten us and lead us toward salvation. Subordinate

profane letters to sacred letters: you must study the latter
more.

The bishop dated his letter 25 November 1690.

Three months later, on 1 March 1691, Sor Juana answered the Bishop of
Puebla with her *Reply to Sor Filotea de la Cruz*. Her reply has two main ideas:
(1) "this, my black inclination" (*inclinación*—fondness, bent, love, inclination)
and (2) *mulieres in ecclesia taceant*. By her "black inclination," Sor Juana
means an all-consuming thirst for knowledge, an overpowering desire to read,
a yearning to know more if only to be less ignorant. She explains that she must
study all the time; when there are no books at hand, she will learn something
somehow; she will examine the beams of a ceiling to see why they converge
and go down, or at least appear to do so, as they go away; she will fry one egg
in oil and another in syrup, to learn that the one unites whereas the other
breaks up; she will put sifted flour under a spinning top to observe its spiral
path; or she will meditate, metaphysically, on the multitude of different
characters who share the one human nature.

Mulieres in ecclesia taceant, the Biblical text she wants to discuss with the
bishop, means, "Let women be quiet in church," and by extension the phrase
could mean "Women should be seen and not heard," or "Books, study, and
learning are not for women." Sor Juana defends the right of women to be
educated, and one critic goes so far as to say "that we might well consider the
Reply to Sor Filotea the Magna Carta of intellectual liberty for women in
America."[14]

The *Reply to Sor Filotea* is a carefully reasoned work which reveals much
about Sor Juana's life. Since she knows that Sor Filotea is the bishop (see the
last two paragraphs of the letter), she discreetly builds up a case for her two
principal ideas: her own inclination toward letters and women's freedom to
cultivate them.

She says that she is grateful to Sor Filotea for publishing her letter on Vieyra,
although she had no idea it was going to be printed. Had she known, she would
have exercised more care in writing it. She agrees with Sor Filotea that she
should read more sacred literature, and promises to do so, adding that one
must exercise a certain caution with books such as the erotic Song of Songs,
which even learned men do not read before they are thirty. Sor Juana displays
a restrained and gentle humor in writing to Sor Filotea, for the *Reply to Sor*

FILI

Copia de otra que de si hizo, y de su mano pintó la R. M. Juana Ynes de la Cruz Fenix de la
America, Glorioso desempeño deste Sexo, Honrra de la Nacion, destre Nuevo Mundo, y argu-
mento delas admiraciones, y Elogios del Antuido. Nacio el dia 12. de Nov. deel año de 1651. a la
onse dela noche. Recivió el Sagrado Habito de el Maximo D. S. Geronimo en su Convento de
esta Ciudad de Mexico, de edad de 17. años. Y murió Domingo 17. de Abril de el de 1695. de edad
40. y 4 años, cinco mezes, cinco dias, y cinco horas. Requiescat in pace. Amin

Filotea, in which she promises to read more sacred literature, is filled with arguments, allusions, and Latin quotations that show how well she knew Holy Writ, the Fathers of the Church, the medieval Scholastics, and the religious writers of her own day.

Sor Juana also says that in all her life as a nun she never wrote anything at her own urging except perhaps the little paper called *The Dream*. She always wrote "under duress and violence," that is, at the behest of others. She says that she does not study in order to write or much less to teach, but rather because she has the craving and inclination to study and wants to be less ignorant. Her inclination toward books persists even though she has tried to check it; once when she was ill the doctors forbade her reading in the hope that this would alleviate her distress, but she had to return to her books since without them she became worse.

She tells Sor Filotea that she learned to read when she was three. In her own words:

> To continue the story of my inclination, which I want you to know all about, I say that I was not yet three years old when my mother sent an older sister of mine to learn to read at one of the schools called *Amigas*, and partly out of affection, partly out of mischief, I followed her; and when I saw that they were giving her a lesson, I became so inflamed in my desire to learn how to read that I told the teacher, whom I thought I was deceiving, that my mother wanted me to have a lesson. She did not believe it, since it was unbelievable, but in a spirit of good-natured fun she gave me the lesson. I kept going and she kept teaching me, but it was no longer in fun since experience had taught her otherwise; and I learned to read in such a short time that I already knew how before my mother found out, because the teacher had kept it from her in order to surprise her and to receive a reward for her services; and I kept quiet about it, thinking they would spank me for doing it without their permission. The one who taught me is still living (may God keep her) and she can testify to what I say (p. 445).

It is in the *Reply* that Sor Juana recounts the anecdotes of refraining from eating cheese as a young girl and of cutting off her hair as an incentive to learn Latin grammar.[15] She was six or seven years old when she heard of the university and of schools where people studied different subjects. As soon as she heard of the university, she begged her mother to change her mode of dress and send her to the home of a relative in Mexico City so that she could become a student. It is also clear that her interest in reading was not always encouraged. In the *Reply* she writes: "I whetted my appetite by reading many different kinds of books that my grandfather had, and punishments and reprimands were not enough to stop me" (p. 446).

After describing her efforts to learn Latin, Sor Juana writes some twenty-two lines that are the most important part of the *Reply*. In these lines she tells the reader much about her religious life, her attitude toward marriage, her studies, and her philosophy. After explaining that she became a nun because she did not wish to marry and was anxious to assure her salvation, she writes:

> My petty whims were such that I would have preferred to live alone, to have no duty or occupation that might interfere with my freedom for study, to avoid the noise of a community about me which might upset the silence of my books: this was my whim, but whim had to bow down and subject itself to the most important consideration of all: salvation. I vacillated for some time in my determination, but finally some learned persons showed me how my whims were a temptation; I conquered them with divine help and took up the state I now so unworthily hold. I thought I was fleeing from myself when I entered the convent, but wretch that I am, I brought myself with me, and I also brought my worst enemy in this inclination to letters which (I am not certain) was sent by Heaven either as a gift or a punishment; for instead of dying down or going out amidst all my religious practices, it blew up like powder, and I was living proof of the refrain *privatio est causa appetitus* [to be deprived of something is to increase one's appetite for it] (p. 446).

This passage is based on the doctrine of vocation to a state in life. Sor Juana says that she was not attracted to the accessories, or accidents, of convent life, particularly the noise a community might make at the very time she wanted to study; nevertheless, she knew she would have to put up with these annoyances. This was the price she had to pay for living in a religious community.

After speaking of her vocation Sor Juana says that she hoped to study the queen of the sciences, theology. But to know the queen one must also know the handmaids, the ancillary sciences, and so she set out to study logic, rhetoric, physics, arithmetic, geometry, architecture, history, law, music, and astronomy.[16] Her inclination, she says, was general rather than particular; she was not what people today would call a specialist. Sor Juana unquestionably had the thirst for learning of a humanistic scholar.

Perhaps the most moving part of the *Reply to Sor Filotea* is the passage in which Sor Juana says she always lacked a teacher and fellow students. To her regret she was a self-educated scholar and a self-taught philosopher:

> What might excuse me is the great difficulty I have had, not only in lacking a teacher but in lacking fellow students with whom to discuss and work on the subject matter. My only teacher was a mute book, my only fellow student an inkwell without feeling; and instead of explanations and exercises I had a great many interruptions, not only those of my religious duties (and these indeed are profitable and useful and do not waste time), but those that are accessory to a community; for example, I would be reading and in the next cell they would decide to play music and sing; I would be studying and two maids would have a squabble and come to me to settle their argument; or I would be writing and a friend would come to visit me, thereby, doing me a bad deed with a good will—naturally I could not show any annoyance, I had to be grateful for the harm done me. And this went on continuously, since the free hours I had for study were also the free hours of the whole community, and the other sisters could come to interrupt me. Only those who have experienced community life know how true this is and only the strength of my vocation could make me be good-natured, that and the great love that exists between me and my beloved sisters, for love is union and where it is there are no opposite extremes (pp. 450-51).

The rest of Sor Juana's *Reply to Sor Filotea* shows that she met considerable opposition to her studies. Curiously, the worst opposition of all came from those who were her friends and wanted her to stop studying for her own good; for example, there was a well-intentioned but unlettered prioress who looked upon studies as something to be investigated by the Inquisition. She forbade Sor Juana her studies, and during the three months she was the superior, Sor Juana did not read a book. As a matter of fact, since Sor Juana could not quiet her intellect and had to apply it to something, it was during this period that she made observations of a scientific nature.

Some of the opposition, however, was not so charitable, and here Sor Juana, rather than name her adversaries, contents herself with pointing out the example of Christ. The more He did, the more He gave, the more He was (Sor Juana identifies perfection with being), the more He was persecuted. And so it must be with others. The more they stand out the more they will wear a crown of thorns, as their Savior did before them. Opposition and persecution are not to be wondered at; they are to be expected.

Perhaps because of the opposition to study which she personally experienced, Sor Juana takes very seriously St. Paul's Biblical text *mulieres in ecclesia taceant* (Let women be quiet in church), a phrase that some people employed to discourage women from learning. Sor Juana acts as a lawyer for the defense and draws up a formidable argument, citing learned women from Jewish and pagan antiquity and then from Christianity itself: Ste. Catherine of Egypt, Ste. Gertrude, Ste. Paula, Ste. Theresa of Avila, and others. Sor Juana concludes that women who have the ability to learn should study in private but not preach in public. She also says that unqualified men would do better not to study, for a little learning is dangerous: it is like a sword in the hands of a madman. Mentioning the example of the heresiarchs, she specifically identifies Pelagius and Arius as early leaders in heresy and then also mentions Luther.

Concerning the *mulieres in ecclesia taceant*, she holds that St. Paul meant women could not preach from the pulpit in church although they could study in private. She quotes parts of the Bible in favor of women's learning and shows by many examples that one cannot place a literal interpretation on every passage of Holy Writ. Why, then, did Paul, the great apostle, say *mulieres in ecclesia taceant?* Sor Juana answers:

> Moreover, that prohibition concerned a historical question, which Eusebius refers to, namely, that in the early Church women began to preach doctrine to one another in the temples; and this noise caused confusion while the apostles were preaching, so that the women were ordered to be

silent. And the same thing happens today, namely, that while the preacher is preaching, one should not pray out loud (pp. 465-66).

Sor Juana closes the *Reply to Sor Filotea* by saying that she has written two devotional works that were published without her name. She was happy to see them published, and she encloses two copies for Sor Filotea (the bishop) to read. Otherwise she has written nothing for publication, least of all *The Athenagoric Letter*.

The *Reply to Sor Filotea* is the work of an intellectual who has taught herself the rudiments of many subjects and has closely examined two, philosophy and theology. Sor Juana is a religious woman who, unlike many Catholics of her day, did not use her faith as an excuse for neglecting her reason. She realizes that arguments based on authority are usually the weakest arguments of all, but she will defer to authority in order to avoid scandal and to increase charity. She is an apostle of union, an enemy of discord: "For love is union and knows no opposite extremes."[17] From a literary perspective Sor Juana's *Reply to Sor Filotea* is "perhaps the most charming autobiography we have in the Spanish language, where this genre is so wanting."[18] Every person who is interested in Sor Juana will want to read it several times.

The events following the incident of the letters are not clear to us today, for there is very little reliable documentary evidence. We know that there was disagreement within the Church over the letters: the Bishop Manuel Fernández de Santa Cruz favored Sor Juana, whereas her own confessor, the Jesuit Father Antonio Nuñez abandoned her. We also know that the lustrum 1690-1695 was a trying period of pestilence, hunger, and insurrection, in which the Indian uprising of 1692 was the most memorable event. Finally, we know that Sor Juana made a total renunciation of the world. We have the general picture and the specific act of renunciation, that is to say, we have certain facts, but the causes underlying these facts are not obvious. It is too much to say, as some critics have zealously asserted, that Sor Juana was the victim of a Jesuit conspiracy, or of her own menopause; there is no documentary evidence to support these theories. After the incident of the letters, in a city suffering from pestilence and violence, this forty-two-year-old woman sold her entire library together with her mathematical and musical instruments and gave the money to the poor. For herself she kept "three little prayer books and many hairshirts and disciplines." With her own blood she signed a renewal of her vows, in which she affirmed that "my lady the Virgin Mary was conceived without stain of original sin." Her confessor returned to her and changed his role, endeavoring to restrain her pious zeal. The last two years of her life, 1693-1695, are a mystery. An epidemic struck the convent, and Sor Juana, helping the other sisters who were older and more infirm than she, "became sick through charity." She received the sacraments and died on 17 April 1695, at the age of forty-four.

Sor Juana Inés de la Cruz has an established place in Latin American literature because of her plays and a score or more of good poems. *The Trials of a Noble House* and *Love the Greater Labyrinth* are *comedias de capa y espada*, plays written in the fashion of Calderón. They contain amorous intrigue, mistaken identities, and entangled plots that are unravelled rather quickly at the end. Her *The Divine Narcissus*, a sacramental play also in the style of Calderón, is usually presented on the feast of Corpus Christi. *The First Dream* is a long baroque poem with an epistemological theme, focusing on intuitive knowledge and the senses.

In modern parlance, Sor Juana was an intellectual, and at a time when freedom of thought, especially for women, was discouraged. Her *Reply to Sor Filotea* shows that she was sharply criticized for opposing the ideas of Father Vieyra; however, she quite simply states: "just as I was free to disagree with Vieyra, so others are free to disagree with my judgment." This insistence upon intellectual freedom is characteristic of her thought.

Sincere in her religious vocation, she sold her library to provide for the poor and sacrificed her life nursing her companions. Not only did Sor Juana brilliantly describe what she calls her own "inclination to letters," she responded as well to the challenge of justifying learning for all women and in so doing contributed to the development of a tradition of female scholarship.

NOTES

[1] Ludwig Pfandl's *Die zehnte Muse von Mexico* was published in Munich in 1946. The reader is referred to the Spanish translation of his book, *Sor Juana Inés de la Cruz. La décima musa de México: Su vida, su poesía, su psique* (México: Universidad Nacional Autónoma de México, 1963). Pfandl presents a Freudian interpretation of Sor Juana's life.

[2] For a comparison of Sor Juana's *gracioso* [figure of fun] with that of Calderón, see Charles David Ley, *El gracioso en el teatro de la península* (Madrid: Revista de Occidente, 1954).

[3] See José María de Cossío, "Observaciones sobre la vida y la obra de Sor Juana Inés de la Cruz," in the *Homenaje a Sor Juana Inés de la Cruz* of the Real Academia Española (Madrid: S. Aguirre, 1952), pp. 18-20.

[4] See Ermilo Abréu Gómez, "Prologue," *Poesías de Sor Juana Inés de la Cruz* (México: Ediciones Botas, 1940) who argues that Sor Juana lacked a religious vocation and was Cartesian in her thought; Elizabeth Wallace, *Sor Juana Inés de la Cruz, Poetisa de corte y convento* (México: Ediciones Xochitl, 1944), who accepts much of the Abréu Gómez school, but does not oppose her so much to the Church; Anita Arroyo, *Razón y pasión de Sor Juana* (México: Porrúa y Obregón, 1952) who follows Abréu Gómez and views Sor Juana as a rebellious woman who entered the convent for worldly reasons. See also Clara Campoamor, *Sor Juana Inés de la Cruz* (Buenos Aires: Emecé, 1944), and the newspaper article of Alfonso Méndez Plancarte, "Sor Juana heterodoxa, histérica y otros piropos," in the newspaper *El Universal* (México, 21 May 1945).

[5] José María Pemán "Sinceridad y artificio en la poesía de Sor Juana Inés de la Cruz," *Homenaje a Sor Juana*, pp. 31-32.

[6] All references to the *Reply to Sor Filotea* are taken from Alfonso Méndez Plancarte, editor, *Obras completas de Sor Juana Inés de la Cruz* (México: Fondo de Cultura Económica, 1951-1957), IV, 440-75, esp. p. 446. Translations are mine.

[7] Antonio de Robles, *Diario de sucesos notables* (1665-1703) (México: Editorial Porrúa, 1946), I, 3-14.

[8] Méndez Plancarte, *Obras completas de Sor Juana*, I, xxviii.

[9] From the biography by Padre Calleja, as quoted by Méndez Plancarte, *Obras Completas*, I, xxviii.

[10] Pfandl, *Sor Juana*, pp. 47-48.

[11] Reported by Ezequiel Chávez, *Ensayo de picologia de Sor Juana Inés de la Cruz* (Barcelona: Editorial Araluce, 1931), but see also Sor Juana Inés de la Cruz, *Poesía, teatro y prosa*, edición y prólogo de Antonio Castro Leal (México: Editorial Porrúa, 1965), p. xxviii. Leal points out that Chávez fails to mention his source for this information.

[12] See Méndez Plancarte, *Obras completas*, I, lxi, and Castro Leal, above, but see also Dorothy Schons, "Some Obscure Points in the Life of Sor Juana Inés de la Cruz," *Modern Philology*, 24 (1926), 141-62, who argues that the "four thousand volumes" should read "four hundred."

[13] Pfandl, *Sor Juana*, p. 76.

[14] Alberto G. Salceda, *Obras completas de Sor Juana*, IV, xliii. Salceda edited the fourth and last volume of Sor Juana's *Obras completas* after the death of Alfonso Méndez Plancarte.

[15] Sor Juana does not mention her childhood friends, games, trips, or any other personal information. To be sure, the *Reply* is an intellectual autobiography and an apology for female learning, but the reader can only regret that she has not told us more about herself.

[16] According to Sor Juana, all the sciences are linked and the comprehension of one helps the comprehension of another. She speaks of a "universal chain of being." For the tradition, see Arthur O. Lovejoy, *The Great Chain of Being* (Cambridge, Mass.: Harvard University Press, 1936).

[17] Questions concerning the primacy of revelation or reason and whether or not the two can be reconciled remain important issues today. Before reading the *Reply to Sor Filotea*, the reader should consult Etienne Gilson's *Reason and Revelation in the Middle Ages* (New York: Scribners, 1938).

[18] José María de Cossió "Observaciones," *Homenaje a Sor Juana*, pp. 18-20.

APPENDIX A:

Sátira Filosófica

*Arguye de inconsecuentes el gusto
y la censura de los hombres que
en las mujeres acusan lo que causan.*

Hombres necios que acusáis
a la mujer sin razón,
sin ver que sois la ocasión
de lo mismo que culpáis:

si con ansia sin igual
solicitáis su desdén,
¿por qué queréis que obren bien
si las incitáis al mal?

Combatís su resistencia
y luego, con graveded,

Philosophical Satire

*The poem argues that the appetite
and the censure of men are illogical;
men accuse in women the very
thing they cause in them.*

Foolish men you who accuse
women without reason,
not seeing you are the occasion
of the very thing you blame:

if with unequalled anxiousness
you solicit their disdain,
why do you want them to act well
when you incite them to evil?

You combat their resistance
and then, very gravely,

decís que fue liviandad
lo que hizo la diligencia.

Parecer quiere el denuedo
de vuestro parecer loco,
al niño que pone el coco
y luego le tiene miedo.

Queréis, con presunción necia,
hallar a la que buscáis,
para pretendida, Thais,
y en la posesión, Lucrecia.

¿Qué humor puede ser más raro
que el que, falto de consejo,
él mismo empaña el espejo,
y siente que no esté claro?

Con el favor y el desdén
tenéis condición igual,
quejándoos, si os tratan mal,
burlándoos, si os quieren bien.

Opinión, ninguna gana;
pues la que más se recata,
si no os admite, es ingrata,
y si os admite, es liviana.

Siempre tan necios andáis
que, con desigual nivel,
a una culpáis por crüel
y a otra por fácil culpáis.

¿Pues cómo ha de estar templada
la que vuestro amor pretende,
si la que es ingrata, ofende,
y la que es fácil, enfada?

you say that it was looseness
that your diligence has wrought.

The boldness of your crazy mind
implores resemblance
to the child who calls out bogeyman
and then has fear of him.

You want, with foolish presumption,
to find in the girl you seek,
at wooing time, Thais,*
and in marriage, Lucrece.

What humor can there be more rare
than that which, lacking counsel,
clouds the mirror itself,
and then is sorry it is not clear?

With favor and with disdain
you have the same condition,
complaining if they treat you ill,
sneering if they treat you well.

A reputation, no woman gains one;
since she who is most prudent,
if she admits you not, is ungrateful,
and if she admits you, she is loose.

You are always so foolish
that, with no consistency,
you blame one for being cruel,
another you blame as easy.

Well, how can she be firm,
she who pretends to your love,
if being ungrateful, she offends,
and being easy, she angers?

*Thais was the proverbial courtesan of Athens, who had many famous lovers.
Lucrece is the prototype of conjugal fidelity in ancient Rome.

Más, entre el enfado y pena
que vuestro gusto refiere,
bien haya la que no os quiere
y quejaos en hora buena.

Dan vuestras amantes penas
a sus libertades alas,
y después de hacerlas malas
las queréis hallar muy buenas.

¿Cuál mayor culpa ha tenido
en una pasión errada:
la que cae de rogada,
o el que ruega de caído?

¿O cuál es más de culpar,
aunque cualquiera mal haga:
la que peca por la paga,
o el que paga por pecar?

Pues ¿para qué os espantáis
de la culpa que tenéis?
Queredlas cual las hacéis
o hacedlas cual las buscáis.

Dejad de solicitar,
y después, con más razón,
acusaréis la afición
de la que os fuere a rogar.

Bien con muchas armas fundo
que lidia vuestra arrrogancia,
pues en promesa e instancia
juntáis diablo, carne y mundo.

But amidst the anger and pain
which your taste reports
there may well be one who doesn't
love you, so go ahead and complain.

Your great suffering in love
gives flight to their liberties,
and after making women bad,
you want to find them very good.

Who has the greater fault
in a passion gone astray:
she who falls being begged,
or he who begs having fallen?

Or who is more blameworthy,
no matter what evil may be done:
she who sins for payment
or he who pays to sin?

Then, why get so astonished
over this fault of yours?
Love women as you make them
or make them as you want them.

Stop soliciting,
and later, with greater reason,
you will accuse the eagerness
of she who might beseech you.

I seek a goodness with many defenses
to fight your arrogance,
since in promising and pressing
you join the devil, the flesh, and the
world.

ELIZABETH ELSTOB: "THE SAXON NYMPH"
(1683–1756)

MARY ELIZABETH GREEN

> There mark what ills the scholar's life assail,
> Toil, envy, want, the patron, and the jail.

If, in her old age, Elizabeth Elstob read these lines by Samuel Johnson, written seven years before her death in 1756, surely she experienced a poignant recognition. In a time when the majority of men, according to Swift, believed it the duty of women "to be fools in every article except what is merely domestic," and, added Swift in his even-handed way, the majority of women apparently agreed, except for those who had "*as little* regard for family business as for the *improvement of their minds*,"[1] Elizabeth Elstob chose to be a scholar. In making such a choice, Elstob faced three formidable difficulties: she was a woman; she wished to be a serious scholar, and she wished to be a serious scholar of Anglo-Saxon.

In the first place, there was something unnatural about women scholars. In an age in which "according to nature" and "the nature of things" were shibboleths, the worst charge to be laid against a person or an idea was that it was "unnatural." If men were to "first follow nature," as Pope wrote, so also were women. When, in 1710, the young Lady Mary Pierrepont, during her self-willed courtship with Mr. Edward Wortley Montagu, sent her translation of Epictetus to Gilbert Burnet, Bishop of Salisbury, she protested the inadequate education afforded women: "We are permitted no Books but such as tend to the weakening and Effeminateing the Mind, our Natural Deffects are every way indulg'd, and tis look'd upon as in a degree Criminal to improve our Reason, or fancy we have any." As if surprised by her audacity in uttering these radical sentiments, Lady Mary assured the worthy Bishop that she could not deny "that God and Nature have thrown [women] into an Inferior Rank," owing "Obedience and Submission to the Superior Sex." Any woman denying this, she said, "Rebells against the Law of the Creator and the indisputable Order of Nature."[2] These remarks by Lady Mary throw into sharp relief the first obstacle Elizabeth Elstob faced in her pursuit of learning: her sex. Throughout her life even the indisputably intelligent and self-educated Lady Mary Wortley Montagu was unsparing in her contempt for bluestockings and self-styled learned ladies and thus provides, a fortiori, a striking illustration of the hostility and ridicule facing any woman who dared to lay claim to the title of scholar.[3]

Even men who took their scholarship too seriously were the subject of ridicule in the early eighteenth century, particularly in the writings of satirists like Swift and Pope, who, along with other possessors of what was often called "polite learning," espoused the basically Platonic synthesis that knowledge and virtue are one. In other words, the intellectual milieu of an influential portion of eighteenth-century society did not value the theoretic sciences, in which knowledge is seen as an end in itself, as highly as the practical and productive sciences, whose value is measured in terms of their effects on the individual and the social and political institutions he creates.

It is significant in terms of one's understanding of the difficulties facing Elizabeth Elstob that a great portion of the widespread satiric attacks on what were then called "abuses of learning" was directed not against the new science and the Royal Academy (as in Shadwell's play "The Virtuoso" and Swift's "Voyage to Laputa"), but against historians, antiquarians, and textual scholars, whose activities were in the humanistic rather than the scientific sphere. In the eyes of their critics, although certainly not in their own, these scholars violated John Locke's injunction: "Our business here is not to know all things, but those which concern our conduct."[4]

In this regard, the eighteenth-century English gentleman or would-be gentleman, who professed "polite learning," was close in spirit to the more conservative of his Elizabethan forebears. The words that William Paulett, third Marquis of Winchester, wrote about knowledge and wisdom in the 1580's would have sounded not at all alien to the reader of the *Spectator* over 130 years later:

The end why men ought to studie is to learne to live well: for there is no surer science in man than to knowe how to order his life well.

What profiteth it me to know much, if thereby I take no profit; what to speake strange languages, if I refraine not my toong from other mens matters; what to studie any books, if I studie not but to beguile my friends; what to know the influence of the stars and course of the elements, if I cannot keepe myselfe from vices?[5]

In 1597, Sir William Cornwallis, the Younger, meditated similarly about "essaies and bookes" in a passage adumbrating Addison's reflections in *Spectator* 10:

Marke but a Grammarian, whose occupation wel examined is but a single-soled trade, for his subject is but wordes, and yet his construction is of great matters resting in himself. *Socrates* was the wisest man of his time, and his ground for that was his turning all his acquired knowledge into morality; of whom one saide, he fetched Philosophy from heaven and placed her in Cities.[6]

Cornwallis expanded his indictment to include not only the studies of grammarians but any intellectual pursuit that does not teach the *gentleman* (and that is the significant word) to live well:

What Bookes or art meddles with a doctrine remote from the use of life is a busie Idleness and a cover of an unprofitable mind, like fiddlers undertaking the use of an Instrument to keepe them from a more laborious trade.[7]

In polite circles, a singular devotion to the scholarly life was considered not only idle and useless, but downright dangerous, as Richard Burton noted in his *Anatomy of Melancholy* (1621):

How many poor scholars have lost their wits, or become dizzards, neglecting all worldly affairs and their own health, wealth, being and well being, to gain knowledge! for which, after all their pains, in the world's esteem they are accounted ridiculous and silly fools, idiots, asses, and (as oft as they are)

rejected, condemned, derided, doting, and mad! . . . Go to
Bedlam and ask. Or if they keep their wits, yet are they
esteemed scrubs and fools by reason of their carriage!

Even if scholars retained their sanity, they still faced social disapproval:

Because they cannot ride a horse, which every clown can do;
salute and court a gentlewoman, carve at table, cringe and
make congies, which every common swasher can do, &c. they
are laughed to scorn and accounted silly fools by gallants.
Yet, many times, such is their misery, they deserve it: a
mere scholar, a mere ass.[8]

It was this attitude toward scholars in general which passed into the Restoration and early eighteenth century, when, as a young woman, Elizabeth Elstob
labored to become a serious Anglo-Saxon scholar.

Yet, for a number of reasons, the seventy years following the Restoration in
1660 witnessed a truly remarkable outpouring of Anglo-Saxon studies; and,
for a few short years at least, Elizabeth Elstob found herself in a small circle
of scholars who encouraged her work. David C. Douglas has written of these
years that "it would not be difficult to defend the opinion that Anglo-Saxon
studies have never progressed with greater rapidity than in the period which
elapsed between the publication of William Somner's *Dictionary* in 1659 and
the death of Humphrey Wanley in 1726."[9] Perhaps it was precisely for this
reason that Pope ridiculed such antiquarian labors in the *Dunciad*:

> But who is he, in closet close y-pent,
> Of sober face, with learned dust besprent?
> Right well mine eyes arede the myster wight,
> On parchment scraps y-fed, and Wormius hight.
> To future ages may thy dulness last,
> As thou preserv'st the dulness of the past!
>   (III. 185-90)

Of all scholarly pursuits, the antiquarian studies of the Saxonists were subject
to particular ridicule. Samuel Butler scorned the antiquarians' "great Venera-
tion for Words that are stricken in Years, and are grown so aged, that they have
outlived their Employments,"[10] and in the last half of the eighteenth century

Horace Walpole—certainly not adverse to polite Gothicizing himself—wrote this opinion of some of his contemporaries:

> The Antiquarians will be as ridiculous as they used to be; and since it is impossible to infuse taste into them, they will be as dry and dull as their predecessors. . . . Their Saxon and Danish discoveries are not worth more than the Monuments of the Hottentots.[11]

The fact remains, however, that the years between 1660 and 1730 saw a major contribution to learning in the discovery and editing of historical records of England's past and in the production of such literally monumental treatises as George Hickes's *Linguarum Venterum Septentrionalium Thesaurus,* · [the Treasury of Northern Tongues], a major contribution to the development of comparative philology, and Thomas Rymer's *Foedera*, planned as a compilation of all the records of England's alliances and foreign transactions. By the time of his death in 1713, Rymer had completed fifteen volumes containing all the available material from 1101 to 1543. Of Hickes's study William Wotton wrote in 1708 that "the learned world never yet saw anything like or comparable to this kind of literature."[12] Yet Hickes's work, like Rymer's and the indefatigable Thomas Hearne's, constitutes only a small part of the production of the great scholars of the age: Thomas Gale, Humphrey Wanley, Robert Brady, Henry Warton, Thomas Tanner, Edmund Gibson, Thomas Madox—to name only the most prolific and outstanding of a group whose work must still command the respect of modern scholars.

Yet if William Dugdale could remark in 1655 that "Man without learninge, and the remembrance of thingse past falls into a beastlye sottishness,"[13] there were those who viewed the scholarly achievement of the post-Restoration years with something akin to alarm: to them the mind and soul of man appeared to be contracting into ever smaller and smaller areas. What was lacking in those who viewed these learned efforts with contempt and ridicule was the historical perspective necessary to trace how the tremendous production of disparate critical editions adorned with learned controversy and commentary was a necessary prelude to the development of a more integrated and sophisticated approach to the study of language, literature, and history. In their search for and preservation of the state documents and the early religious and secular literature of England's past, the Anglo-Saxon and Anglo-Norman scholars left a rich legacy to their intellectual descendants, who could more easily separate the prefatory dross of outworn controversy from priceless texts. Moreover, in some quarters at least, an intense interest in England's pre-Elizabethan history and language seemed less and less relevant to a nation apparently approaching a new classical age:

> Every civilized Nation has, I believe, sooner or later, such an Age; how far we may be in it, or what Approaches we have made towards it, I need not go about to ascertain: However, it seems to me plain, that the *English* Language is not capable of much greater Perfection, than it has already attain'd: We have trafficked with every Country for the enriching it; the Moderns and Ancients have both contributed to the giving it Splendor and Magnificence; the fairest Scyons, that could be had from the Gardens of *France* and *Italy*, have been grafted on our old Stocks, to refine the Savageness of the Breed; we have laid aside all our harsh antique Words, and retain'd only those of good Sound and Energy; the most beautifule Polish is at length given to our Tongue, and its *Teutonic* Rust quite worn away.[14]

Leonard Welsted wrote this assessment of the English language in 1724, but he was saying nothing startling or new. The antiquarians had long since been forced to a defensive position about their studies. George Hickes had prefaced an Apology for Saxon learning to his *Thesaurus*. Elizabeth Elstob felt compelled to answer the questions: "What is this Saxon? what has she to do with this barbarous antiquated Stuff?"[15] And Thomas Madox wrote in 1711: "I know . . . the Lovers of Antiquities are commonly looked upon to be men of Low unpolite genius fit only for the Rough and *Barbarick* part of Learning."[16]

One must remember that in his *Letters on the Study and Use of History* Pope's friend Lord Bolingbroke had warned that the misuse of the study of history "may serve to render us mere antiquarians and scholars" and argued that the end of the fifteenth century was the proper beginning for the useful study of England's past:

> To be entirely ignorant about ages that precede this aera would be shameful. Nay some indulgence may be had to a temperate curiosity in the review of them. But to be learned about them is a ridiculous affectation in any man who means to be useful to the present age.[17]

(We may place this thought next to Voltaire's belief that there were only four ages worth studying: "the four happy ages," he called them—of Pericles, Augustus, the Renaissance, and his own enlightened eighteenth century.)

Yet despite such strictures, there was a great Anglo-Saxon revival after the Restoration, and it paralleled in may ways the Elizabethan interest in English antiquity as a means of justifying the Anglican establishment. What has been called the first English literary society was founded in 1572 by Matthew Parker, the Archbishop of Canterbury, who had been instrumental during the previous decade in the publication of *A Testimonie of Antiquity* (1566), the first book ever printed in Anglo-Saxon type. Similarly, a century later, ecclesiastics like Edward Stillingfleet and William Wake, also an Archbishop of Canterbury, turned to history to defend the Anglican Church against both "Papists" and "Presbyters"; and a dedicated group of Non-jurors, those who refused the oaths to William III or George I, men like Hickes and Hearne, Jeremy Collier and William Lloyd, were instrumental in the preservation and revival of interest in the learned and literary documents of English antiquity. The firm dedication to religious principles that informed these endeavors often resulted in an almost missionary zeal and single-mindedness of purpose which admitted of no compromise with those who disdained their labors. Elizabeth Elstob brought a typically crusading spirit to her studies of Anglo-Saxon. "Those who please themselves with an Opinion of their own extraordinary Wit or Learning," she wrote in 1709, "usually think themselves obliged to overlook all they do not know themselves, as useless and impertinent. So that it is not a difficult Matter to foresee, what kind of reception a Work of this Nature will meet with, from this kind of Persons."[18]

Against this background, that is, the fact that both learned women and Anglo-Saxon scholars were, more often than not, the subject of ridicule in "polite" society, we may turn to the life and career of Elizabeth Elstob. It should not surprise any student of the eighteenth century that the earliest printed account of Elizabeth Elstob is to be found in the *Bibliotheca Topographica Britannica* of that inexhaustible compiler John Nichols, who published in the first volume a paper about Elizabeth Elstob and her brother William, which had been presented by Samuel Pegge at a meeting of the Society of Antiquaries in 1767.[19] Of great interest also is the brief "Autobiography" written in Elstob's own hand in November, 1738, when she was fifty-five years old, yet containing regrettably little information about the difficult years following her brother's death in 1715. Written in the third person, this memoir is deposited with the papers of George Ballard in the Bodleian Library. (The Ballard MSS. are an invaluable source, containing letters to, from, and about Elizabeth Elstob.) Other important sources of information about Elstob are to be found in the six-volume *Autobiography and Correspondence* of Mary Delany [Swift's Mrs. Pendarves] and the *Diary and Correspondence* of Ralph Thoresby, who has been somewhat overenthusiastically referred to as the "Samuel Pepys of the North." It was Thoresby who called Elstob "the justly celebrated Saxon nymph," a phrase that caught on in her own lifetime. Invaluable also are the *Remarks and Collections* of Thomas Hearne (eleven volumes of marvelous scholarly gossip), Nichols' *Literary Anecdotes of the Eighteenth Century*, and M. A. Richardson's *Reprints of Rare Tracts*, of which only 100 copies were printed in Newcastle in 1847. These works supply the principal sources for the appreciations of Elizabeth Elstob which have appeared in the twentieth century[20] and for Sir Leslie Stephen's account of her life in the *DNB*.

Elizabeth Elstob was born in Newcastle-on-Tyne in September, 1683, lost her father when she was five and her mother only three years later. With the death of her mother, Elizabeth was sent to live with her uncle, the Rev. Charles Elstob, D.D., prebendary of Canterbury. Writing of her early years—the memoir is to be found in the Ballard MSS.—Elstob says of herself: "From her childhood she was a great lover of books, which being observed by her mother, who was also a great admirer of learning, especially in her own sex, there was nothing wanting for her improvement, so long as her mother lived." Life with her uncle, however, was in this regard at least more difficult, for he "was no friend to woman's learning, so that she was not suffered to proceed, notwithstanding her repeated requests that she might, being always put off with that common and vulgar saying that one tongue is enough for a woman."[21] Despite this lack of encouragement, and, as Elstob writes, "in obedience to her mother's desire," she spent her time reading extensively in English and French, "which last language," she writes, "she with much difficulty obtained leave to learn." By the end of her life Elstob was credited with having mastered seven languages, in addition to English and Latin.[22] How and when this mastery was effected is difficult to ascertain. It was in 1691 that Elstob was sent to live with her uncle, and in 1702 she was living in London, in Bush Lane, with her brother William, with whom she lived until his death from consumption early in 1715. William, ten years his sister's senior, had spent five years at Eton and then, after a short attendance at Cambridge, entered Queen's College, Oxford, well-know at this time as a center of Saxon learning. It was from her brother that Elizabeth most likely obtained her first interest and training in Old English. William himself was no mean Saxonist, and Elizabeth eventually equalled him in mastery of the tongue.

All that is known for certain about Elstob's life between 1691 and 1702 is that she lived with her aunt and uncle "the space of a few years." Her brother William, in the meantime, was elected a Fellow of University College, Oxford, in June, 1696, and six years later was presented with the united parishes of St. Swithin and St. Mary Bothaw, London. It is certain that his nineteen-year-old sister joined him at this time, but it is tempting to speculate about the years preceding this move to London. Some evidence suggests that she may have spent time with her brother at Oxford. In 1938 a special exhibit at the Bodleian of the works of two learned ladies—Margaret Cavendish, Duchess of Newcastle, and Elizabeth Elstob—occasioned an article in *The Oxford Magazine* entitled "The First Home Student?"[23] Its author cites the antiquarian Edward Rowe Mores's description of Elizabeth Elstob as "a female student in the university."[24] Alas, however, the author also states, on the basis of no evidence, that Elizabeth "lived in lodgings" with her brother from the time he came to Oxford in 1691—clearly an impossibility for an eight-year-old girl and a contradiction to the few facts she records of her early life. There is, however, a delightful tradition at Oxford that she owns the title of "First Home Student." At any rate, Elizabeth Elstob has more than a courtesy relation with Oxford today: the Oxford University Press has in its possession punches and matrices of a font of Anglo-Saxon type known as the "Elstob" font, presumably cut for Elizabeth Elstob when the one used for her Anglo-Saxon Grammar, printed in 1715, was found to be unsatisfactory. When the *Authors' and Printers' Dictionary* was published in 1905, its author wished to give the Anglo-Saxon alphabet in Elstob type because of its elegance, but a complete alphabet in type did not exist, and the Delegates of the Oxford University Press would not incur the expense of casting from the matrices.[25]

For Elizabeth Elstob, the thirteen years between 1702 and 1715 were the most productive and happy of her life. In 1702 she came to London to live with her brother. The Leeds antiquary Ralph Thoresby recounts finding the two in their house on Bush Lane busily copying and editing Anglo-Saxon texts. A letter from Elstob to Thoresby, dated London, 7 February 1710, apologizes for not having written sooner, thanks him for the subscription he has sent, and relates that she is beginning work on the Saxon Homilies, "of which I at present have by me two very ancient manuscripts from the Cottonian library."[26] The year 1715 saw the deaths of both her brother William and George Hickes, the greatest Old English scholar of his age and a man who had enthusiastically supported her work. The years from 1715 unil her death in 1756 were years of trial and tribulation. As Samuel Pegge wrote of these years in the paper he read before the Society of Antiquaries in 1767: "But this excellent woman, her profound learning, and masculine abilities notwithstanding, was very unfortunate in life."[27]

Yet this is to anticipate. While she enjoyed the intellectual and financial support of her brother, Elstob's work flourished. Indeed, the relationship between brother and sister reminds one of the deep intellectual and emotional kinship of Dorothy and William Wordsworth. During her years at Bush Lane, Elstob enjoyed the life of a productive scholar. Her first printed work was a translation of Mlle. de Scudéry's *Essay on Glory*, which appeared in 1708. This is notable in the light of the Duchess of Portland's later remark that she would have to employ a tutor other than Elizabeth Elstob to teach her children French. Apparently, and not at all surprisingly, Elstob never learned to speak the language fluently. The following year, in 1709, her first significant contribution to Anglo-Saxon studies was published: Aelfric's *An English-Saxon Homily on the Birthday of St. Gregory*. It was Thomas Hearne's *bête noire*, Dr. John Hudson, Bodleian Librarian, who gave Elstob access to the manuscript; and it was George Hickes, the "great Patron of Septentrional Studies," who urged her, as she wrote in her Preface, to publish "somewhat in *Saxon*, [as] I wou'd invite the Ladies to be acquainted with the Language of their Predecessors, and the Original of their Mother Tongue" (p. vii).

As was then the custom, the *English-Saxon Homily* was published by subscription. Of the 260 subscribers whose names are appended to the work, nearly half are women, including Lady Elizabeth Hastings, granddaughter of Lucy, Countess of Huntingdon, who had employed Bathsua Makin to tutor her children, and Lady Winchelsea's friend Mrs. Thynne, who was later to write: "I am determin'd to be on a par with this Mrs. Elstob, if the Expence of an Hour or two's Morning Study will enable me to conquer the Difficulties of the Saxon Tongue."[28] Among the dukes, duchesses, university and church dignitaries, relatives, and plain folk who make up the list of subscribers are Henry Aldrich, Dean of Christ Church; Sir Richard Blackmore, of the *Arthurs* infamy; Joshua Barnes, Professor of Greek at Cambridge; and Thomas Hearne, who, nevertheless, referred to the finished product as a "Farrago of Vanity," with its lengthy preface and "Bedrol" of subscribers.[29] The Bishop of Carlisle had written from Westminster to Ralph Thoresby, enclosing subscriptions "to our Saxon nymph" and remarking that he had "procured a few from my brethren of the bishop's bench, and some of my countrymen in town."[30] Apparently her uncle had reconciled himself to his niece's mastery of more than one tongue, as the name of the Rev. Charles Elstob, D.D., also appears among the subscribers.

147

Elstob's lengthy Preface to the *Homily* captures the attention of modern scholars on two counts: her spirited defense, first, of women's studies and, second, of St. Gregory and St. Augustine, Apostle of England, to advance the argument that "the Polity and Discipline of the *English Saxon* Church . . . was settled in Episcopacy" (p. xiv). Elstob knew she faced formidable criticism not only from those who ridiculed women's learning and antiquarian studies, but also from those antiquarians who denigrated Gregory and Augustine for their ties with Rome. She tackled the first set of opponents first. Dismissing the despisers of Anglo-Saxon studies as beneath contempt—"Those who please themselves with an Opinion of their own extraordinary Wit or Learning, usually think themselves obliged to overlook all that they do not know themselves, as useless, and impertinent"—she turns to the feminist issue:

> For first, I know it will be said, What has a Woman to do with Learning? This I have known urged by some Men, with an Envy unbecoming that greatness of Soul, which is said to dignify their Sex. . . . Where is the Fault in Womens seeking after Learning? why are they not to be valu'd for acquiring to themselves the noblest Ornaments? what hurt can this be to themselves? what Disadvantage to others? But there are two things usually opposed to Womens Learning. That it makes them impertinent, and neglect their household Affairs. Where this happens it is a Fault. But it is not the Fault of Learning, which rather polishes and refines our Nature, and teaches us that Method and Regularity, which disposes us to greater Readiness and Dexterity in all kinds of Business (pp. i ff).

What learning really makes most women neglect, says Elstob, is "the Theatre, and long sittings at Play [i.e., gaming], or tedious Dressings, and Visiting Days." Because Elstob the scholar was well aware of the tradition of female learning to which she belonged, she refers those gentlemen who are "eager to deny" women the privilege of learning to the elegant Latin discourse on the subject by "that Glory of her Sex, Mrs. *Anna Maria a Schurman*," and turns her scorn on her own sex: "I shall not enter into any more of the Reasons why some Gentlemen are so eager to deny us this Privilege: I am more surpriz'd, and even ashamed, to find any of the Ladies even more violent than they, in carrying on the same Charge." Turning from this kind of woman as "a being in love with [her] own Ignorance, which justly renders [her] contemptible," Elstob chooses "rather to converse a little with those who have some degrees of

Learning, and know how to value it in themselves . . . [those women who] admire a Play, a Romance, a Novel, perhaps entertain themselves a little with History, [who] read a Poem gracefully, and make Verses prettily, [who] rally and repartee with abundance of Wit and readiness"[31] in an attempt to convince them that the study of Anglo-Saxon is neither useless nor contemptible:

> What is this Saxon? what has she to do with this barbarous antiquated Stuff? so useless, so altogether out of the way? But how came they to know that it is out of the way, and useless, who know nothing of it? and they seem to have forgot the Sentiments of their polite Masters, who judg'd not any part of Learning to be out of the way. I fear, if things were rightly consider'd, that the charge of Barbarity would rather fall upon those who, while they fancy themselves adorn'd with the Embellishments of foreign Learning, are ignorant, even to barbarity, of the Faith, Religion, the Laws and Customs, and Language of their Ancestors (p. vii).

The major portion of Elstob's Preface, however, is concerned with Anglican rather than feminist apologetics, and her contributions in this area have been admirably discussed by Michael Murphy in his essay, "The Elstobs, Scholars of Old English and Anglican Apologists."[32] The Preface concludes with Elstob's acknowledgment of the generosity of her many subscribers and her happiness "to find so many of the Ladies, and those, several of them, of the best Rank: favouring these Endeavours of a Beginner, and one of their Sex" (p. lviii) and with a return to a theme already announced in her Dedication to Queen Anne: "It were endless to repeat all the Instances of illustrious Women, that might be enumerated, as contributing to the Advancement of Religion, in their several Ages." She cites Helena, mother of Constantine; Bertha, the first Christian Queen of England; Edelburga, her daughter and consort of King Edwin; Chlodesuinda, Queen of the Lombards; Ingundis, sister to King Childebert, as well as "two of the greatest Monarchs that the World has known: for Wisdom and Piety, and constant Success in their Affairs, *Queen Elizabeth*, and *Anne Queen of Great Britain*." She adds: "And I think it some further Apology for me, to the Ladies of *Great Britain*; that this is publish'd in the Reign of so highly Excellent a Lady" (pp. lix-x).

Shortly after the publication of the *English-Saxon Homily*, Elstob visited Canterbury, where she made the acquaintance of a young lady whose desire to learn Anglo-Saxon prompted Elstob to begin work on *The Rudiments of Grammar for the English-Saxon Tongue*. Although a specimen of the grammar was published in 1712, the entire work did not appear until 1715.[33] It bears on its title page Hickes's words to the author: "Our Earthly Possessions are truly called a *Patrimony*, as derived to us by the Industry of our *Fathers*, but the Language that we speak is our *Mother-Tongue*; and who so proper to play the criticks in this as the *Females*." Like its predecessor, the *Grammar* is dedicated to a royal lady, this time Caroline, Princess of Wales and future Queen of England.[34] The Preface to this work is addressed to her friend and patron the Reverend Dr. Hickes and bears the title "An Apology for the Study of Northern Antiquities." Though considerably shorter than the Preface to the *Homily*, it is written in the same lucid style and fighting spirit. This time, however, Elstob takes on a more formidable opponent than all the dilettantes in England put together, Jonathan Swift, who in 1712 had written his *Proposal for Correcting, Improving and Ascertaining the English Tongue*, in which the Dean fired a few more rounds in his lifelong battle against what he considered the lamentable tendency of the English to become monosyllabic and in which he made slighting remarks upon the so-called Septentrional or northern languages. Another recipient of Elstob's scorn was John Brightland, whom Hearne, relishing Elstob's attack, called a "vain, flashy person," one whom he "look'd upon . . . as the most unfit Person I knew of [as] a Scholar"; as for Mrs. Elstob's "Apology," Hearne found it "judicious, learned & elegant."[35]

Elstob scoffs at Swift's admission that, with the exception of German, he knew nothing of the northern tongues, and "neither is there any occasion to consider them." She writes that "it must be very difficult to imagine how a Man can judge of a thing he knoweth nothing of" (p. ix) and confesses herself filled with "admiration" that "those Persons, who talk so much, of the Honour of our Countrey, *of the correcting, improving and ascertaining of* our Language" would think to improve it by "separating it from the *Saxon* Root, whose Branches were so copious and numerous" (p. iv). Elstob next challenges the assertion that the northern languages "were made of nothing else but Monosyllables and harsh sounding Consonants" (p. x). What follows is a bravura display of vast learning and wide reading, in both ancient and modern literature, turning even Dryden's assertion that "he had a great Aversion to *Monosyllables*" (p. xiv) against him by citing the opening lines of his translation of the *Aeneid*: "Arms and the Man I sing, who forc'd by Fate."[36] Happily, the entire book is readily accessible to modern readers in facsimile.[37] The *Grammar* itself, as its author acknowledges, draws heavily on the pioneering work of Hickes and Thwaites and is principally notable for being the first grammar to be written in English for "those whose Education, hath not allow'd them an Acquaintance with the Grammars of other Languages" (p.iii).

The "Apology" and the *Rudiments of Grammar* to which it was prefixed appeared in 1715, a year that marked a dramatic change in Elstob's fortunes. Before turning to the events of these later years, however, it is necessary to consider briefly Elstob's attempt to publish a Saxon Homilarium. The reception afforded the single Aelfric homily published in 1709 undoubtedly whetted her enthusiasm, and in 1713 Elstob published a letter addressed to her uncle, Charles Elstob, D.D., Prebendary of Canterbury, entitled *Some Testimonies of Learned Men, in Favour of the Intended Edition of the Saxon Homilies, concerning the Learning of the Author of those Homilies.*[38] Consisting for the most part of testimonies to the usefulness of such a Homilarium by such noted scholars as William Cave, Jeremy Collier, George Hickes, John Leland, William Lisle, Humphrey Wanley, Henry Wharton, and Abraham Wheloc, the letter nevertheless sheds interesting light on the activities and attitudes of Elizabeth Elstob during the productive London years.

Her pleasure in all aspects of the preparation for the *Anglo-Saxon Homily* must have been immense. In March, 1709, writing to Thoresby to present him with the frontispiece of that work, Elstob talked about the "ornaments and border letters, which will make the book somewhat dear, but I will willingly have it as beautiful as possible."[39] Other letters to Thoresby in the same year relate her plans to edit the Saxon Psalms,[40] a plan graciously abandoned a few months later when she learned that Wanley was preparing the entire Bible: "I cannot allow myself to interfere with so excellent a person, though he has been so generous as to offer me all the assistance he can give."[41] In the later months of 1709 Elstob apparently fixed on the Homilarium as her next major venture, and she was working on the transcriptions early in 1710. In this work, Elstob received the usual support and encouragement of Hickes, who had himself at one time planned such an edition, yet who now, according to Ballard, derived "no small pleasure . . . to see one of the most considerable of them attempted, with so much success by Mrs. Elizabeth Elstob, who with incredible industry hath furnished a *Saxon Homilarium* . . . which she hath translated, and adorned with learned and useful notes."[42]

Some Testimonies of Learned Men, written as an appeal for subscribers to the Homilarium, is of biographical interest because it is addressed to Elstob's uncle and former guardian, who had, according to her memoirs, not supported his

151

niece's desire for learning as a child. The *Testimonies* reveals a warm and supportive relationship in 1713, recording Elstob's

> sincerest Testimonies of my Gratitude to you, and others of my Benefactors for your extraordinary Zeal and Forwardness, in procuring Favourers of my Design. In which you will share with me this Satisfaction, that you concur with the two Universities in favour of me. The University of *Cambridge*, which hath indulg'd me with the use of the Manuscript from which I take my Copy, hath been already very liberal of her Subscriptions, and promiseth me the Favour of farther Encouragement. And the University of *Oxford*, besides some Subscriptions, and the like kind Promises, hath done me the Honour to cast a new Letter, to engage me to print the Homilies with them (pp. 4-5).

In spite of Elstob's best efforts, the Homilarium on which she had worked so industriously never reached her subscribers. Only thirty-six folio proof pages of the Homilarium are preserved in the Lansdowne collection at the British Library, along with the manuscript note: "For reasons now unknown the Press was stopped."[43] The title page, apparently never printed, was to have borne the title *The English-Saxon Homilies of Aelfric, Archbishop of Canterbury, who flourished in the latter end of the tenth century. Being a Course of Sermons collected out of the Writings of the antient Latin Fathers, containing the Doctrines &c of the Church of England before the Norman Conquest, and shewing its Purity from many of those Papist Innovations and Corruptions which were afterwards introduced into the Church. Now first printed, and translated into the Language of the present time by Elizabeth Elstob.*[44]

One can only speculate as to why the Homilarium proceeded so far and no further: lack of sufficient funds to complete the printing, most likely. Elstob's preference for books "as beautiful as possible" perhaps led her to conceive a work whose production costs far surpassed the income from subscriptions. A letter from her dated at Bush Lane, 13 May 1713, addressed "To the most honourable Robert earl of Oxford and Mortimer, Lord High Treasurer of Great Britain, present," enclosing specimens and entreating his interest in obtaining the Queen's bounty toward printing the homilies, was apparently not successful, although another letter, written the next year, acknowledges her obligations to Harley for his personal support.[45] Certainly Harley's fall from power and the subsequent political upheavals occasioned by the death of Queen Anne in 1714 dramatically altered the careers of many statesmen, churchmen, and scholars.

For Elstob 1715 was a year of personal disaster as well. At the age of thirty-two she lost both her brother William and her mentor and friend Dr. Hickes. Very little is known about the next twenty years of her life. Nichols records that "after the death of her brother, and the ill success of her studies, she was obliged to depend upon her friends for subsistence, but did not meet with the generosity she might expect; Bishop Smalridge being the only person from whom she obtained any relief."[46] Had her uncle also died, or had his enthusiasm for Elizabeth's scholarly endeavors waned with William's death? Was her association with so many prominent Non-jurors now an even more distinct disadvantage? One can only guess. Hearne's Diaries contain scattered references to Elstob's financial problems over the next few years. In July, 1716, the Oxford antiquary received a letter from one of his correspondents expressing concern that Aelfric's Homilies were not yet published, and on 15 November 1716, Thomas Baker, of St. John's College, Cambridge, wrote that he was "sorry I am disabled from doing you so much service as I am desirous to do, for I am so deep with Mrs. Elstob and Mr. Stryke that I have no other answere to give to my Subscribers, but that I will trouble them no more till I have made good these Proposals, which I doubt I shall not be able to do in hast."[47] Not two weeks later Hearne received word that Mrs. Elstob's book was "going" at last, and then he was silent on the subject until he received another letter from Baker on 30 November 1718: "If I hear of any Subscriptions I will acquaint you, tho' I have been so bit by Mrs. Elstob of late, who is lately gone off for debt, that tho' I am very safe with you, yet I am almost come to a general Resolution never to collect more Subscriptions, as I give out to all my Friends."[48]

Was it fear of imprisonment for debt that drove Elizabeth Elstob from London sometime about 1718? There is some evidence to suggest that she might even have changed her name for a while after leaving London. As late as 1738, writing to her sister Ann Granville, Mrs. Pendarves refers to the kindness of her mother in inviting Mrs. Elstob and adds, "I almost fancy she will not accept of it, because of having been there in a disguised way; the Duchess has now a thousand fears, least my Lord and Lady Oxford should have any objections against taking her. . . ."[49] Margaret Cavendish Harley, Prior's "lovely little Peggy," daughter of Edward, second Earl of Oxford, had married William, second Duke of Portland, and in 1738 engaged Elizabeth Elstob "to instruct her children in the principles of religion and virtue, to teach them to speak, read, and understand English well, to cultivate their minds as far as their capacity will allow, and to keep them company in the house, and when her strength and health will permit to take the air with them."[50] Mrs. Elstob's income from the Portlands of thirty pounds per annum was to commence on Christmas Day, 1738, and on 22 December, Mrs. Pendarves wrote her sister: "I think your advice to Mrs. Elstob quite right about *paying debts*; a person of such principles as hers cannot enjoy any advantages without doing justice when it is in her power to do it."[51]

From the time that she left London until a few years before her going to Bulstrode in the employment of the Duchess of Portland, the story of Elstob's life becomes vague and uncertain. The memoir she sent Ballard glosses over these years with the brief statement that she was "unhappily hindered" in her learned pursuits "by a necessity of getting her bread, which she [had] endeavoured to do for many years, with very indifferent success." Her story picks up again at Evesham, in Worcestershire, sometime around 1735, where she appears as a schoolmistress. It is evident from her letters to George Ballard that the duties of a schoolmistress were not totally uncongenial to her, although the demands of the position left her little time for scholarly pursuits. A letter to Ballard states that "when my School is done, my little ones leave me incapable of either reading, writing, or thinking, for their noise is not out of my head until I fall asleep, which is often late."[52]

The reason why the story of Elizabeth Elstob continues after 1735 is that it was in this year that she made the acquaintance of George Ballard, himself a remarkable man, remembered in the main for his *Memoirs of several Ladies of Great Britain who have been celebrated for their writings or skill in the learned languages, arts and sciences*, which appeared in 1752, four years before Elstob's death. Since the memoirs excluded lives of ladies yet living, Ballard's work unfortunately contains no account of Elizabeth Elstob, who assisted him with many details in his preparation of the work. When she first became acquainted with Ballard in 1735, he was about twenty-nine years of age and Elstob then fifty-two; they became lifelong friends. At the time of their first acquaintanceship, he must have still been following his trade as a ladies' tailor in the place of his birth at Campden, Gloucestershire. It was not until 1738 that his antiquarian learning brought him to the attention of Lord Chedworth and other patrons of the hunt, who pursued their sport in the neighborhood of Campden and who afforded the unusual tailor an annuity of one hundred pounds to enable him to pursue learning. It is always remarked of Ballard that he accepted only sixty of the hundred pounds, and with this eventually went up to Oxford and became a clerk at Magdalen College at the age of forty-four.

It was through Ballard that Elstob was brought once more to the notice of scholars and antiquarians, and through Ballard that she made the acquaintance of Mrs. Sarah Chapone, the future mother-in-law of the even more famous bluestocking, Harriet Chapone. Learning of Elstob's situation from Ballard, Mrs. Chapone initiated a fund-raising among her acquaintances and obtained for Elstob a tentative offer from Lady Elizabeth Hastings to teach in a charity school. Nichols records Elstob's reaction to this possibility:

> As to your [Ballard's] objection on the meanness of the scholars, I assure you, Sir, I should think it as glorious an employment to instruct those poor children, as to teach the children of the greatest. But I must tell you that mine may be termed a life of disappointments from my cradle till now, nor do I expect any other while I live. This, and hearing no more of that affair, makes me think her ladyship is provided with a mistress before now, there being many more deserving than myself, that are in want of such an employment. Nor do I repine; for I am so inured to disappointments, that I expect nothing else, and I receive them with as much easiness as others do their greatest prosperity.[53]

Mrs. Chapone's childhood friend Mary Granville, later Mrs. Pendarves, and finally Mrs. Delany, proved more helpful, for it was she who finally obtained Elizabeth Elstob her position with the Duchess of Portland. In addition to her introduction to Mrs. Chapone, Elstob was also indebted to Ballard not only for his friendship and appreciation of her scholarship, but for the interest he aroused on her behalf among his antiquarian friends, some of whom corresponded with Elstob and occasionally visited her at Evesham and, later, Bulstrode.

Through the good offices of Mrs. Chapone and her more socially prominent friend Mrs. Pendarves, the fortunes of Mrs. Elstob were set before Queen Caroline, to whom, as the Princess of Wales, Elizabeth had dedicated *The Rudiments of Anglo-Saxon Grammar* in 1715. Once again Elstob experienced disappointment of her hopes, for the Queen died in 1737, before the money promised Elstob to establish a school for young ladies of higher rank had been paid. At last, however, despite Mrs. Pendarves' fear that Lord and Lady Oxford might object, Elstob became a member of the household of the Duchess of Portland, where she resided from 1739 until her death in 1756. Interesting insights into her life during these years are afforded by her correspondence with Ballard and in the correspondence of Mary Delany. I myself find a sadness in these letters, despite Elstob's protests of her good fortune. Her letters to Ballard indicate she was active in her attempts to secure subscriptions for his *Memoirs of Learned Ladies*, but without much success:

> I am sorry to tell you the choice you have made for the Honour of the Females was the wrongest subject you cou'd pitch upon. For you can come into no company of Ladies or Gentlemen, where you shall not hear an open and Vehement exclamation against Learned Women, and by those women that read much themselves, to what purpose they know best. . . . The prospect I have of the next age is a melancholy one to me who wish Learning might flourish to the end of the world, both in men and women, but I shall not live to see it.[54]

Her letters to Mrs. Pendarves and Mrs. Dewes, Mary Pendarves' sister, strike the modern reader as pathetically abject and grateful in their repeated expressions of humble gratitude.

Yet none of this is surprising, considering the circumstances in which Elizabeth Elstob was placed. One recalls Lady Mary Wortley Montagu's attitude toward learned ladies, and reflects that Mary Delany "never associated with Mrs. Thrale [wife of a brewer] or Dr. Johnson, having a disinclination to make the acquaintance of one and a *horror* of the occasional bursts of rudeness of the other" and that she admitted Fanny Burney, already the author of *Evelina* and *Cecilia*, into her social circle only after being assured of the "sweetness of [her] manners."[55] Nor is it surprising that after years of exhausting labor and uncertainty about her future, Elizabeth Elstob would feel grateful to find no small measure of peace and security among her young charges at Bulstrode. Yet despite this, the sadness persists. The letters of Mary Delany put before the modern reader a vague vision of a superannuated English nanny, tucked away in her proper place in the household, cherished and somewhat tolerated like an old family pet. It does not seem the most fitting ending to the life of a scholar.

[1] *Correspondence*, ed. Harold Wilson, 5 vols. (Oxford: Clarendon Press, 1965), IV, 258. Granted, Swift wrote these lines to Mrs. Pendarves (Mary Delany) complaining about the Anglo-Irish and urging her to visit him in Dublin. But one can just as well imagine Swift writing these lines had he lived in England. The Dean enjoyed the company of intelligent and well-educated women.

[2] *Complete Letters*, ed. Robert Halsband, 3 vols. (Oxford: Clarendon Press, 1965-67), I, 44-45 et passim.

[3] As an old woman, Lady Mary was deeply concerned that her granddaughters receive proper educations. Writing on this matter to her daughter, the Countess of Bute, she confessed an inclination "to think (if I dare say it) that Nature has not plac'd us in an inferior Rank to Men, no more than the Females of other Animals, tho I am persuaded if there was a Common-wealth of rational Horses (as Doctor Swift has suppos'd) it would be an established maxim amongst them that a mare could not be taught to pace" (*Letters*, III, 27). Concerned about the education of her eldest granddaughter, Lady Mary urged the Countess to be unsparing in the child's education, but warned "a caution to be given her (and which is most absolutely necessary) . . . to conceal whatever Learning she attains, with as much solicitude as she would hide crookedness or lameness" (III, 22-23). Perhaps Pope was right: "Woman's at best a Contradiction still."

[4] "An Essay concerning Human Understanding," in *The English Philosophers from Bacon to Mill*, ed. Edwin A. Burtt, The Modern Library (New York: Random House, 1939), p. 246. Cf. Adam's realization in *Paradise Lost* (VIII. 191-94):

> . . . not to know at large of things remote
> From use, obscure and subtle, but to know
> That which before us lies in daily life,
> Is the prime Wisdom.

[5] *The Lord Marques Idleness: Conteining manifold matters of acceptable devise, as sage sentences, prudent principles, &c.*, 2nd. ed. (London, 1587), pp. 13-14.

[6] *Essayes*, ed. Don Cameron Allen (Baltimore: The Johns Hopkins Press, 1946), p. 191. Cf. *Spectator* 10 (12 March 1711): "It was said of *Socrates*, that he brought Philosophy down from Heaven, to inhabit among Men; and I shall be ambitious to have it said of me, that I have brought Philosophy out of Closets and Libraries, Schools and Colleges, to dwell in Clubs and Assemblies, at Tea-Tables, and in Coffee-Houses."

[7] Ibid., p. 200.

[8] Ed. Floyd Dell and Paul Jordan-Smith (New York: Tudor Publishing Co., 1949), p. 261.

[9] David C. Douglas, *English Scholars, 1660-1730* (London: Eyre and Spottiswoode, 1951), p. 15.

[10] *Characters*, ed. Charles W. Daves (Cleveland and London: The Press of Case Western Reserve, 1970), p. 76.

[11] John Nichols, *Illustrations of the Literary History of the Eighteenth Century* (London, 1817), I, 684-85.

[12] Preface, *Brevis Conspectus*. Cited by Douglas, p. 89.

[13] Quoted by Douglas, p. 14.

[14] "A Dissertation concerning the Perfection of the English Language, the State of Poetry, &c." in *Critical Essays of the Eighteenth Century, 1710-1725*, ed. Willard Higley Durham (New Haven: Yale University Press, 1915), p. 358.

[15] *An English-Saxon Homily on the Birth-Day of St. Gregory: Anciently used in the English-Saxon Church. Giving an Account of the Conversion of the English from Paganism to Christianity* (London, 1709), p. vi. All further citations to this work are given in text when possible.

[16] *Exchequer*, p. ii. Cited by Douglas, p. 276.

[17] (London, 1779), pp. 162-63.

[18] *English-Saxon Homily*, p. ii.

[19] "Memoirs of the Learned Saxonists Mr. William Elstob and his Sister," in *Bibliotheca Topographica Britannica* (London, 1790), I, 1-32.

[20] Three of the most important of these appeared in the 1920's: Myra Reynolds, *The Learned Lady in England, 1650-1750* (Boston and New York: Houghton Mifflin, 1920), pp. 170-85; Margaret Ashdown, "Elizabeth Elstob, The Learned Saxonist," *MLR*, 20 (1925), 125-46; Ada Wallas, *Before the Blue-Stockings* (London: George Allen & Unwin, 1929), pp. 133-89.

[21] The Ballard memoir is printed by Reynolds, pp. 170-71. Future citations in the text are from this transcription.

[22] John Nichols, *Literary Anecdotes of the Eighteenth Century* (London, 1812), IV, 129.

[23] (24 Nov. 1938), pp. 212-13.

[24] In his *Dissertation upon Typographical Founders and Founderies* (1779), Rowe Mores referred to Elstob as "a female student in the University and a great favorite of Dr. Hudson [Bodleian Librarian] and the Oxonians" (Nichols, *Lit. Anec.*, IV, 130).

[25] G. S. Hinds, "The Saxon Nymph," *TLS*, 5 Oct. 1933, p. 671.

[26] *Letters of Eminent Men, Addressed to Ralph Thoresby, F.R.S.*, 2 vols. (London: Henry Colburn & Richard Bentley, 1832), II, 226-27. Hereafter cited as Thoresby.

[27] *Bibliotheca Topographica*, I, 26.

[28] Cited in *The Oxford Magazine* (24 Nov. 1938), p. 212.

[29] *Remarks and Collections of Thomas Hearne*, 11 vols. (Oxford: Printed for the Oxford Historical Society, Clarendon Press, 1885-1921), I, 289-90. Hereafter cited as *Remarks and Collections*.

[30] Thoresby, II, 160.

[31] p. iv. Women like Lady Winchelsea, perhaps, whose name does not appear among the subscribers, although those of her friends do?

[32] *Durham University Journal*, 58 (1966), 131-38.

[33] William and Elizabeth Elstob, the Learned Saxonists," in *Reprints of Rare Tracts*, imprinted by M. A. Richardson (Newcastle, 1847), p. 51. Hereafter cited as *Reprints Rare Tracts*. The full title of Elstob's work is *The Rudiments of Grammar for the English-Saxon Tongue, First given in English: With an Apology for the Study of Northern Antiquities. Being very useful towards the understanding our ancient English Poets, and other Writers*. Like her other works, this was printed by W. Bowyer. Page citations are given in text.

[34] In a letter to Thoresby (13 July 1715), Elstob tells of having had the honor of being introduced to the Princess (Thoresby, II, 301).

[35] *Remarks and Collections*, IV, 83.

[36] In a letter dated 29 June 1737, George Ballard wrote of the "Apology": "Indeed I thought the bad success Dean Swift had met with in this affair from the incomparably learned and ingenious Mrs. Elstob, would have deterred all others from once opening their mouths in this affair" (Nichols, *Illustrations of Literary History* [1822], Ch. IV, p. 212). Cited by Wallas, p. 138.

[37] (Menston, England: Scholar Press, 1968).

[38] The title continues *And the Advantages to be hoped for from an Edition of them. In a Letter from the Publisher to a Doctor of Divinity*. Page citations are given in text.

[39] Thoresby, II, 147.

[40] (6 May 1709), Ibid., p. 163.

[41] (10 Oct. 1709), Ibid., p. 198-99.

[42] *Bibliotheca Topographica*, I, 26.

[43] Ashdown, p. 133.

[44] *Reprints Rare Tracts*, p. 56.

[45] Harl. MS. No. 7524.

[46] *Lit. Anec.*, IV, 133.

[47] *Remarks and Collections*, V, 271, 337.

[48] Ibid., VI, 14.

[49] *The Autobiography and Correspondence of Mary Granville, Mrs. Delany*, 3 vols. 1st series, 3 vols. 2nd series, ed. Rt. Hon. Lady Llanover (London: Richard Bentley, 1861-62; rpt. New York: AMS Press, 1974), II, 1st series, 14.

[50] Ibid., pp. 14-15.

[51] Ibid., p. 18.

[52] Cited by Wallas, p. 160.

[53] *Lit. Anec.*, IV, 137.

[54] Cited by Ashdown, p. 144.

[55] Delany, *Correspondence*, III, 2nd series, 348 n. 279. No wonder Edmund Burke called Mary Delany "the highest bred woman in the world."

MERCY OTIS WARREN: PLAYWRIGHT, POET, AND HISTORIAN OF THE AMERICAN REVOLUTION (1728–1814)

JOAN HOFF WILSON and SHARON L. BOLLINGER

In 1775 when Thomas Paine argued that American female patriots deserved "an equal right to praise" and to "the sweets of public esteem" his suggestion was probably as appalling to the women of the revolutionary era as it was to the men.[1] Because of wholesale acceptance of the philosophical concept of "separate spheres," women of Mercy Otis Warren's time lived physically and intellectually circumscribed lives. European Enlightenment theories strictly maintained the inferiority of the private, and by definition "natural," sphere which women occupied. However, upper-class American women like Mercy Otis Warren and her friend Abigail Adams aspired to intellectual equality with men, and they insisted that their separate sphere of activity was equal—a claim their male colleagues never accepted. Thus, Abigail Adams wrote to her sister in 1799 that she would "not consent to have our sex considered in an inferior point of light," saying: "Let each planet shine in their [sic] own orbit. God and nature designed it so—if man is Lord, woman is *Lordess*—that is what I contend for."[2]

Despite these brave words few well-to-do daughters of Columbia escaped being formed and educated for the world of fashion, and even those who did fully accepted the limitations of living within their "proper sphere." Warren, for example, wrote that "appointed subordination" of women to men had to be outwardly accepted "for the sake of Order in Families" until "these temporary gender Distinctions subside and we may be equally qualified to taste the full Draughts of Knowledge & Happiness prepared for the Upright of every Nation and Sex. . . ." Abigail Adams sounded even more resigned about sex-segregated functions when she finally stated in 1796: "Government of States and Kingdoms . . . I am willing should be solely administered by the lords of creation. I should contend for Domestic Government, and think that best administered by the "female."[3]

This claim to intellectual equality, while acquiescing to an inferior, exclusively private sphere of activity, caused a creative and assertive woman like Warren no end of psychological anguish and insecurity. Nonetheless, she advised young women that "it may be necessary for you to seem inferior, but you need not be so. Let them have their little game, since it may have been so willed. It won't hurt you; it will amuse them."[4] Warren not only gave such advice to young women, but she also practiced it herself. Like Margaret Fuller a half-century later, Warren thrived on praise from a close circle of male contemporaries and resorted to a variety of "feminine wiles" in order to function in male-dominated intellectual circles without assuming a threatening posture. The enormous psychic price exacted from her as a result of being forced by prevailing patriarchal standards to be an intellectual by subterfuge can only be surmised. A review of Mercy Otis Warren's circuitous career as a late eighteenth-century literary figure and historian represents a striking example of the high aspirations of the fettered female mind in the last quarter of the eighteenth century.

It is possible that Mercy Otis Warren faced greater psychological and social obstacles in developing her mind than did her sixteenth and seventeenth-century counterparts. Since Warren scarcely ever traveled from her home in Plymouth during the War of Independence, and since she worried about moving outside the bounds of her "proper sphere" every time she wrote for public consumption, it is ironic to find her referred to as the "Pen woman of the American Revolution." Even so, in the most important aspects of her life and writing, she stretched the limits of her societal conditioning as far as she could. As one biographer wrote of her last years: "Life to a less vivacious, less personally cheerful temperament, might now have seemed hopelessly circumscribed."[5] In spite of poor eyesight and the death of her favorite son, Winslow, she continued to write until her death in 1814. Only the written words of Abigail Adams, who lived until 1818, have outlasted those of Mercy Otis Warren among the generation of women who lived through the revolutionary era.

The third of thirteen children, Warren was born on 9 September 1728 into the family of James Otis and Mary Allyn Otis.[6] Although she received no formal schooling, she grew up in an environment that stressed intellectual achievement and political activity. In addition to this stimulating family life, she attended the lessons that her older brother James took with their uncle, Reverend Jonathan Russell, a religious and intellectual leader of the Cape Cod community of Barnstable. Although she continued to perfect skills considered necessary for accomplished women, such as needlework and embroidery, Mercy preferred reading. This preference led her to borrow from her uncle's collection of works on theology, history, philosophy, and poetry, thus providing her with reading materials that exposed her to contemporary ideas. Attracted to history, she particularly enjoyed reading Sir Walter Ralegh's *History of the World*.

Warren grew up in a farm house which was often visited by leaders of the English colonies, and she had access to a wide selection of the latest pamphlets, journals, and newspapers. She formed a close bond with her brother James. They frequently exchanged letters after he left home to attend Harvard, and James guided her reading, recommending that she study Milton, Shakespeare, Dryden, Pope, and John Locke. Later her poetry would be as reminiscent of Pope as her prose was of Ralegh. Warren combined such reading with experiments in writing verse and lessons in household skills, such as making soap, cheese, and candles. While she appeared well-trained in all traditional domestic duties, her efficiency as a household and land manager never approached that of Abigail Adams. Also, unlike her friend, Warren led a secluded life, keeping in touch with the world at large vicariously. She rarely left her home in Barnstable except for a trip to Harvard in 1744 at age fifteen to attend the graduation ceremonies for her brother James. During this visit to Cambridge, she met the man who would be her future husband, James Warren of Plymouth.

Not until ten years later did she marry James Warren at what many of her contemporaries would have regarded as the advanced age of twenty-six. Mercy Otis was a small woman with expressive eyes. No one ever referred to her physical appearance as beautiful, but she had wit, intelligence, and a charm that attracted people. The Warrens made their home on the Warren family farm for three years; James, however, inherited the job of County Sheriff after the death of his father, and so they considered moving to the city. When Warren became pregnant with the first of her five sons, they decided to purchase a house in Plymouth where she was to spend the rest of her life. This house would later be described as the "breeding place" of the American Revolution.

The Warrens welcomed to their home many of the most radical leaders of colonial society. Because of her frequent contact with these leaders, Warren had the opportunity to gather letters, newspapers, and books which outlined the political position of many colonial rebels. Much of the information she collected would later be incorporated into her three-volume *History of the American Revolution*. As early as December, 1775, for example, she unsuccessfully attempted to obtain from Abigail Adams "[c]ertain private Journals as you dare trust me, With. I have a Curiosity to know a Little More about Certain public Characters and perticular [sic] transactions than I am in a Way of being Acquainted with. It Would be an agreeable Entertainment to my Lonely hours."[7] Adams later refused to turn over her husband's diary volumes to Warren saying that she could not comply with the request because "unless I knew the hand by which I sent them I am afraid to write any thing which ought not to come to the public Eye."[8] Undaunted, Warren continued to solicit confidential information about American leaders from the Adamses and other prominent revolutionary families. That she succeeded more often than she failed in obtaining information in this fashion is proved by the personal insights and characterizations contained in her *History*.

As the independence movement gathered strength, the Warren home often served as a focal point for revolutionary plans. They participated in the meetings where strategies were developed, and possibly some of the 1765 demonstrations demanding repeal of the Stamp Act were planned in their home. These demonstrations included not only parades, but also burning the stamp officer in effigy and vandalizing the Boston home of the Massachusetts Royal Governor Hutchinson. Other members of their family undoubtedly took part in planning these protests, and after the repeal of the Stamp Act, her brother James Otis held an open house to celebrate the success of the demonstrators. The years immediately preceding the American Revolution found Warren closer to the center of political action than she would be following the war, because neither her husband nor her sons achieved prominence in the new government.

Responding to rising anti-British sentiment, Mercy Otis Warren took up her pen and did not lay it down again for the next thirty-five years. Her correspondence included numerous letters to Abigail and John Adams. She and Abigail Adams also corresponded with a number of male revolutionaries. The formation of the Committees of Correspondence by the Boston town meeting in the early 1770's has been attributed to the example set by Mercy Warren and Abigail Adams. Whatever their direct influence, however, the idea for the

Committees of Correspondence probably originated from discussions in the Warren household.

While continuing to keep her duties as a wife and mother foremost in her life, Warren began composing poems and plays which voiced her political philosophy. Warren had been composing poetry since 1759, but in the early 1770's turned more and more to political satire. Her first revolutionary verses reflected what would later become a major theme of her interpretation of American independence, namely, the absence or presence of virtue. Thus, in "A Political Reverie," a poem about how the colonists vacillated over whether or not to resort to arms, she predicted revolution because freedom no longer existed in England; its people had stopped emulating Locke: "Virtue turned pale, and freedom left from the isle."[9]

When she wrote about the Boston Tea Party, John Adams urged Warren in a letter to her husband to write about the "equity" of the event which he described as the "late frolic among the Sea Nymphs and Goddesses." Adams even sketched the highly classical outline he had in mind for such a work, and on 21 March 1774, "The Squabble of the Sea Nymphs; or the Sacrifice of the Tuscararoes" [sic] appeared on the front page of the Boston *Gazette*. In an unusually positive reference to the contemporary attitudes of women she wrote that "The virtuous daughters of the neighboring mead, / In graceful smiles approved the glorious deed" (p. 205). Usually she chided women in these propaganda poems "to check [their] wanton pride / And lay [their] female ornaments aside." At the instigation of Dr. John Winthrop, the husband of her friend Hannah, she urged women to support the various boycotts of British goods. Accordingly, she once proclaimed: "[A]nd be it known unto Britain, even American daughters are politicians and patriots, and will aid the good work with their female efforts."[10]

Warren's reliance upon both the encouragement and praise of men, such as her husband, John Adams, Alexander Hamilton, and later Thomas Jefferson, emerged as an early pattern in her literary career. After publishing her poem about the Boston Tea Party, she was not disappointed because John Adams praised "the skirmish of the sea deities" excessively. Warren ingeniously expressed surprise claiming that she never realized that she could "amuse, much less . . . benefit the world by [her] unstudied composition." Of course she disclaimed any desire for public esteem or eminence. Her correspondence contains many apologies for going "so much out of the road of female attention" because she realized it was "not altogether consonant with Female

Genius." Private approval, however, she constantly sought from her male friends. This tendency was particularly evident in her early correspondence with John Adams during the height of her poetic output before and during the American Revolution.

Virtue, however, remained uppermost in her mind. Thus, she advised a young American male residing in France during the War for Independence to remember to practice private virtue in the midst of foreign corruption. In 1778, after her eldest son had lost a leg in the fighting, she began to lament the disappearance of virtue from the revolutionary cause. On 5 October 1778 her poem "O Tempora! O Mores!" made the first page of the Boston *Gazette* with a prose comment which read: "This piece was written when a most remarkable depravity of manners pervaded the cities of the United States, in consequence of a state of war; a relaxation of government; a sudden acquisition of fortune; a depreciating currency; and a new intercourse with foreign nations." In the course of this poem, she asked: "Shall freedom's cause by vice be thus betray'd? / Our country bleeds and bleeds at every pore, / Yet gold's the deity whom all adore; / All public faith, and private justice dead, / And patriot zeal by patriots betray'd" (pp. 225, 246, 249, 250).

Warren's growing disillusionment with what she perceived as the diminished virtue of American political leaders is reflected in the satiric focus of her plays. In *The Adulateur* (1772) and *The Defeat* (1773) she castigated Governor Hutchinson, attacking him as mediocre and unprincipled. In *The Group* (1775), her best-known play, she attacked the British-appointed officials ruling Massachusetts. After the war began, she published *The Blockheads* (1776), her only prose play, which satirized the grand treatment Loyalist Bostonians gave the captured British general, John Burgoyne. In this play, Warren startled her readers by using rough street language to emphasize her disenchantment with those who did not support the Revolution. By 1779, in *The Motley Assembly*, she had turned her satire on another group of Americans, the moderate Whigs, who were beginning to emerge as leaders of the new nation.

Her stultified, classical style, although highly regarded at the time, seems unduly artificial to the modern reader. Later her three-volume history was to read like a narrative prose version of these early poems. In retrospect, it is difficult to perceive any significant literary development in her writing. Her style has been described as a pseudo-elegant "flowery mode of expression." Only *The Blockheads*, renowned at the time for its "vulgarity," stands out from the rest because she used terms such as "prig," and "pimp," and described one character as having "shit his breeches." As a result, some scholars question her authorship of this play and of *The Motley Assembly*.[12] However, the sentiments in both plays are surely hers. Their vocabulary and broad sexual humor afford a glimpse of a considerably less staid and protected homebody than her portraits and private correspondence would lead us to expect.

The Blockheads, interesting because of its sexual innuendos, is distinguished by unusual demographic insight. As in all her satires, she portrayed the British as more degenerate and avaricious than they were; however, she also depicted American Loyalists as stupid, pretentious, lower-class farmers mainly interested in rising socially among their new-found British friends. Until very recently, accounts of the Loyalists stressed their wealth, education, and cultural refinement. While she exaggerated both their social ambitions and uncouthness, she was demographically correct in describing the American Loyalists as primarily poor farmers, dissatisfied with their lot in life. For what it is worth, Warren's satire comes closer to the collective biographical truth about rank and file native American Loyalists than most standard accounts since that time. Thus, Mr. and Mrs. Simple and their daughter Tabitha leave their "filthy farm" because "it is all dirty stuff, only fit for Yankees," in response to false promises from the British (including the propositioning of their daughter by Lord Dapper). Their humiliation and suffering as refugees is approved by a woman in good radical Whig—later Jeffersonian Republican—fashion in the last soliloquy of the play.

> Good enough for them, they have brought it upon them-
> selves; they had better have minded their farms. . . . If I had a
> good farm, I would see government to the devil, before
> they should catch me here, to be froz'd, famish'd, ridiculed'd
> —curse them and their spiritless protectors, and let's con-
> clude with huzzas for America.[13]

The Group is more traditional in both style and subject matter. Concentrating on wealthier Loyalist leaders, Warren paints a devastating picture of ambitious, greedy, petty traitors. The origins of the play are in many ways more interesting than its contents, because it represented another of her male-inspired projects. Although she wrote it upon the "particular desire" of her husband, Warren worried that she might have violated good taste and her proper sphere with her "satirical propensity." So she asked John Adams on 30 January 1775 if she should curb her talent and remain entirely within her proper sphere. Adams, who had already been sent a partial manuscript by her husband and

167

had published it anonymously in the Boston *Gazette* on 23 January, replied through James Warren "it would be criminal to neglect" her talent, and he concluded with words he would not remember later when she dared to criticize him in her history of the American Revolution: "The faithful Historian delineates Characters truly, let the Censure fall where it will. . . ."[14]

Abigail Adams also reassured Warren that she need not worry about her writing being incompatible with her "female character" because "when it is so happily blended with benevolence, and is awakened by the love of virtue and the abhorrence of vice . . . it is so far from blameable that it is certainly meritorious." Indicating the way the two women viewed the approaching revolution, Abigail Adams reminded Warren that "who combats virtue's foe is virtue's friend." Nonetheless, after the entire play had been published as an anonymous pamphlet in April, 1775, Warren was upset by the immediate rumors that she had written it. Her claim to anonymity, always tenuous at best, disappeared after the play had become a success. John Adams even drew up a list identifying the characters in *The Group* as leading Tories.[15]

It must be remembered that plays written in the eighteenth century were for readers, not theater-goers, since a law in Massachusetts actually prohibited all public performances. The authorities believed the theater to be "the highway to hell." Warren's plays, however, appeared in newspapers and reached a wide audience. Although she wrote anonymously, her friends knew which works she authored. Both they, and a large segment of the public, also knew which fictional characters represented actual Bostonians.

Warren's two dramatic poems, *The Ladies of Castile* (1784) and *The Sack of Rome* (1785), were both written immediately after the War for Independence had ended, but were not published until 1790 in a collection of her poetry. On 4 January 1787 she had asked John Adams if he could get *The Sack of Rome*, which was then dedicated to him, published and, if not, she wanted him to, "dispose of this little WORK to the most advantage of your friends." This letter clearly reflected Warren's use of feminine flattery at its best (or worst depending on one's point of view). Lauding his judgment, his national prominence as U.S. Minister to England, and his friendship, she disclaimed any serious desire to see the work in print and any attempt to influence him with undue praise. Most important for their later relationship, she casually informed him at the end of this classic example of female persuasion that she had begun to write "a concise History of the American Revolution."[16]

Although Adams heartily approved of the work he failed to get it produced or printed in London.

Both tragedies were inspired by her son Winslow, and both focus upon the conflict between love and duty, virtue and corruption, responsibility and ambition. Both contain introductions which anticipate the rather gender-conscious, semi-apologetic way Warren would twenty years later introduce her history. *The Ladies of Castile*, the first of the two tragedies, concerns the tyrannical successors of Charles V in Spain; however, it begins with unadulterated praise of the uniqueness of the newly created United States:

> America stands alone:—May she long stand, independent of every foreign policy; superior to the spirit of intrigue, or the corrupt principles of usurpation that may spring from successful exertions of her own sons . . . whose valour completed a revolution that will be the wonder of the ages. What a field day for genius: What a difference of capacity . . . in science, in business, and in politics does this revolution exhibit! Certain enough to fire the ambition, and light every noble spark in the bosoms of those who are in the morning of life (pp. 100-01).

In spite of these confident words, Warren apologized because *The Ladies of Castile* was a dramatic poem rather than an epic, saying that "the candor of the public will be exercised not so much for the sake of the sex, as the design of the writer, who wishes only to cultivate the sentiments of public and private virtue in whatsoever falls from her pen" (p. 101). *The Sack of Rome* begins more pessimistically, focusing on the intrigues of the Roman court under Petronius Maximus. Here, Warren claims that her aim is to improve morals in the United States "by an exhibition of the tumult and misery into which mankind are often plunged by an unwarrantable indulgence of the discordant passion of the human mind." She asks to be forgiven if the play is distasteful, and in an epilogue she describes herself as a "female bard" asking the public for a "candid eye" (pp. 10-11, 95).

Between the writing of these two dramatic poems Warren's evaluation of the American Revolution changed as did perhaps her estimation of herself. She seems more self-assertive and desirous of public approval in the second tragedy. Both poems have stronger female characters than her previous play, even though the most virtuous women are doomed to suffer and often die with

their virtuous fathers, husbands, lovers, brothers, or sons. Nonetheless, strong women emerge in the two poems, and both end with either death scene statements by or about them. Thus, *The Ladies of Castile* concludes with the words: "To virtue bend the wayward mind of men," which *The Sack of Rome* echoes with "[v]irtue, sublim'd by piety and truth, now beckons to the skies" (pp. 94, 178).

By 1785, when *The Sack of Rome* was written, Warren's poetry already showed that all was not well with the new American republic. Soon she would find herself swept into postrevolutionary politics. Finally she would write a three-volume history, in part, to justify those politics. During the hostilities with Britain, American political leaders formed a government under the Articles of Confederation. When the Articles were judged to be unworkable and the Constitution of 1787 was subsequently written, Warren found herself ideologically upon the side of the Antifederalists. In 1788 anonymous objections to the Constitution were published as a pamphlet entitled *Observations on the New Constitution and on the Federal and State Conventions. By a Columbian Patriot.* Originally attributed to Elbridge Gerry, scholars now assign authorship to Warren.[17]

The opinions expressed in *Observations* certainly correspond to the political and ideological stance taken by Warren in her previous literary works and in her unfinished *History.* The author calls the Constitution a degradation and views loss of liberty as the probable consequence of ratification. After reiterating the Lockian doctrines regarding sovereignty and inalienable rights, the author warns that the new document may promote tyranny and points out critical omissions from the Constitution.

The author noted the lack of provisions for direct annual elections, freedom of the press, clear separation of executive and legislative power as well as a bill of rights. Equally important, certain provisions in the document seemed dangerous. Included in the list of objectionable provisions are the power over a standing army given to the President, the elimination of state resources for taxation, the appellate jurisdiction given to the Supreme Court, the excessive length of the term of office for Senators, and the power of the Electoral College to take freedom of choice from the people. Finally, the author questions the practicality of the Constitution, arguing that the United States is too large to be governed by one legislative body. The legality of the Constitution is also questioned with the author charging that the Constitutional Convention went beyond its authorized duties. In conclusion, the author points out that the mode of ratification appeared to deny the people enough time for reasonable consideration of the new document and objects as well to the provision which stipulated ratification by only nine states before becoming effective (pp. 6-11).

Warren's passionate Antifederalist attitudes, first exhibited in the 1788 debates over the ratification of the Constitution, later led her to emphasize her political philosophy in the last section of her *History*.[18] She began writing the three-volume work in 1775 and labored over the text intermittently until it was nearly finished in 1791. The delay in completing the manuscript was perhaps fortunate, because during this period publishers worked from subscription lists, taking orders from those who indicated a willingness to purchase a forthcoming publication. There is little doubt that Warren's political stance would have precluded a healthy subscription list during the decade of the 1780's when conservative Federalist views tended to dominate national politics. Although three of her contemporaries had already published their views of the Revolutionary period, notably William Gordon, David Ramsey, and John Marshall, they had championed the Federalist cause. *This work of Mercy Otis Warren remains the only multi-volume Antifederalist history of the Revolution written by an eye witness.*[19]

As in the case of her other publications, Warren felt compelled to apologize for her intrusion into a public sphere, a world reserved for men. She acknowledges overstepping proscribed boundaries, stating in her introduction to the *History*: "It is true there are certain appropriate duties assigned to each sex; and doubtless it is the more peculiar province of masculine strength . . . to describe the blood-stained field, and relate the story of slaughtered armies" (I, iv). Her preoccupation with the preservation of virtue and her belief in the duty of all citizens to combat vice led her to write: ". . . yet, recollecting that every domestic enjoyment depends on the unimpaired possession of civil and religious liberty, that a concern for the welfare of society ought equally to glow in every human breast, the work was not relinquished" (I, iv).

The encouragement of both her husband and son played an important role in the completion of the *History* as Warren admitted, "the trembling heart has recoiled at the magnitude of the undertaking, and the hand often shrunk back from the task" (I, iv). James Warren, Jr., her eldest son, copied the manuscript before it went to press and probably compiled the index. She also received critical assistance and praise from the Reverend James Freeman who conducted negotiations with the publishers and arranged for proofreading.[20]

Thus, once again private approval and encouragement from men gave Warren the courage to step outside the domestic sphere.

Through the years comments upon Warren's *History* have fluctuated from praise to criticism, from enthusiasm to boredom. In their evaluation of the work of American historians, Mary and Charles Beard discussed Warren's work with even-handed and fair criticism and concluded that her attempts to give meaning to the history of an emerging nation deserve attention, even praise. As they pointed out, Warren found herself placed between debaters, Thomas Jefferson and John Adams, espousing the ideal of progress, but realizing that valor and patriotism would be necessary if democracy were to endure and civilization were to advance.[21]

From our vantage point it is easy to see in Warren a precursor of the late nineteenth-century historian Frederick Jackson Turner who developed the "Frontier Thesis." In 1779, long before she composed her *History*, she had written Abigail Adams about the United States with sentiments very similar to those made famous by Turner:

> America is a theatre just erected—the drama is here but begun, while the actors of the old world have run through every species of pride, luxury, venality, and vice—their characters will become less interesting, and the western wilds which for ages have been little known, may exhibit those striking traits of wisdom, and grandeur and magnificence, which the Divine economist may have reserved to crown the closing scene.[22]

From this letter and her other writings it is clear that Warren, like Turner a century later, saw America as distinctly different from European society and attributed the democratic principles evident in the emerging American society to the equality of conditions which existed on this continent, especially on the frontier. She warned her readers that freedom may be lost as it was in other democratic experiments and urged them to oppose the Constitutional provision of a standing army. More idealistically, she called for the conquest of poverty, end of servility, and respect for the dignity of native Americans.[23]

Although Warren concentrated upon the divine plan for humankind and the religious aspects surrounding both the Revolution and the formation of the new nation, she also emphasized a unifying patriotic theme. In this way, she thought she had provided the vehicle by which Americans could gain a sense of their nationality through a common history and tradition, despite her serious doubts about the conservative nature and undemocratic potential of the Constitution of 1787. She almost succeeded in synthesizing two basic ideas— republicanism in the national character and the special destiny of the nation— into a portrayal of not only a new nation, but a new society.[24] She failed in this attempt because of her commitment to radical republicanism, natural rights, and the essential equality of human beings. This persistent commitment to individualism ultimately contradicted her patriotic appeal to national unity.

The development of the new nation required a patriotic commitment to national unity. Warren's insistence on the rights of individuals was out of step with the times, however in tune it may be with the present. She advocated individuality and humane treatment of native Americans, for example, at the expense of western expansion (II, 120-22). No wonder her *History* so quickly became obsolete for those Anglos interested in conquering the continent. Thus, she prophetically wrote:

> But if the lust of domination, which takes hold of the ambitious and the powerful in all ages and nations, should be indulged by the authority of the United States, and those simple tribes of men, contented with the gifts of nature, that had filled their forests with game sufficient for their subsistence, should be invaded, it will probably be a source of most cruel warfare and bloodshed, until the extermination of the original possessors (III, 206).

Warren's *History of the Rise, Progress and Termination of the American Revolution* is the work of a keen mind and a painstaking scholar, but it is neither a brilliant nor an astute historical document. She never perceived the modern political system that evolved from the Revolution; nor did she accept the vision of a pluralist society developed by James Madison in *Federalist Papers*, Number Ten, during the fight over the Constitution of 1787. It is ironic that John Adams was to accuse her of having written for the nineteenth century; if anything, her belief in virtue and conviction that God or Providence had used the American experiment to further His ultimate plan for humankind seems closer to that of the seventeenth century. Accepting the Lockian concept that men are created equal in nature as well as in the sight of God, she believed that each man must search his inner being, overcome selfishness and act in accordance with God's will. She viewed the Revolution as a defense of divinely inspired principles that Americans had discovered and practiced through their colonial experience. That other countries had learned from the American example and instigated their own revolutions was evidence of the success of God's plan.[25]

Although she acknowledged that men were basically selfish, she remained convinced that, if they allowed reason and conscience to control their actions, they could further God's plan and thereby promote equality and ensure their own happiness and virtue. Because she argued that merely revising the Articles of Confederation would have been sufficient and regarded those who conspired illegally to write the Constitution as monarchists, she believed that they were attempting to undermine the original principles of the Revolution. In contrast, she saw those who opposed ratification, herself included, as republicans who were continuing to carry on those principles.[26] In her *History* she reluctantly concluded that although the Constitution was thought by many to be too strongly marked with the features of monarchy, it was, after much discussion, adopted by a majority of the states (III, 340-43, 356-57).

Warren had praised George Washington and the Patriot forces during the War for Independence, but she became critical of many of the peacetime leaders who emerged after the fighting stopped. During the administrations of both Washington and Adams she felt that there was a decline in the principles of republicanism because of the influence of Hamilton's policies; his views seemed to her to violate both Constitutional law and God's plan. Each attempt by the Federalists to increase the power of the central government in the 1790's appeared to her an assault on republicanism and a movement toward the establishment of an American monarchy. Although John Adams had encouraged Mercy Warren to write her *History*, he was enraged by her evaluation of him and his political allies.

Fortunately, the letters which passed between John Adams and Warren have survived, for from them we get the full impact of her formidable and independent mind. Adams began the correspondence on 11 July 1807 by taking issue with Warren's assessment of his temperament: "Mr. Adams was undoubtedly a statesman of penetration and ability; but his prejudices and his passions were sometimes too strong for his sagacity and judgment."[27] Fixing only upon the last part of Warren's sentence, Adams asks her to supply instances when his "passion" and "prejudice" were ever too strong for his "sagacity" and "judgment." Not in the least mollified by Warren's tribute to the unimpeachable character of his private life, he was furious with her for suggesting that he had returned from Europe with a partiality for monarchy. Asserting that he had always opposed "despotism, absolute monarchy, absolute aristocracy, and absolute democracy," Adams adds that "a mixed government is the only one that can preserve liberty" (p. 392).

It is possible to read the first few letters which passed between Adams and Warren with some detachment, but by 27 July Adams begins to sound so condescending and petulant that one is tempted to conclude that Warren's assessment of his temperament, in light of remarks that today would be viewed as sexist, was overly flattering. In this letter he objects to her statement that "John Adams, one of the negatived councillors, a barrister at law, of rising abilities" appeared on the "Theatre of politics" in 1774:

> . . . I ought to have been considered in your History as a figure on the state from 1761 to 1774, call it the figure of a doorkeeper, a livery servant, a dancer, a singer, or a harlequin, if you will; but I ought not to have been shoved off the theatre and kept behind the screen for fourteen years (p. 358).

Later, he took even greater offense at her suggestion that he was happy while living in the Dutch Republic and found the French court less congenial. He insisted that he was ill for a while in Holland and that he found the French court exactly to his taste. Infuriated by her statement that he lacked the *je ne sais quoi* so necessary in polished Parisian society, he announced that Benjamin Franklin had no more *je ne sais quoi* than he did and indignantly stated that he might write a volume explaining why he and Franklin did not get along (pp. 407-10).

In his letter of 3 August 1807 he attacked her on the very issue she had dreaded and confided to him years before—transgressing her proper womanly sphere —by insisting that she had exposed herself to "eternal ridicule by her unladylike insinuations and assertions." Warren replied calmly, considering her lifelong anxiety on this point. Perhaps this response represents her use of feminine reserve and intellectual subterfuge at its best:

> On what point of ridicule would Mrs. Warren's character stand, were she to write her History over again and correct her *errors.* . . . She must tell the world that Mr. Adams was no monarchist; that he had no partiality for the habits, manners, or government of England; that he was a man of

fashion, that his polite accomplishments rendered him completely qualified for the refinements of Parisian taste . . . that he was beloved of every man, woman, and child in France; that he had neither ambition nor pride of talents, and that he 'had no talents to be proud of'; . . . that he was a favorite of the administrators of the affairs of France; that they loved him for his yielding, compliant temper and manners; that he was always a republican, though he has asserted that there was no possibility of understanding or defining the term republicanism; that in France he was always happy . . . (p. 423).

Warren concluded her list of the corrections which would be necessary to take account of the errors he had pointed out with a sarcasm as just as it was devastating:

. . . that his name was always placed at the head of every public commission; that nothing had been done, that nothing could be done, neither in Europe nor America, without his sketching and drafting the business, from the first opposition to British measures in the year 1764 to signing the treaty of peace with England in the year 1783.
Mr. Adams might indeed think this was a very pleasant portrait, but I doubt whether the world would receive it as a better likeness than the one drawn in the 'copious stream of Mrs. Warren's historical eloquence,' which appears to be so unacceptable to Mr. Adams (p. 423).

Provocatively, she quoted at length from letters in which he had praised her earlier work, but most of the time Warren was content to point up the inconsistency of Adams' criticism in brilliant satirical style. It would be difficult to improve upon sentences that read: "It was not the design of my historic work to write a panegyric on your life and character, though fully sensible of your virtues and your services. You may do that yourself in some future memoir, as I observe you contemplate writing your own life . . ." (p. 449).

The breach between Mercy Warren and John Adams was finally healed in 1812 by a mutual friend and arbitrator Elbridge Gerry, Governor of Massachusetts at the time. The correspondence between Abigail Adams and Mercy Warren resumed and continued until Warren's death in 1814. The reconciliation between the families seems to have pleased both Abigail Adams and Mercy

Warren, who wrote in January, 1813: "A visit from two such aged friends would be gratifying indeed. Mr. Adams with yourself will accept the respect and regard of your friend" (p. 350).

Mercy Otis Warren was not a feminist, nor should we expect her to be one, because of her historical context. Indeed, she opposed many of the views of Mary Wollstonecraft, whose *A Vindication of the Rights of Women* did advocate political and economic equality for women. She supported education for women only as long as it did not interfere with their domestic duties, and in her letters she repeatedly stated that care for husband and family must remain a woman's prime objective. Although she did not always practice what she preached, there is no evidence that her liberal politics included even as much moderate concern and commitment to civil rights for women as that demonstrated by Abigail Adams.[28]

Convinced that women and men were equal in intelligence and that all people should have an education, she seems never to have envisioned a society in which women could actively engage in public life. Nevertheless her own willingness to concern herself intellectually with the history of the American Revolution and the ratification of the Constitution suggests the intensity of her interest in public life. Although female novelists later in the nineteenth century were frequently to sign their works with male names, she signed her three-volume history with her own name. Likewise, her political philosophy, characterized by an ardent radical republicanism, was by no means a reflection of the prevailing views of her time and class. Her criticisms of the electoral college and of a standing army have been voiced again in the twentieth century, but her *History* is now rarely consulted.

Warren consciously regarded herself as an annalist of her time, but there is considerable poignance in her realization that her work might never be read:

> The virulence of party spirit shuts up the avenues of just information and until *truth* has a chance for fair play, the annalist . . . may as well seclude her observations to the cabinet. If they never come . . . to public view, the manuscript . . . may be a pleasant amusement to her children.[29]

Inevitably one admires the character and perseverance which enabled her to write a three-volume work which she realized might possibly serve only as an amusement to her children. Limited in her opportunities for education and her access to materials, Mercy Warren had the mind and industry of a scholar. Her *History*, although of historical interest because it preserves an eighteenth-century critique of Federalism, is remarkable principally because it was written by a woman at a time when it was necessary to justify interest in politics and history on the part of a woman. It was in her private correspondence with John Adams that she revealed the wit and sense of self which make her of interest today.

Unfortunately, her reputation remains marred by her gender. While some mistakenly attempt to revive her as a bona fide feminist, others continue to regard her work as antiquated. Perhaps Clifford K. Shipton has supplied the most incisive description of her plight as a bright and ambitious woman living at a time when such attributes and aspirations were not readily assigned to the private sphere of females. In 1933, he said in a sketch of her husband:

> She was a woman whose strong character and never-quiet pen made her more famous than her husband. Untroubled by logic, reason, or perspective, furious in her prejudices, she poured upon the leading men of the times a confident and assertive correspondence which caused many a pitying glance to be cast toward her husband.[30]

Today, as then, Mercy Otis Warren is still judged by male standards, and, like most women, she falls short of the mark. Only when viewed from the circumscribed situation in which she found herself does she emerge as a truly remarkable mind and personality of her time.

NOTES

[1] See "An Occasional Letter on the Female Sex," and "Reflections on Unhappy Marriages," in *Life and Writings of Thomas Paine*, ed. Daniel Edwin Wheeler (New York: V. Parke, 1908), V. Both articles appeared in the *Pennsylvania Magazine* for August, 1775.

[2] Adams quoted in Page Smith, *John Adams* (Garden City, New York: Doubleday & Co., 1962), II, 1006. Other independent positions taken by

Abigail Adams include her opposition to slavery and her indirect responsibility for John Adams' using "citizen" instead of "male" when he drafted the constitution for the state of Massachusetts.

[3] For a study of the status of American women before and after the Revolution, see Joan Hoff Wilson, "The Illusion of Change: Women and the American Revolution," in *The American Revolution: Explorations in the History of American Radicalism*, ed. Alfred F. Young (DeKalb: Northern Illinois Univ. Press, 1976), pp. 385-445. Quotations are from pages 428 and 431.

[4] Alice Brown, *Mercy Warren* (Boston: Charles Scribners, 1896), p. 242.

[5] Charles and Mary Beard, *The American Spirit* (New York: Macmillan, 1942), p. 120; Brown, *Warren*, p. 302.

[6] For biographical details see the following: Brown, *Warren*, pp. 1-66, *passim*; Katharine Anthony, *First Lady of the Revolution: The Life of Mercy Otis Warren* (Garden City, New York: Doubleday & Co., 1958), pp. 19-61, *passim*; Jean Fritz, *Cast for a Revolution, 1728-1814* (Boston: Houghton Mifflin Co., 1972), pp. 6-32, *passim*; Annie Russell Marble, "Mistress Mercy Warren: Real Daughter of the American Revolution," *New England Magazine*, 28 (1903), 163-74; Maud Macdonald Hutcheson, "Mercy Warren, 1728-1814," *William and Mary Quarterly*, 10 (1953), 379-402; Elizabeth F. Ellet, *The Women of the American Revolution*, 3 vols. (Philadelphia: George W. Jacobs & Co., 1853-54), I, 91-126.

[7] Mary Beard, ed. *America Through Women's Eyes* (New York: Macmillan, 1935), p. 59; Lawrence J. Friedman and Arthur H. Shaffer, "Mercy Otis Warren and the Politics of Historical Nationalism," *New England Quarterly*, 48 (1975), 206; Ellet, *Women of the Revolution*, I, 94; Hutcheson, "Mercy Warren," p. 384; Anthony, *First Lady*, pp. 77-78; Charles F. Adams, ed., *Correspondence between John Adams and Mercy Warren* (1878; rpt. New York: Arno Press, 1972), p. 482.

[8] L.H. Butterfield, ed., *Adams Family Correspondence*, 4 vols. (Cambridge: Belknap Press of Harvard University Press, 1963), I, 338-39, 423-24; II, 377 [hereafter cited as *AFC*, vol., page].

[9] Unless otherwise noted all references to her poetry (including her two long poetic tragedies) are taken from Mrs. M. Warren, *Poems, Dramatic and Miscellaneous* (Boston: I. Thomas & E.T. Thomas, 1790), pp. 188-94.

[10] Hutcheson, "Mercy Warren," pp. 386-87; Ellet, *Women of the Revolution*, I, 113; *AFC*, I, 91-94, 97-99.

[11] Hutcheson, "Mercy Warren," pp. 378, 386, 395; Ellet, *Women of the Revolution*, I, 104-05; Friedman and Shaffer, "Mercy Otis Warren," p. 209; Anthony, *First Lady*, p. 202.

[12] Only two scholars categorically deny she wrote either *The Blockheads* or *The Motley Assembly*: Worthington Chauncey Ford, "Mrs. Warren's 'The Group,'" *Massachusetts Historical Society Proceedings*, 62 (1928-1929), 20-21, and Fritz, *Cast for a Revolution*, pp. 318-19. Most of her biographers, especially Anthony, simply assume she did write both plays or indicate that the evidence is not conclusive on one side or the other. For comments on her prose and poetic style, see *AFC*, III, xxx, 290; Hutcheson, "Mercy Warren," pp. 339-40; Brown, *Warren*, pp. 67-70; Anthony, *First Lady*, pp. 78-80, 148-49.

[13] Warren, *The Blockheads or, the Affrighted Officers, A Farce* (Boston: John Gill, 1776), pp. 4, 10, 11, 17-19.

[14] *AFC*, I, 186, n. 5; Hutcheson, "Mercy Warren," p. 388; Anthony, *First Lady*, pp. 94-95; Brown, *Warren*, p. 165; Ford, "Mrs. Warren's 'The Group,'" pp. 15-22.

[15] *AFC*, I, 185; Warren, *The Group* (1774; rpt. Ann Arbor: University of Michigan Press, 1953), Foreword; Anthony, *First Lady*, pp. 95-96.

[16] Letter quoted in Brown, *Warren*, pp. 174-75.

[17] Charles Warren, "Elbridge Gerry, James Warren, Mercy Warren and the Ratification of the Federal Constitution in Massachusetts," *Massachusetts Historical Society*, 64 (1932), 143-64. It is this article which attributes the authorship of *Observations* to Mercy Warren. Although Charles Warren's arguments have been accepted by most scholars, it should be noted that he was a direct descendant of the Warren family. Unless otherwise noted, all references to the *Observations* are taken from Richard Henry Lee, ed., *An Additional Number of Letters from the Federal Farmer to the Republican* (1788; rpt. Chicago: Quadrangle Books, 1962).

[18] Friedman and Shaffer, "Mercy Otis Warren," pp. 194-215. Unless otherwise noted, all references to Warren's *History* are taken from Mercy Otis Warren, *History of the Rise, Progress and Termination of the American Revolution* (1805; rpt. New York: AMS Press, 1970).

[19] Anthony, *First Lady*, pp. 204-10.

[20] Hutcheson, "Mercy Warren," pp. 396, 399.

[21] Charles and Mary Beard, *The American Spirit*, pp. 120-22. For detailed criticisms and interpretations of the work, see Judith B. Markowitz, "Radical and Feminist: Mercy Otis Warren and the Historiographers," *Peace and Change*, 4 (1977), 15-19, and Friedman and Shaffer, "Mercy Otis Warren," pp. 194-215.

[22] *AFC*, III, 191, n.5.

[23] Markowitz, "Radical and Feminist," pp. 10-15.

[24] Kenneth A. Lockridge, "Social Change and the Meaning of the American Revolution," *Journal of Social History*, 6 (Summer, 1973), 425-26; William

R. Smith, *History as Argument: Three Patriot Historians of the American Revolution* (Paris: Moulton & Co., 1966), pp. 118-19; Friedman and Shaffer, "Mercy Otis Warren," pp. 197-99; Markowitz, "Radical and Feminist," pp. 13-14, 19.

[25] Smith, *History As Argument*, pp. 73-75; Adams, *Correspondence between Adams and Warren*, p. 463.

[26] Smith, *History As Argument*, pp. 110-19.

[27] Unless otherwise noted, all reference to their letters is taken from Adams, *Correspondence between Adams and Warren*, p. 392.

[28] Friedman and Shaffer, "Mercy Otis Warren," p. 208. In fact, Abigail Adams unsuccessfully urged Warren to champion the cause of removing certain common law restrictions on married women during the first months of the American Revolution. Years later she also privately approved of suffrage for women. See Wilson, "Illusion of Change," p. 427; Smith, *John Adams*, p. 225; and Abigail Adams to Mary Cranch, 4 July 1797, in Stewart Mitchell, ed., *New Letters of Abigail Adams, 1788-1801* (Boston: Little, Brown and Co., 1947), p. 112.

[29] Anthony, *First Lady*, pp. 202-03.

[30] *AFC*, I, xiv.

NOTES ON CONTRIBUTORS

Leslie Altman completed the research for her essay on Christine de Pisan while she was lecturing at the University of Southampton. Author of articles in such diverse areas as Middle English linguistics and eighteenth-century satire, she is currently doing research on women in Chaucer's *Canterbury Tales* in connection with a book she is writing on the images of women in medieval romances and early English narratives.

Louise Buenger Robbert has published studies on the Venetian money market, coinage, and the import and export of bullion and coins from the twelfth to the fifteenth centuries. Her monograph on Venetian colonies and the crusades and her study of a twelfth-century Venetian merchant's inventory will soon be published. She is currently analyzing the Venetian response to overseas expansion, 1205–1261.

Charmarie Blaisdell has been working for several years in the area of roles of women in early Modern Europe, especially as the patronesses of heretical and reforming movements in France and Italy. In addition to her work on the circle of Marguerite of Navarre, she has completed a biography of Renée de France, Duchess of Ferrara, and articles on political and religious turmoil in Ferrara, 1534–1559. Recently, she has been moving in the direction of cross-cultural studies and working on the problems and changing roles of women in developing countries.

Sandra M. Foa was reared in London and then completed her education in the United States and Spain. Her full-length study of María de Zayas, *Feminismo y forma narrativa: un estudio del tema y las técnicas de María de Zayas y Sotomayor* is forthcoming (Chapel Hill: Estudios de Hispanófila).

183

Currently, she is examining both dramatic and nondramatic discussions of the model Christian prince as background for a study of the ideal prince in Lope and Calderón.

Joyce Irwin works primarily on the history of religious life and thought in the sixteenth and seventeenth centuries. In addition to publishing articles on theology and liturgy, she has edited a book of sources entitled *Womanhood in Radical Protestantism: 1525—1675* (New York: The Edwin Mellen Press, 1979). She is now embarking on a study of attitudes toward music in sixteenth and seventeenth-century Protestant churches.

Jeanie R. Brink works in the area of English Renaissance literature and has published extensively in sixteenth and seventeenth-century literary biography and bibliography. She became interested in Bathsua Makin and other female scholars when she discovered some of Makin's unpublished poems and letters in the Hastings Collection at the Huntington Library. Her principal current interest is in the longer philosophical poem as it developed in England during the sixteenth and seventeenth centuries.

Jeanne A. Ojala is a French historian working in the seventeenth and the eighteenth centuries. Her book entitled *Auguste de Colbert: Aristocratic Survival in an Age of Upheaval, 1793—1809* was published by the University of Utah Press in 1979. She has published articles on the regulation of prostitution in Paris during the Revolution, 1789—1793; Auguste de Colbert; and Ira Allen and the French Directory, 1796. In the fall and spring of 1979 she traveled in Europe, doing research for her current project, the memoirs of Princess Aglaida Pavlovna Galitzine Unkowskoy.

Gerard Flynn has published numerous articles and several books including biographies in the Twayne World Authors Series on *Sor Juana Inés de la Cruz, Manuel Tamayo y Baus,* and, most recently, *Manuel Bretón de los Herreros* (Boston: G. K. Hall, 1978). Currently, he is working on the nineteenth-century novel of ideas (*novela de tesis*), especially Luis Coloma's *Pequeñeces* (1891). He attributes his interest in books to the love of learning he acquired at the famous grammar school, P.S. 11, in his native Highbridge, the Bronx, New York.

Mary Elizabeth Green works in eighteenth-century English literature, especially with Scriblerian satire and the history of ideas. As a result of her research on Augustan satires of learning, she has developed a special interest in the history of English scholarship and antiquarian studies. Currently, she is working on the correspondence of Mary Delaney and the longer philosophical poem in the eighteenth century.

Joan Hoff Wilson has authored a number of articles and books including *American Business and Foreign Policy 1920–1933*, awarded the Bernath Prize from the American Society of Historians of Foreign Relations in 1972; *Ideology and Economics: United States Relations with the Soviet Union 1918–1933* (1974); *Herbert Hoover: Forgotten Progressive* (1975); and co-authored with Albie Sachs *Sexism and the Law: Male Beliefs and Legal Bias in Britain and the United States* (1978). Her important theoretical article in women's history, "The Illusion of Change: Women and the American Revolution," received the Berkshire prize in 1977. At present, she is working on the impact of the American Revolution on the legal status of women and on a biography of Henriette Martin, militant western suffragist.

Sharon L. Bollinger has just completed a study of *Women in the American Revolution* (1976) and is currently working on a dissertation entitled "Failure to Persuade: The People's Party in Arizona, 1890–1896." Previously, she has worked extensively in the area of historical archaeology and published theoretical articles on the role of the historian in archaeology as well as co-authoring a study of the historical archaeology of Old Town, San Diego, entitled *The American Hotel, Casa de Alvarado, 1820 to 1880*.